PRACTICE AND PEF
IN VALIDAT

ᵓUS

# PRACTICE
# &
# PERSPECTIVE
# IN VALIDATION

## Edited by
## Clive H. Church

**SOCIETY FOR RESEARCH INTO HIGHER EDUCATION**

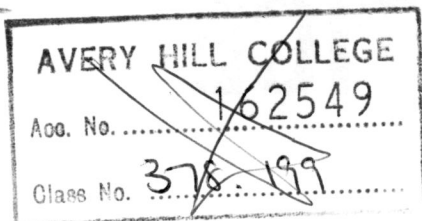

SRHE Proceedings

The Society for Research into Higher Education,
At the University, Guildford, Surrey GU2 5XH

First published 1983

© 1983 The Society for Research into Higher Education

ISBN 0 900868 94 5 ✓

Printed in England by Direct Design (Bournemouth) Ltd. Printers
Butts Pond Industrial Estate, Sturminster Newton,
Dorset DT10 1AZ

# CONTENTS

# CONTRIBUTORS

ROBIN ALEXANDER is Lecturer in Education at the University of Leeds

RON BARNETT is an Assistant Registrar in the Council for National Academic Awards

DAVID BILLING is Associate Director of the West London Institute of Higher Education, on secondment from the CNAA

CLIVE H. CHURCH is Senior Lecturer in European Studies at the University of Kent at Canterbury

ROY COX is Lecturer in Education at the University Teaching Methods Unit, London University

BRIAN GENT is Deputy Director of Leeds Polytechnic

ROGER HARRISON is Lecturer in Education at the Open University

JOHN HEYWOOD is Professor of Teacher Education at Trinity College, Dublin

ROBERT G. MURRAY is Head of Humanities at Oxford Polytechnic

ROY NIBLETT is Emeritus Professor of Higher Education in the University of London

EILEEN WORMALD is Academic Dean at Worcester College of Higher Education

This volume is the somewhat altered and delayed outcome of a research project originally initiated in 1978 by the Society for Research into Higher Education. Late in 1977 discussions in its Governing Council revealed that some institutions of higher education had to try and satisfy the requirements of a large and growing number of external bodies with rights to control the launching, financing, running and content of the courses they offered. It was felt that this situation, which was inherently likely to produce conflicts and contradictions within institutional management, needed detailed investigation. It therefore charged a group consisting of David Billing of the CNAA, Clive Church, then of the University of Lancaster, Colin Flood-Page of the University of Aston and Robin Alexander of the University of Leeds, to whom was later added Roy Cox of the UTMU in London, to consider the matter. After some discussion, the group suggested to the Council that SRHE should embark on a research project on validation, aimed at producing a book which would contain both an outline of the structures of validation — administrative, external academic, professional, internal academic — and some analysis of the costs, criteria, conflicts and consequences of validation, whether for students or for staff.

The proposal was accepted by the Council in May 1978 and the group was established as a Steering Committee (later to become a Study Group) to oversee the project. The intention to launch such a project was publicized in the educational press that summer, eliciting a number of helpful comments and offers of assistance. In due course the Steering Committee agreed a list of contributors, drawn from those who had volunteered and from others, with known expertise in the field. In order to give the enquiry as wide a base as possible it was decided, perhaps unwisely, to entrust each area of interest to two writers working in collaboration, so that no chapter would be too tied to the experience of any one institution. It was also intended that those engaged on the first, more descriptive, sections would be able to circulate synopses of their papers by the end of November 1978. This was so that unnecessary overlaps and repetitions might be avoided when first drafts of all papers were circulated during 1979, prior to discussions amongst the contributors and other interested parties during the following winter. After such critical review it was planned to publish the volume as part of the new *SRHE Proceedings* series.

However, as was no doubt to have been expected, these plans proved too optimistic. Thus, it proved impossible to find people able to work on all the areas originally envisaged, particularly when attempts to obtain outside funding failed. Moreover, a disproportionate number of those who did get involved came from the universities and polytechnics, and although a wide spectrum of people from administrators, through educational research workers to practising academics was obtained, there was obviously a lack of familiarity with both the administrative and professional sides of validation. Some contributors also found it difficult, and in certain cases impossible, to find the time for research amongst many other commitments. Nonetheless, despite such problems a start was made. Questionnaires were drawn up and circulated, some visits were made and some synopses distributed.

Yet, by the spring of 1980, things had still not advanced greatly, so that an approach from the Foundation for the Study of Values in Higher Education, as it then was, offering to share in the organization of a conference on validation was extremely opportune and welcome. The Foundation, which was to be renamed the Higher Education Foundation after its subsequent merger with the Higher Education Group, is a charitable body supported by a large number of people interested in higher education, both inside and outside universities and colleges, from a position best described as 'Christian-compatible'. Its purpose is to analyse and understand the fundamental values and objectives of higher education, operating mainly through a series of small conferences or 'Consultations' on issues which cause current concern and spring from, or lead to, deeper value questions. It felt that validation fitted into this programme, offering a means of looking at the intellectual presuppositions of a crucial area of higher education and possibly also a means of arriving at both an agreed position and an agenda for future research into validation. Their offer to organize and help fund a consultation on validation, providing chairmen, extra speakers and participants, and also providing a transcript, was put to the SRHE contributors and then, following their consent, accepted with gratitude. The liaison with the Foundation, of course, added a new practical and philosophical dimension to the enquiry's basic concerns for the provision of basic information and its evaluation.

The actual consultation, bringing the two together, took place at the Froebel campus of the Roehampton Institute of Higher Education in July 1981. The efforts of Sinclair Goodlad of Imperial College, the Secretary of the Foundation, in organizing it, together with the financial and technical assistance of the St Luke's Trust, an anonymous Roman Catholic trust, and the Sony Corporation, who together provided the material means for holding and recording the discussions, must all be gratefully acknowledged. The discussions were based in part on a number of SRHE draft papers, circulated in advance, together with new contributions both written and verbal. From the former came papers by Alexander and Wormald, Billing (with West), Church and Murray, Harrison (with Evans), and Heywood (with Webb), together with invited notes on internal validation from Brian Gent of Leeds Polytechnic and thoughts on validation and objectivity from

Roy Niblett. A paper by Rox Cox on evaluation and its relationship to validation was tabled at the meeting.

The discussions, which were chaired throughout by Hugh Sockett of UEA, were divided into plenary sessions on the impacts, structures, functions and philosophical assumptions of validation on the one hand, and study groups which tried to clarify agreement and future options on the other. The former were led by Kevin Keohane, Neil Merritt, Jerry Ravetz and Ron Barnett respectively, while general focussing sessions were introduced by Tony Becher and David Edge. The working parties also reported their deliberations and the proceedings ended with a general review in which Hugh Sockett sought to sum up the debate as a whole. As his remarks were directed primarily to the philosophical and policy interests of the Foundation rather than to those of the SRHE project they have not been included here save in so far as they figure in Roy Niblett's afterthoughts. However, extracts of a subsequent version of Sockett's paper are to be found on pp. 28-31 of the *Higher Education Newsletter* 2 (December 1981). Similarly, although a transcript of the discussions was drawn up and circulated, it has not been possible to reproduce it here. Copies may be consulted on application to Sinclair Goodlad.

However, although the interests of the two parties did diverge somewhat, preventing a consensus about the present situation of validation and future policy thereon from emerging, it is perhaps worthwhile to indicate the main lines of the debate. These can best be described as a process of mutual, and often painful, education. The Foundation was reminded of the complex realities of validation — often unappreciated by many outside the public sector — in which values have to exist, realities documented in the pages that follow. The SRHE members were reminded of assumptions often overlooked in the hurly-burly of everyday educational life.

Thus, the consultation ranged somewhat wider than the present volume, seeing validation as a crucial mechanism not limited to higher education but visible in such things as the consumers' movement. While there was relative agreement on the value of existing validation practices as a means of defending academic standards, there was disagreement as to their wider implications. Some saw them as a *de haut en bas* imposition of uncertain and often dubious criteria, parallel to ministerial control in other countries, and posing a threat to academic freedom, institutional autonomy and general educational innovativeness. Though such criticisms were resisted where the CNAA was concerned, and the positive effects of its scrutiny urged, there was some common feeling that there was an element of mystification in validation, in so far as it rests on somewhat naive views of secular perfectability and an asymmetrical distribution of power. Yet while all would agree that further research was needed, for instance on validation by universities and professional bodies (which were not subject to much scrutiny at the consultation), not all were convinced that ways forward could be found either through such things as process consultation, dialogue style validation, and evaluation of teaching or by fundamentally rethinking the status of institutions in the public sector. Here it was suggested that the existing system of external validation was the product of rather special historical circumstances and might now have outlived its usefulness. Hence, it could give way to something more akin to simple licencing or accreditation. However, all participants agreed in wishing to see further investigation of case studies, criteria, alternative structures, comparative career patterns, rituals, the organization of validating bodies, and the philosophical questions raised by the whole exercise.

It is to be hoped that some of these gaps may be filled, at least in part, by the present volume, the publication of which owes much to the selfless generosity of the CNAA in making available an interest-free loan to the Publications Committee of SRHE. The help of Gerald Collier, who not merely advised so helpfully at all stages of writing but who also, with Sally Kington, laboured mightily in preparing the volume for the press, and all those who contributed to the project is also acknowledged with thanks. Some contributions of the volume obviously arise out of the consultation, notably that by Barnett and, to a lesser extent, that by Niblett. For the rest, the authors cover some of the ground etched out in the original project. This is true of the chapters on definitions and comparative aspects — although there is a great deal more to be said on both — on academic validation by CNAA and universities respectively, on professional involvement — which again takes up the question of values and rights — and on internal practices. Unfortunately, it has not been possible to cover the administrative mechanisms of course approval, which remain significant even though rendered nugatory by recent government fiscal policy; on the impact of validation on academics; on the systematic comparison of CNAA and university validation and the criteria they use; and, most ironically, on the conflicts of validation. Where the analytical aspect of the original proposal is concerned, the impact of validation on students and teacher education has been covered, along with questions of costs and the issues raised by practices of validation. Finally, the whole scene is brought into focus by Roy Niblett.

Despite the gaps the work, as it stands, does provide more basic information than has been available heretofore on what validation means, on what structures it works through, on what effects it has and on what issues it raises. In other words the book offers some insight into the setting and meaning of four major areas of validation practice and into that of as many important perspectives. In both sections however, the stress is as much on the questions arising and the queries which need to be resolved about validation and its place in higher education, as on mere description. Perhaps this as well, if it is true that the British are essentially pragmatic, preferring to avoid reflection wherever possible. The ultimate aim of both consultation and study group has been to make people reflect on what they are doing in validation since such reflection is doubly necessary in the uncertain times in which we live. It will all have served its purpose if it succeeds in raising as many questions as it answers, and especially if it pulls practice into perspective.

To put it another way, *Practice and Perspective* is not so much the end report originally intended, but more of a beginning. So, if it is outdated and rebutted by responses, then it will have served its purpose, particularly if such rebuttal is based on the depth of empirical enquiry which is so urgently needed. At least the issues raised by British validation practices have been fairly and seriously posed. It is to be hoped that the future will see them answered more completely, and in a more considered way, than has so far been the case thanks to the plethora of polemic and prejudice which surrounded the subject in the seventies.


Clive H. Church
Editor

# 1  OF DEFINITIONS, DEBATES AND DIMENSIONS

*Clive H. Church and Robert Murray*

For many people working in higher education 'validation' is a well understood practice which has recently become part of daily life. Yet, for equally as many others, it is a word which either signifies nothing concrete or, more rarely, something more methodological, a theoretical concern involved in educational research in general, not just at the tertiary level. Indeed when used in relation to tickets on British Rail the word has been described as an example of official obfuscation by supporters of good English. Although this book is devoted to the meaning and practice of validation as understood by the first school of thought, the fact that it can be so unfamiliar, or so differently understood, by some people demands that the emergence and context of the new practical understanding of validation be made clear at the outset. To do this and, it is to be hoped, eliminate one kind of misunderstanding, is the purpose of the present chapter. However, before even this can be essayed some kind of working definition of what validation has come to involve in practice is necessary.

Validation can be defined as the consideration of a course of study which leads up to and includes the decision on its approval or re-approval. To be more explicit, as the term is commonly used, 'validation' means the process of scrutinizing a proposed degree scheme, and of deciding whether or not it should be approved as being of an appropriate standard for the award to which it is intended to lead and, if this proves to be the case, of then specifying the conditions which must be fulfilled if the course is actually to run. Some argue that there is a legal and substantive difference between the examination of a proposal in order to determine whether its implementation would result in an acceptable course and the actual act of approval (Newcastle 1980). However, most usages seem to embrace the two.

It should also be noted that the process is, to a large extent, carried out prior to the running or re-running of a course, and whether validation signifies that proclaimed objectives have been met is open to question. It has been said that validation does not and can not be based on proclaimed objectives being met. Its objectives can be examined and the likelihood of the course achieving those objectives can be discussed but the discussion must by its very nature be based on inspired (or uninspired) conjecture — furthermore, the way the documentation is presented makes it difficult to discuss and judge whether the course will meet its proclaimed objectives, since the course is not described in the documents as a learning process. It could be argued that CNAA initial validation is the beginning of a process that includes external examiners and renewal of approval and, more recently, review visits. This is nice in theory but does the process really explore if those subjected to the course have reached the objectives of the course? However, all such problems of definition and feasibility will be examined later. For the moment the basic idea of validation as a process of scrutinizing and approving degree schemes in higher education can serve.

Validation in this sense became a familiar word in the early nineteen seventies (Davis 1980). It was soon seen as a key concept and practice, almost inseparable from much thinking about some parts of higher education. Indeed, it is perhaps not an exaggeration to say that validation became the central focus for the organization and identity of the developing public sector of academic higher education in Britain. Validation became virtually a way of life.

AIMS AND OBSTACLES
There is today resistance to criticism of validation in some quarters. However, since it is now so widely used and well established those who believe in the process ought to welcome a critical analysis of validation, not least because the rhetoric surrounding validation has gone well beyond the facts. Because this happened validators have been placed in an unnecessarily exposed position. Some thought about what it all means and why it has come about should help to shed light on a valued and valuable practice in higher education.

Indeed, for all the ink and effort devoted to the term, its meaning has rarely been probed or studied. In good empirical English academic fashion, the job has been done without a great deal of theoretical consideration, let alone much research. And although some of these omissions are remedied in the chapters which follow, it would not be right to plunge straight into the labyrinth of structures and values which have resulted from validation. It is worthwhile taking a preliminary tour through the semantic and comparative bunkers into which protagonists in the 'Great Game of Validation' have so often strayed.

There has indeed been a good deal of discussion of the subject. This has indicated the rudiments of a definition of validation, but we can best hope to place the later chapters in context by exploring these problems of definition and debate, and setting them in the context from which they emerged. The concern is as much, if not more, with what has been said about validation as with what actually happens when validation takes place. But even such conceptual or rhetorical discussion raises questions and issues of relevance to practice which need to be answered. By thus listing the things whch really need to be remembered in any conceptual analysis of validation, whether semantic, historical, or comparative, attention can be directed away from empty claims towards more profitable research into the realities of validation.

The aim of this chapter then, is to provide a background to the rest of the book by sketching in the things whch have been so often omitted from the debate on validation. Perhaps the key element here is the foreign dimension, since validation has been treated in an extremely insular as well as in an empirical way. Furthermore there is a need to touch on some aspects of the world of validation which it has not been possible to cover by separate chapters, for instance the administrative underpinnings. In a word, there is a need to situate validation in its specific historical and geographical context, and this is something which requires both analysis and comparison.

The starting point for all this must of course be the emergence of a specific concept of validation and the way in which this has so far been debated in British higher education (Church 1976). This debate has been an undistinguished one, orientated by hidden issues, unsubstantiated by research, over concentrated on limited aspects of the work of the Council for National Academic Awards, and oblivious both of parallel developments, and, particularly, of the precise historical time and climate in which the concept evolved.

Validation acquired its new meaning in the vocabulary of higher education some ten years ago. It originated as a practice a little earlier. It was the creation of the National Council for Technological Awards in 1955 which first set up a public body with the task of ensuring that courses mounted by new institutions were comparable to those in universities and other established institutions, so that the public could have equal confidence in them (Davis 1980b). After the Robbins *Report* (1963), with its argument that 'in any properly co-ordinated system of higher education the academic grading of individuals should be dependent on their academic accomplishments rather than upon the status of the institution in which they have studied', this role was passed on to the Council for National Academic Awards. Its task was to raise standards in extra mural institutions, some of which might ultimately become universities. In the early days this meant that major stress was laid on conformity to existing models. Much also depended on the empirical development of expertise in course scrutiny. The pragmatism of the process perhaps explains why the term 'course approval' was then used as a description.

Validation as a term first seems to have been used after, and probably because of, the James *Report* (1972) which mentions the willingness of the University of Wales to 'validate' the Dip.H.E. in the Principality. Since then the rise of the term has been meteoric. By the end of 1972 the White Paper was confidently talking about validation and the habit spread like wildfire in the public sector, even though some CNAA officers still prefer to avoid it and there is some evidence that the DES has dropped the word from its list of approved terms. This sudden explosion was not just because validation was a nice sounding word. It was because the concept filled a vacuum; it provided a term to describe the burgeoning role of the CNAA and the problems of status and role change faced by the old colleges of education as they diversified (CNAA 1977). The desire of many other institutions to escape from what they perceived as the straight-jacket of external degrees of the University of London went hand in hand with diversification. To gain validation was proof of successful institutional adaptation and survival.

And, since the Charter precludes the devolution of actual approval to institutions, the re-emerging desire for autonomy was conveniently handled under the concept of 'Partnership in Validation', that is to say the evolution of appropriate structures and procedures for the devolution of responsibilty for course approval which has much concerned both institutions and Council throughout the second half of the seventies. Although the result was new proposals in 1979 for a greater emphasis on assessment of institutions and greater power sharing in the process of course validation, it is not clear that operation of these has resolved the matter (CNAA 1979). Validation is therefore likely to remain a central concern of the public sector, at least in the near future. The desire of the DES to relinquish the recognition of language schools in favour of the British Council and the feeling that changes are needed in the way private further education and even Correspondence Colleges are scrutinized also points in this direction.

THE DANGER OF DEBATE

Over the last ten years the practice, if not the concept, of validation has been much debated. The debate began a year after the term was first used, in connection with the fate of the colleges of education, and the question of whether their diversified degrees should be awarded by the CNAA or the universities. Charges of lack of standards, rigour, and seriousness were flung out broadcast in the course of this. Universities in particular were accused — and doubtless not always without justice — of passing un-thought-out schemes without real inspection and subject to no time limit. This phase of the debate petered out inconclusively about 1975, when economic and other pressures had forced many universities to withdraw from external validation, often without reluctance. By then too, the CNAA had settled down and had absorbed responsibility for an increasing number of colleges so that attention focussed on the way in which it and better established colleges reacted to newcomers. There were those outside who complained of the Council's imperialistic ambition to corner the public sector higher education market. And those inside began to argue that it was institutions rather than courses which counted, and that those institutions deserved greater status and respect. It was this feeling, especially amongst polytechnic administrators and those who, like the Association of Polytechnic Teachers, shared the directorates' status anxieties, that helped to start the 'Partnership in Validation' discussions.

There continued to be some use of earlier themes, such as the way that 'CNAA scrutiny of all degree courses is a guarantee that they are academically sound, thoroughly prepared, and of a comparable standard to university degree courses' (Gold 1979), but these were now used less to attack universities than to defend CNAA against attacks on two fronts. Firstly, such attacks came from those who complained that the public sector offered silly subjects, provided poor facilities or taught essentially university reject students. Secondly, and more significantly, they came from inside the public sector where the size and demands of the CNAA began to seem a burden, especially in an age of recession, by when institutions had, in any case, produced parallel internal validating systems. Concern over bureaucratization began to emerge along with the suggestion that validation did as much to inhibit as it did to encourage innovation. Where once there had been talk of the CNAA insisting on traditional patterns for degrees, an exponentially increasing number of schemes — often of new styles — were then gaining approval.

This prompted a concern about administrative overload which was probably intensified by early experiences with the 'Partnership in Validation' proposals. These did not always produce the hoped for simplifications and decentralization. Often, some claimed, it led to the imposition of new layers of activity between teaching and course approval, and made internal planning and management of institutions more difficult than before. Yet, apparently oblivious of all this, there now seems to be a new twist in the debate: universities and colleges savaged by the UGC and internal committees of enquiry, which seem to proceed on no clear or public criteria, have begun to ask whether the creation of something like the CNAA, which operates openly and on the basis of peer review by acknowledged experts, might not be a way of preserving their strengths (Crequier 1982). Indeed, not merely has it been noted that the University of California uses programme evaluation to determine who should lose tenure or office as universities contract there, but Chelsea College has already created its own validation panel to answer the critiques of Swinnerton-Dyer's committee report. The determination of the Thatcher government to reduce the total number of places in higher education has exposed a hitherto hidden problem associated with validation: can validation be used to rank courses or can it (and should it) only make the gross distinction that course $x$ is comparable in standard to similar schemes?

The fact that the idea of validation, if not actually the term itself, can be produced like a rabbit out of a hat with no apparent awareness of what has been said previously about the problems of the process is typical of the weaknesses of the debate. For although a great deal of heat and energy have been generated by the debate, the latter has been blinkered, superficial, and not addressed to the real issues. This does not necessarily imply that the practice of validation suffered from the same faults. Rhetoric and reality rarely coincide. But, since so many people in the debate see the rhetoric as reality, one has to start here.

To begin with, the debate has been semantically confused. The word obviously lacks precise definition. Hence what was supposed to be a debate about validation often turned out to be about something else. A second point, and this is perhaps more important, the debate lacks any historical dimension. Not merely has it ignored most precedents for validation, whether in previous generations, or more recently, but it has ignored the setting of the debate. Validation has not been conceived as the product of a precise and changing educational situation.

This is particularly surprising when one considers that the third weakness of the debate has been its over-concentration on the CNAA. This is itself a major product of the historical configuration in question. People seem to have ignored not merely the importance of the state administrative side of validation, through the Regional Advisory Councils for example, but also the fact that validation-like activities are not confined to the down market end of the Gray's Inn Road world. There may not be so much activity as at the CNAA, and it may be no better, but it does happen elsewhere.

Thus not merely do universities validate but so do other bodies such as the Technician Education Council (TEC) and Business Education Council (BEC) and the professions. The National Council for Drama Training of 1976 is one of the latest recruits to a panoply of bodies who influence, direct and approve courses in higher education. The Central Council for the Education and Training of Social Workers and the Royal Town Planning Institution have enjoyed, if that is the right word, relationships with institutions and courses very similar to those between CNAA and public sector colleges. Mention could also be made of the General Optical Council and the General Nursing Council in this context. Even the Historical Association now uses the term to describe its relation to refresher courses it sponsors at various public sector colleges. And such relationships do not exist in vacuo. They can often make difficult and conflicting demands on institutions who may have to deal with a plethora of such bodies.

Fourthly, the debate has too often ignored the informal side of validation. Little attention has been paid to the social role it fills. Nor have the vested interests it has created once it became a continuing reality been openly admitted. Furthermore, the methodological, philosophical and political issues the practice poses need examination.

Fifthly, it has been an immensely insular debate in a second sense. It has wholly ignored the fact that other countries have evolved similar mechanisms for such purposes. Perhaps less importantly, it has been carried on in cheerful unawareness of the fact that it is really part of a much wider debate on the role and nature of evaluation throughout higher education, evaluation including, of course, exams. Sixthly, and lastly, there has been virtually no research on the realities of validation. Its effects on courses, its role as a means of accountability, and its objectivity, have never been seriously examined. Too often the beneficial effects of validation have been taken on faith. Rhetoric has been no friend to the strengths of validation, any more than it has been to its weaknesses.

To try and remedy this, and to put validation more concretely into a context where it will be better understood, both by those for whom it is a way of life, and by those who may be quite unacquainted with the way the term is now used in the United Kingdom, is the purpose of the rest of this paper. Three aspects of validation are especially concentrated upon: the conceptual problem, the historical dimension and particularly the comparative aspect. It is to be hoped that this will help to show that validation is not something which can just be done without being thought about. In fact, although the process is trans-national, the sudden emergence of the practice in this country is historically and structurally specific. Failure to realize this robs much discussion about validation of any real value. A revised definition is therefore called for.

## SEMANTICS

Although the current attitude seems to be 'never mind the semantics just feel the documentation', there are at least three obstacles to a proper understanding of validation. Firstly, 'validating' has a perfectly clear and well-known meaning in educational research and other areas, as reference to any reputable dictionary of education published before 1980 will show. It there means testing the results from experimental enquiry so as to establish their reliability, usually in a mathematical sense. The same kind of process can be found in philosophical argumentation. This is the meaning one finds in ordinary dictionaries too (OED 1933). 'Valid' is 'the quality of being well founded and applicable to the case or circumstance: it can also be used to denote soundness and strength of argument, proof of authority, etc.' The term 'validation' has affinities with the OED definition of 'valid', something which has been validated is valid because it does, on inspection, have the quality of being well founded and applicable to the circumstances.

One can see how this is immediately relevant to detailed or statistical educational or philosophical argumentation. There is something of a case for it being partly relevant to course submission and approval as well. Yet there are a number of problems which make this the second obstacle. To begin with, the CNAA Charter nowhere mentions the term, following the Robbins *Report* in talking about 'approval of courses of study'. Hence, in part, the recent attempt to discriminate between approval, registration, and validation. Moreover, a reading of some current documentation quickly reveals that these key words, not to mention 'accreditation', 'analysis', 'assessment', 'evaluation', 'monitoring', 'review' and 'vetting', are rarely clearly defined. Indeed at times they appear to be used quite interchangeably and indiscriminately. Some people have tried to discriminate between validation, whereby whole courses are individually scrutinized, approval, where only outlines are submitted, and registration, where the only control is by examiners, but there are no agreed usages. Hence, the education correspondent of *The Times* recently added insult to injury by claiming that validation was the new jargon word for 'allowing for inflation that is higher than suspected' (Geddes 1981).

The lack of clarity and conviction in public sector usage is also demonstrated by the fact that other organizations use different terms to describe much the same process. The National Council for Drama Training, like the Institute of Chartered Accountants in England and Wales, describes the course approval process as accreditation. This, apparently, was at the suggestion of the DES (Barnes 1980). In Australia the term registration is sometimes used, while in British Columbia the preferred term is 'articulation'. However, accreditation is the term most frequently used in similar contexts. There has been a great deal of discussion about accreditation which many interested parties like the Committee of Polytechnic Directors see as an alternative, which they would like to replace validation in order to boost their status, autonomy, and integrity (Tolley 1974). However as might be expected, this pressure is not based on a sound knowledge of accreditation, as will be shown later. For though accreditation usually results in the approval of an institution, this approval can be reached by a process very close to course validation, and can often impose the same costs and strains as CNAA validation. Here again the semantics are confused, even if the political imperatives are clear.

Even if one overlooks this and accepts validation as the scrutiny of proposals, the concept itself is not a simple one, hence the third bunker. The concept operates on at least three levels of meaning (Church 1977). Firstly, it implies concern for resources and organization. Secondly, it presupposes a scrutiny which ensures that proposals are in line with prevailing norms or assumptions, and thirdly, it implies an underwriting of the end product of the course in question. It is rarely clear which, if any, of these facets is being referred to when the term is so loosely used. All this is not to suggest that there is one 'proper' meaning of validation, only that the meaning given to the term must always be considered. As it has rarely been thought out it can often have very diverse meanings, and there is no compelling reason as to why it was, or should be used.

This must surely indicate that the term emerged to fill a particular role in a specific situation. It also no doubt explains why, although one foreign observer can say that the practice is an essential part of the 'university tradition' in British higher education, the debate has also been carried on with virtually no reference to earlier practices, and indeed largely without any historical dimension at all (Jones 1978). The process was implicit in the ideas of Mark Pattison and others who thought about the organization of the early provincial universities, underlay the first university dealings with Training Colleges and was present in the work of HM Inspectors (HMIs) who advised the Treasury when the first government grants to universities were made. And, if the role of the University of London as a sponsoring body for the University Colleges of the inter-war years was a little different, the initial sponsorship of the University College of North Staffordshire was not. Even more relevant was the way the National Certificate systems worked for advanced but non-degree vocational qualifications, from the nineteen twenties onward. There are also some precedents in secondary education, such as the Mode 3 Certificate of Secondary Education (CSE) examinations.

Then in 1955, when industrial demand for more technological and other graduates was not being met by the universities, the NCTA was set up. This was founded as an 'independent and self-governing body to create and administer technological awards having a national currency' (Davis 1980b). It operated in what was, for higher education, a somewhat new way. It did not act as an examining body supervising syllabuses and setting examinations. Instead it let colleges construct courses and conduct examinations, but only after an extremely rigorous scrutiny of the colleges and their proposals. Much was inherited from the NCTA by the CNAA in terms of personnel and practices, even though it had previously been applied to a narrower spectrum of disciplines. The roots of the CNAA and its validating systems are therefore much deeper and more orthodox than some of its proponents have wished to claim. However, to be fair, the CNAA itself in its documents has always recognized that it built on foundations laid by NCTA.

## THE HISTORICAL IMPERATIVE

If a practice which was not unknown before has thus been given a new name the reason lies in another aspect of history. The debate has often treated validation, as has already been suggested, as something abstract, divorced from normal constraints of time and space. The impression is given that it 'just happened' to be conveniently available when the polytechnics emerged. The relationship with the actual development of British higher education is in fact far closer than this. Any discussion of validation such as that at the recent consultation makes it blindingly clear how much the development of validation was historically contingent and conditioned. This does not mean that validation has no relevance or value outside the context which gave it birth. It does mean, however, that its actual role cannot be fully understood without reference to the historical situation.

In fact although the growth of a public sector was encouraged by Robbins and particularly by Anthony Crosland when Minister of Education, no thought was given to the internal cohesiveness and self-respect of the public sector. Robbins saw colleges pulling themselves into the University sector by their own bootstraps, a kind of acquisitive individualism amongst institutions. Crosland, on the other hand, believed in a public sector in which service to society provided equivalent motivation and satisfaction. In practice the two not merely proved uneasy bedfellows, but both isolated new institutions. Promotion was not welcomed by those above and society was less hospitable than might have been hoped.

The CNAA offered reassurance and community to teachers in new institutions. Although its value was usually seen as reassuring the public about the value of their degrees, it seems likely that it was as much the teaching staff who needed convincing that what they were doing was right and acceptable. They, after all, were products of an extremely hierarchical educational system and, not surprisingly, they had internalized its pervasive elitism. That about half the members of the CNAA boards came from the universities ensured that the chain of authority was securely maintained: once approved by a professor you knew where you stood.

CNAA validation therefore came to serve as the thing which unified and differentiated the public sector. It served as much as a means of fostering self-confident adaptation to new circumstances as it did as a means of quality control. In this it may not have had the support of the universities as a whole but it was critically important that it enlisted the enthusiasm of many respected university academics. Since no overall plan or system of control was laid down by state or society, the CNAA came to fill the role. It provided a forum, a means of development and, increasingly, a pressure group in academic politics which had a vested interest in the expansion of public sector higher education. This was, and still is, immensely praiseworthy. The trouble is that, as is the way with all institutions, validation could become an all absorbing operation. Teachers could, in a paradoxical way, become isolated from their subject colleagues in universities because of the way they had to concentrate their energies on the processes of approval and monitoring rather than on the actual pursuit of the subject itself.

As the progress of the debate shows, once the public sector had been converted and rightly encouraged to stand on its own feet, the situation changed. Moreover, whereas the CNAA started out life in a period of relative prosperity and optimism, as part of the triumphalist rationalism of the white hot technological revolution and with easy access to funds, it now faces a period of decline (Lane 1975). Many of the assumptions which guide it are dependent on expansion, and this is presently not feasible. The recession and the rise of more directive governments have changed the rules of the game. Unless we widen our vision to take in these facts much discussion of validation will be little more than blinkered verbiage. The hermeneutics of validation, as examination of its role as a form of accountability has shown, are not what the debate might lead us to expect (Church 1981).

THE WIDER PERSPECTIVE

This lack of historical perspective, like the semantic confusion, help to explain the third weakness of the debate, the way it has concentrated on the CNAA, to the exclusion of the wider spectrum of validation. This is not to suggest that the CNAA is either unworthy or unimportant, simply that it is in practice, if not in rhetoric, only a piece in the puzzle. To begin with, the debate has focussed largely on external forms of validation. This obviously has implications for what happens inside institutions, but the extent to which validation-like activities are carried out inside institutions, even those in the public sector, has rarely been given the attention it deserves. Every institution, in fact, goes through some process of ratiocination in deciding what courses to put on and whether they are working satisfactorily or not. Questions of enrolment, wastage, and external examiners' reports will usually figure in the making of decisions.

Increasingly such procedures have become formalized either because of the growing stress on evaluation in higher education or, as in the public sector, because of the twin demands of accountability and the CNAA. The latter, particularly since the adoption of the 'Partnership in Validation' proposals, tends to require that there should have been an internal validation of any schemes which are submitted to it (CNAA 1979). The working of such internal practices has not really been investigated. It is well known that internal validation and the academic monitoring of courses took place before *Partnership in Validation* but one suspects that it was at very different levels of sophistication across public sector higher education. There does seem to be some evidence that over-dependence on external validation was a positive disincentive to rigorous internal validation. It has been suggested that the latter can concentrate on things for which internal authority is available like resources, admissions, assessment and staff student ratios, rather than academic matters. And, since there is often not enough subject expertise apart from those people involved in mounting the course it has been argued that internal scrutiny must always be deficient so that in the end external validation is essential. Yet even this may not work, unless the values from outside can be internalized.

Whatever the truth of this, it is certainly the case that validation cannot be considered as an external factor alone. Attention, and indeed, research needs to be directed to the way in which course control procedures operate internally: how ideas are devised, developed, resourced and assessed, and on what grounds and values this is done. Similarly the way courses are monitored needs to be considered. Unless we are aware of the internal forces at work, estimates of the efficacy of external validation cannot be realistically made.

Talk of external validation, whether via the CNAA or universities, can often also overlook the fact that they are only one part of the course control system. Most academic validating bodies in the public sector of this country do not have the authority to authorize the launching of a course, only to approve its content. The actual decision to launch a course, involving as it does resource questions, is an administrative act. This is not the situation in the universities although the UGC is now seeking to circumscribe their freedom of action in this field. And although the procedures in the public sector have effectively been frozen by recent government policy in

principle they still exist and need to be remembered. The separation of
resource and academic questions is a fundamental characteristic of the
British way of validation.

The administrative approvals system varies as between England, Wales
and Scotland. In the first, assuming that permission had been granted by
the funding body, whether LEA, Church or government, proposals must be
directed to one of nine Regional Advisory Councils set up in 1947 after
earlier experiments in Yorkshire and the Midlands (Cantor 1979). In Wales
the same role is filled by the Welsh Joint Education Committee. The
Councils, which have a small staff and a council consisting of representatives
of administration, colleges themselves, universities and others have to
address themselves to the question of whether there is a need in the region for
a course of the type proposed. If the need is conceded then the proposals
will be forwarded to the DES who will act on the advice of the Council
and the Regional Staff Inspector. In Scotland the two stages are both
handled by the Scottish Education Department. It is rare for the
Departments to overrule the RAC although the decisions of the latter have
been said to be based on the self interest of existing colleges rather than
on any objective assessment of demand or need.

As a result, it has been argued that the system fails either to exercise
real control or to promote innovation. Need, it has been claimed, is never
satisfactorily elucidated. Nor does the practice encourage institutions to
devise radically new schemes of study. Perhaps because of this, whereas
in the sixties governments tended to urge RACs to take a more active
and positive role, the tendency of late has been to circumscribe their
actions so that only in very special cases, like microprocessing, can any
courses at all be approved. Nonetheless, as in the France of the *ancien
régime*, the fact that the Councils' functions have atrophied has not led to
their being wound up even with the issuing of Circular 1/82 and the coming
of the National Advisory Body and its legions. They therefore remain as
a constraint in the validation process, at least in the public sector.

The Councils used to deal, of course, not only with colleges validated
by CNAA but also with those related to universities and other academic
agencies. Institutions themselves also have to look to a wider range of
bodies with power over their courses whether at higher or further education
level. The university role in all this is discussed elsewhere in the book but
again needs to be remembered. It offers an alternative way of validation
to that of the CNAA, in which academic grounds tend to be the starting
point rather than resources. Here again, in practice at least, it is not a
question of better or worse, but of simple difference, and difference arising
from varied circumstances at that. Yet perhaps even less visible and less
discussed in the debate has been the role of other such bodies like TEC
and BEC. They have played a large role in developing new courses
at sub-degree level and in so doing have used evaluators rather in the
same way that universities have used assessors. Such alternative modes

have never been seriously examined, although they are of interest in themselves as well as counting for a lot in the impact of validation at the institutional level, as will be seen.

Yet the fact that the debate has so ignored the existence of so much validation by professional bodies is strange. As Heywood demonstrates in Chapter 4, they deserve a great deal of attention, for they too have evolved ways of proceeding which are parallel to those of the CNAA, and ways which affect universities as well as public sector institutions. They also pose somewhat different issues. This is not to suggest that all professional bodies are the same (Perkin 1981). Some like the General Medical Council are basically registration or accreditation bodies, in so far as they recognize the graduates of particular medical schools on general grounds, and do not interfere with syllabi (Council 1977). Others like the Central Council for the Education and Training of Social Workers (CCETSW) and the Institute of Chartered Accountants of England and Wales (ICAEW) take a great deal of interest in what goes into college courses and will withdraw approval in cases where their conditions or standards are not met (CCETSW 1977).

Recent conflicts over admissions policy such as the Vyas case at North East London Polytechnic show the potential strength of such professional bodies. The fear of not meeting the requirements of the British Psychological Society or the Council on Legal Education has dominated many curriculum discussions in universities and polytechnics. To some extent academic traditionalism may take refuge behind such external constraints, but it is true, especially where there are professional examinations which have to be taken before progress in professional careers is possible, that the need for exemption to be secured by undergraduate courses is a very pressing one. Even where professions show a willingness to let higher education provide the educational facilities which used to be provided by specialist training schools or even in house, they rarely surrender all their influence. This has probably been both overlooked and underestimated. It really is urgent that some comparative study be done on the extent to which various course approval bodies are more or less directive, more or less encourage innovation, more or less obscurantist. A sophisticated analysis of these bodies in the theoretical context of social reproduction would, one can confidently predict, be extremely revealing.

The issues professional control poses are manifold. Obviously in the case of things like architecture, dentistry or medicine society must know that those who graduate in such fields have basic skills, and that their buildings will not fall down or that they can manipulate a dental drill safely. Yet beyond this point, and certainly in the sub-professions or where skills are judgemental and not manual as they are, for instance, in social work, there is a question about the way professions use educational influence and authority to defend their social position. Validation here can serve as a gatekeeper for access to social status and relative influence, often underwritten and financed by the state of course. This is rather less obviously the case in more academic areas, but the logic of validation as a means of underwriting social status needs to be remembered.

When the chips are down it is, of course, the professional bodies who have the upper hand. There are cases in which CNAA Boards have approved courses only to find them peremptorily rejected by a professional body. Such conflicts do not exist in secondary education where the academic validating bodies are themselves the professional credentialling agencies. However, there are conflicts between academic and professional visions inside both CNAA and other validating bodies. The most corrosive effects of conflicting ideals, powers and demands tend to come within institutions which can find themselves facing a variety of often mutually exclusive requirements from different validating bodies. The debate, by regarding things so much in the abstract, tends to overlook these harsh realities in its enconiums of the value of external validation.

INFORMAL NORMS
This is characteristic of the way the informal role of validation, already hinted at here, has been neglected in general terms. To borrow Becher and Kogan's (1980) happy distinction, the debate has concentrated on the operational mode at the expense of the normative. In fact validation has a very obvious social role in general terms, and also functions significantly in a similar way at a more personal level. Both roles throw up a lot of issues which affect the actual functioning of the process. While validation, to begin with, has been described as if it were a form of disembodied quality control, it has often really been a major influence on the resource and general management of institutions, altering internal balances on the one hand, and changing the distribution of courses between colleges on the other. And, while it was never designed as a policy instrument, it seems clear that at some times, for instance during the 'diversification' period it has been used as such, so that the CNAA was allowed to squeeze colleges which the DES was unwilling or unable to control.

Latterly, with the decline of reliance on demand as a criterion for course provision, validation has been called in to fill the breach. Since institutions can informally manipulate rather than merely follow the CNAA, which has a fund of fellow feeling for its member institutions, and can be used to create policy or at least attempt to create policy in the way in which in earlier days it could create resources. Public sector validation therefore has a social, not to say political, function which is not always realized. It would be instructive to trace the development of the CNAA Academic Policy Committee and the withering away of opposition to the idea that the CNAA had a legitimate role as the spokesman for public sector higher education vis-à-vis the Government and the DES. The CNAA did not have this role exactly thrust upon it, but it did seem to be generally recognized there was no one else to speak for the interested parties (polytechnic and non-polytechnic) in public sector higher education.

A second and related facet of the informal functioning of validation is the effect it has had on the balance of power and careers in the public sector. On the one hand, the existence of the CNAA, and particularly of its subject boards, has provided a defence for academic interests against what they see as the depredations of technologically inclined top management. The demands of CNAA have to be met if anything is to happen in that area, whether or not it fits in with general plans or aims. And since decisions are made by subject specialists these are likely to be more favourable to the area in question than might otherwise be the case. The reaction to the initial proposals on 'Partnership in Validation' was an eloquent testimony to the extent to which CNAA subject boards were prized by teachers in the public sector, not merely as a forum for disciplinary discussion or a source of advice, but as a political defence (CNAA 1975). Of course, subject boards enjoy their power and, even now, some are very reluctant to see their share in validation whittled down to the benefit of arrangements between the Council itself and institutions.

To some extent the reason for this is a genuine belief in the importance of the subject area in question. But, on the other hand, there are other sides to the phenomenon. Firstly, the CNAA can be a source of personal advantage. For those inside institutions this can mean trips to Gray's Inn Road and a useful source of contacts. For some, moreover, it can mean access to CNAA boards themselves which can offer entrée to a potentially vast network of information and influence. A large amount of informal consultation goes on and participation in this can give members influence and prominence and, perhaps, an inflated sense of self-importance. On the other hand, it can give to those who seldom experience it the satisfaction of successful and creative consultancy. This can change their real position inside institutional hierarchies, raising up the humble and threatening the mighty in their seats. Internal discipline can therefore be subverted by such 'gatekeepers', as Alexander and Wormald call them later in this work. Secondly, as well as the influence which can increase if one gets into the inner circles involved, access to the CNAA can offer both a boost to one's standards of living while on visitations and a chance of supplementing one's income through access to publications, consultancies, and especially, external examining, which is markedly better paid in the public than in the university sector. Finally, success in steering courses through the CNAA, in making a name on a subject board, and in other ways advancing one's career, can lead to movement and promotion. Colleges are keen to have those experienced in 'submissionsmanship' as their course leaders, deans or assistant directors. Such members indeed seem to have a much greater buying power than the permanent officers of the Council.

Validation then cannot, by any means, be said to be an abstract activity. And obviously it is hardly value free in intellectual terms either. It is ultimately a charge on the public purse and not a costless exercise. Similarly it also has an influence in social, political and personal terms. The inquisitorial mode, of which people often complain, can be explained in structural as well as academic terms. It has also been said to rest on a particular, and slightly mechanical, view of the curriculum. While ostensibly embracing the primacy of the academic subject, it actually forces the latter to conform to a rather mechanistic paradigm. It is assumed that courses can be understood in terms of precise aims and objectives and that certain structures will end in certain outcomes. The actual uncertainties of teaching and learning can easily be overlooked. As in many other things the model betrays the time of its creation. Consideration of the norms and values implicit in validation, together with their academic power as well as their social influence, need to be remembered when thinking about validation in practice.

## ISLAND APPROACHES

Things like this would have been more obvious had the debate not been so insular. It was insular both in the way it overlooked the existence of similar practices elsewhere in British life, like the jury system, the functioning of the Burnham Committee and particularly the other educational parallels and precedents. It was also insular in not merely being excessively empirical but also totally restricted to Britain. Roy Niblett (1981) has argued that validation is really a two stage process of approval and determination. Attention has usually focussed on the former of late, whereas previously it had been on the latter, with exams for instance. Others have argued that validation in fact implies that courses have achieved their objectives and never really proves that this is so. It can therefore be seen basically as a form of accreditation, if that means approving an institution rather than monitoring a course.

Certainly, there needs to be consideration of both input and output if validation is to be convincing. The role of external examiners also needs more scrutiny. However, even the input/output models can be dangerous in themselves. This is because they divert attention away from what happens to students as they negotiate the course. Input/output models are a convenient way to guarantee that the often bogus 'imperatives' of the discipline are preserved at the expense of the development of genuine knowledge and understanding.

Given the implicit appeal to objectives it is doubly strange that the debate on validation should have so neglected the growing stress on evaluation in educational research. The development of the social sciences, the need for accountability in the ever expanding educational world, and the need to test the claims and responsibilities of education have led to a great growth in the amount of evaluation which has been directed at education. In America this has become a veritable state supported industry —albeit sometimes dominated by professionals — whereas in Britain it has often suffered in public expenditure cuts so that it is more of a professional activity.

Perhaps the institution in Britain which is doing the most intensive evaluation of what it teaches is the Open University. It has a budget for evaluation of approximately £500,000 per annum. The Open University started off attempting quantitative systems based analysis but now has moved to qualitative illuminative analysis. The Open University must for a number of reasons engage in evaluation at a number of different levels, e.g. course design, course delivery, student response, tutor perception and marking standard. But however financed, evaluation has been a movement for the study and measurement of change in education, for assessing how far objectives have been met. And although there are a variety of approaches and not a few technical problems in some of these, the attempt to regularize measurement is a laudable one always providing that such quantification does not become a mere disguise for ideology. The attempt to standardize measurement is not laudable if what it proposes to measure can only be measured through a grossly distorting reductionism.

Cox (1981) has, moreover, argued that not merely should the whole movement for evaluation be an inspiration to validation but that specific types of evaluation have precise lessons to offer. Illuminative evaluation with its preferences for description and interpretation rather than measurement and prediction offers many insights. Notably these are the need for sensitivity to, and familiarity with, the wide environment of the thing under scrutiny, and the necessity for participation by those evaluated if the process is to be accepted. Since much validation is really just one variant of peer group or professional evaluation, these insights could well be useful to help eliminate some of the obvious weaknesses of such an in house system. It is regrettable that disciplinary and administrative boundaries have so far apparently prevented this.

## FOREIGN HORIZONS

The motivation for the spread of evaluation can also be seen in the development of similar practices to validation in other parts of the world. Generally speaking the expansion of higher education in the post-war world has meant that the state has become increasingly concerned not just with its cost but also with its content. The thing has become too big to be left to the professionals. Obviously the precise motivation varies from country to country. In France *habilitation* seems to have been brought in to try and curb graduate unemployment and the political and social anomie this was creating in the ranks of the relatively unfavoured university students, by reshaping output to meet social needs. In New Zealand the motivation was much more straightforwardly financial, as the UGC there intervened on fiscal grounds to limit the development of courses which had emerged in response to perceived and tangible social needs. In British Columbia the motivation was directed more to ensuring government control of an educational system which had been less successful than those in other provinces, prior to the Act of 1970, because of the slowness in devising a plan for higher education (McTaggart Cowan 1979). And in Australia the mixture is closer to Britain with questions of cost and content being associated in a desire for more coherence in a rapidly changing and multi-layered system of higher education rather like the public/private divide here. The list could easily be extended, to the Japanese University Accreditation Association and related bodies and the Federal Council for Education in Brazil for example; but enough is as good as a feast. Given that these practices have emerged and have something to say about both the role and the possible forms of validation it is again sad that this foreign dimension has been so neglected.

It is therefore worth noting, to begin with, that the nearest equivalent to the CNAA is the National Council for Educational Awards in the Irish Republic (NCEA 1975). After a somewhat changeable career it is now a statutory body with a perhaps more positive sounding role than the CNAA in relation to a smaller and much less well-established non-university sector. For not only is it required to see that degrees should be comparable to those in universities but it has to encourage the provision of various kinds of learning opportunities, lays down strict guidelines which encourage courses to be designed in terms of work units — defined as three hours of active participation in the course by a student — and has to take resource considerations into account in making its decisions, although ultimate economic control lies with the Higher Education Authority. The NCEA thus seems to combine the validation role with an attempt to co-ordinate Irish higher education (White 1979).

Its working procedures start with the submission of an application, in a prescribed order, to the appropriate Board of Studies. If the Board decides there is a prima facie case for consideration of the submission it is submitted to a Panel of Course Assessors, along with a detailed analysis by the Academic Registrar of its strengths and weakness. The visit to the college will follow the agenda then drawn up by the Panel. This usually consists of five persons: one each from the colleges of higher education, the universities, the professions and industry and the user sector, together with an Assistant Registrar. The Panel conducts visits rather along the lines of a CNAA visiting party, but it is difficult to determine whether the Panel is sufficiently stable in membership to make comparisons between one course and institution and another. An odd variation from CNAA procedures comes at the end of the "visitation": the latter concluding with a meeting between the Panel and the Principal in which, while the Panel must *not* give any indication of likely recommendations on the course, it is essential for the Panel Chairman to 'indicate any weaknesses or negative findings to the Principal at this end-of-visitation meeting'.

In January 1977 the NCEA reminded colleges that the Council 'is obliged to consider new courses from the point of view of planning and co-ordination'. This means that some twenty-one months before the starting date of a new course the Council must have an outline proposal in respect of new courses an institution intends to offer. 'Preparation of the appropriate documentation will enable the institution to obtain outline approval to offer the course before committing major resources to its initiation'. The categories under which the need for the course must be established are as exhaustive as are those on employment outlets. This is yet another case where course recognition, as validation is called there, includes not only academic judgement on a submission, but also consideration of the course in terms of demand and manpower needs. Courses are not approved on their academic merit alone and then made to compete for students in a free market economy, an economy in which, if supply exceeds demand, there will be an over-provision of courses, with perhaps no course operating at its optimum level of academic effectiveness and resource efficiency and thus not fulfilling the expectations of the institution or of the organization which validated the course.

The Irish thus follow the British habit of using quangos to undertake the validating function. This is also the case in West Germany where the General Framework Law created a hierarchy of course reform committees composed of representatives of government and industry to make recommendations for changes in courses and curricula aimed at producing basic principles and simpler regulations. Here too there is a more positive and regulatory tone to its functions. On the other hand, as one would have expected of France, at least until the Decentralization Law of September 1981, *habilitation* in France is a centralized function largely carried out within the Ministry of Education (Secrétariat d'Etat 1975). A submission, submitted in conformity with ministerial formulae, is considered by the relevant *groupe d'étude technique*, a subject panel composed of representative university specialists, ministerial delegates, people from industry and commerce and even some  students. Each *groupe* reports to the National Council for Higher Education and Research, although the final decision rests with the Minister who can withdraw *habilitation* if he so chooses. To gain approval requires that proposals fit in with national priorities and be based on confirmed regional demand and employment opportunities. As a result of this ministerial power and sensitivity to market conditions, proposals can be rejected and existing approvals axed without notification or explanation, as happened in June 1980 to the University of Amiens amongst others. The actual mechanism of course approval is thus very much secondary to an attempt to reshape the whole of the university sector, excluding as always, the *Grandes Ecoles*.

In New Zealand response to social demand seems to have been found too costly and the local University Grants Commission has been authorised to approve all new courses and course alterations (New Zealand UGC 1978). It has designed a kind of 'early warning' system of new developments and its Curriculum Committee insists on taking resource use into consideration when assessing the need for a new course. The committee has power also to defer consideration of a proposal until it has sought expert opinion on projected manpower needs. It also expects both major and minor changes in curricula to be reported to it. Hence it has far wider powers than the British UGC, or at least uses its powers formally and openly. Australian universities have also had the practice extended to them in recent years, as part of the development of a tripartite control system for higher education (Anwyl 1978). Under the overall responsibility of the Tertiary Education Commission, the Universities Commission now has to approve and renew course offerings just as do its sister bodies for colleges of advanced education and for technical and further education. Australia being a federal state these Commonwealth bodies, which have been introduced to monitor the way the rapidly increasing sums of public monies provided by Canberra are being used, are paralleled by state accreditation agencies as well (Williams 1978).

If there is an element both of cost control and academic direction at the federal level, the state boards are more concerned with academic concerns. The Williams Committee recommended the continuance of such boards and the adoption of differential procedures according to the level of development of the institution concerned (Houston 1976). Thus in South Australia there are three stages for an institution to go through. First it must have its organizations, standards and practices accepted. Then it must submit a sufficient summary of the nature and resources of the course. If this hurdle is cleared the institution then submits a complete description of the course and its operation to one of four subject based Core Assessment Committees which then visits in a manner quite reminiscent of the CNAA. This provides the registration and public underwriting of the degree while the rest of the institutions provide a means of co-ordinating the growth of a tripartite higher educational system increasingly reliant on Commonwealth funding. On the other hand, one part of the public sector in Victoria, the State College of Victoria (1978) has a much more varied set of procedures based on a Senate of its own. Such diversity explains Federal desires to co-ordinate such activities.

This desire for co-ordination, not to say control, is also clearly visible in the British Columbia Higher Education Act of 1974 (British Columbia 1974). This gave the Universities Council power to approve the establishment of new faculties and degree programmes, provided that universities consult to ensure the elimination of duplication. Hence all proposals must be signalled in a letter of intent and, if approved, are then carefully costed and evaluated. One concern underlying approval is credit transfer between the province's three universities and fourteen two-year colleges, the students of which demand access to universities. This necessitates assurances that standards are equivalent and that there is a proper system of 'articulation' to facilitate this access, and, behind it government control of higher education as a whole. Interestingly too, provision for public access to, and scrutiny of, the validation process is also made.

In most of these countries it appears that validation and the bodies that carry it out are more closely locked into general systems for controlling and co-ordinating higher education than is the case with the CNAA. The division between the scrutiny of academic content and approval of the use of resources in specific courses is rarely so clear cut as it has become in this country. Some of the practices also appear to combine scrutiny of course and institutions too without the degree of polarity that has developed in the public sector here. This is certainly true of accreditation in Australia, where CNAA-like practices are very common too. Accreditation in the United States has indeed been held up as an alternative to validation because it recognizes institutions in a free market situation. This, in fact, is not so.

## ACCREDITATION IN THE UNITED STATES

Accreditation has been defined as 'the process of recognizing educational institutions and the various programmes they offer for performance, integrity and quality which entitles them to the confidence of the educational community and the public' (Journal of Higher Education 1979). This is done mainly through voluntary non-governmental institutions and professional associations. Sometimes these are general in coverage, whether national or regional, and sometimes they are subject specific. There have been recent cases of some faculties and courses losing recognition, leaving the institution otherwise untouched. They function in co-operation with institutions, requiring that the latter subject themselves to self-study and especially self-evaluation. Prior to a visit an accreditating agency will require a full general and student evaluation of staff and courses. The strictures previously made on the separation of validation and evaluation could not be fairly directed against accreditation.

All this requires a great deal of work inside the institution and just as much paper is required. Visits can be equally arduous, often lasting three days and involving the sampling of exam papers (there being no external examiner system in the States). Those who have been through the mill of accreditation give the impression that it is as demanding as that involved in validation. The stress on self scrutiny, however, does strike a balance between institutional autonomy and public accountability. And accreditation tends to show not that programmes are comparable but that they have reached a minimum standard. It is often said that these standards are unnecessarily low, so that anything can get accredited, whereas validation is much more rigorous. But when we remember the greater need there both for defence against degree mills and for continent wide assurance of quality for credit transfer, the approach is at least understandable, and not totally different from validation as practised in the United Kingdom.

In recent years this stress on market and educational forces has somewhat waned. Two trends have produced co-ordination and evaluation of the accreditation process (Warren 1977). The rise of consumerism thus has encouraged the agencies themselves to undertake the same self scrutiny as they demand of institutions. Hence the creation in 1976 of the Council on Post Secondary Accreditation which recognizes, co-ordinates and periodically reviews accrediting agencies. It does this not according to absolute criteria but according to the agency's own view of its aims and scope. However, with the granting of massive funds through the Korean War Veterans Scheme and the Nursing Training Act of 1965, the Federal government has felt that this is not enough. This obviously suggests the possibility that the accreditation system has not been successful or rigorous enough.

Since accreditation is tantamount to eligibility for government funds, the efficiency of accreditation is a major concern in Washington. Thus there is a Division of Eligibility and Agency Evaluation in the Office of Education which carries out its own checks. Self study and market forces are no longer enough and the United States has, albeit in its own decentralized way, a similar web of state co-ordination to the other countries mentioned. So accreditation on the one hand can be contrasted with chartering or licensing on the other hand. This reinforces the feeling that while there are some differences in emphasis and operation, accreditation cannot be seen as something wholly divorced from validation. The fact that Britain and America are countries divided by the same language has apparently misled those who were seeking to make a point against the present organization of the public sector. Thus, if there are lessons to be drawn from abroad, they are not always as clear cut as one would like.

The foreign dimension obviously has its own pitfalls too. No absolute answer can be obtained from looking abroad or to other models of course approval, any more than historical and conceptual analysis can make people put aside their own usages and accept an agreed position established outside. The process of making rhetoric harmonize with reality is a slow one. At least Derek Rowntree's new *Dictionary of Education* (1981) has now accepted that validation is not just a term for testing items in programmed learning, but can also mean 'the process whereby an educational institution may submit formal plans to the scrutiny and approval of an outside body'. Yet there is a long way still to go before the full complexity of the practice, as revealed here, is widely appreciated.

Validation is often a good thing. It is not good *a priori*. We do, however, know that it is a much more complicated, and a much more hit-or-miss thing than has often been assumed. It is replete with conceptual pitfalls, very firmly rooted in the particularities of Britain's recent educational development. It is one answer to a set of problems affecting advanced industrialized countries the world over. It is a process designed as a means to an end, and can therefore be assessed in terms of those ends and compared to other means, whether in the professions or in the UGC, where peer group reviews with overt resource implications obviously take place. But because aims and methods are unclear, it is doubtful whether we can either improve the working definition, or, assuming we can, persuade people, including ourselves, to stick to a single definition. Whatever the nature of the historical situation which gave rise to validation and the problems this poses, it did happen and one cannot hope to conjure it out of existence with a wave of a verbal wand. Validation has thus come to be regarded as a process, almost as an end in itself, and its original meaning and impetus have been largely forgotten.

Validation is a process which, if it finds that a proposal for a degree scheme is well provided with resources, justifiable in theory and capable of successful application, gives credibility to its status and operation. This may not be objective or even sufficiently incontrovertible to allow any absolute predictions of its future to be made, but it is a serious and considered verdict. Yet it is doubtful whether such a verdict really commands wide social understanding or consent. Notwithstanding its many virtues validation is a form of elaborated discourse shared by those working in the public sector, and as such not readily comprehended by others in higher education let alone by the public at large. Large rhetorical claims for its general value and applicability therefore are best eschewed. At all events we should try and get to grips with the realities of costs, catalytic role in curriculum development and social function which lie behind the claims.

NEW PASTURES

Many of these questions cannot presently be resolved. They are among the many areas where research is needed. As has been implicit in the discussion of internal validation, one cannot really assess external validation properly without taking these things fully into consideration. Otherwise it becomes simply a matter of faith, especially where validation is only performed prior to the running of a course, or as some would say in 'a prophetic mode'. There are a whole range of concepts, practices and questions which need to be examined. Claims, for instance, that validation can serve as a form of accountability at the tertiary level has not really been explored (Burgess 1977). Without examination of ideas such as accountability, accreditation and autonomy the whole thing remains a semantic minefield and more basic forms of research will be handicapped.

Secondly, a great deal more needs to be known about the actual ways in which courses are evolved and scrutinized, whether here or overseas. Unfortunately such research seems to rate very low both amongst ordinary academics and educational researchers. Is the whole thing a ritualized paper exercise or does actual change take place? Alternative modes and inputs have also rarely been considered. Finally, there are a lot of questions to be resolved, such as the possibility of objective decisions, the feasibility of equal relationships inside the validating relationship and the nature of the historical and socio-political setting of validation. So far rhetorical mystification about validation remains largely unsullied by contact with reality.

How then do we do this? Whatever course of action we adopt should, as has become clear, embrace all areas in which validation takes place and not just the limited parts of the public sector previously studied. Nor should such investigation limit itself to formal structures nor even to actual procedures. The whole set of issues carried by validation have to be investigated if it is to make any sense. This means that the basic questions of political control and co-ordination of higher education have to be asked. What form should such control take and what place has validation at the course level in it and why? We need to investigate and evaluate the other possible systems rather than just start from the curiosity of the historical present.

Thus as well as looking at research on case studies of validating agencies and practices, particularly as these affect the actual teaching act, there needs to be consideration of broader political questions and issues. These could well include the training of validators so that they can grasp the issues and values involved, which are very often hard for people to deal with. The role of career change, the place of rituals and group dynamics in validation could all repay attention. The fact that validation is a form of evaluation should also be borne in mind, by treating the claims of validation to change the actual experience of education within the context of the kinds of methods and proofs usually required in evaluations. Validation will have to be treated as an internal activity as well as an externally imposed one. Whether this will leave the question of institutional standing and recognition as quite so permanent an issue as it now seems to be in the 'Partnership in Validation' debate remains to be seen. The effects of a declining market also need to be taken into account. Things like process consultation may offer a way of improving the actual practices of validation. There are thus a huge range of questions to be answered. It is to be hoped that some of these will be answered on the pages which follow, beginning with a detailed analysis of the CNAA itself, given its centrality to the debate.

REFERENCES

Anwyl, J. (1978) Towards a co-ordinated national system of tertiary education. Unpublished cyclostyled paper for the 4th International Conference on Higher Education, Lancaster

Barnes, M. (1980) Private communication from the Secretary of the National Council for Drama Training

Becher, T. and Kogan, M. (1980) *Process and Structure in Higher Education* London: Heinemann

British Columbia (1974) *Universities Act* (Vancouver)

Burgess, T. (1977) *Education After School* Harmondsworth: Penguin

CCETSW (1977) *Guidelines for Courses leading to the Certificate of Qualification in Social Work* CCETSW Paper 15: 1 February 1977

CNAA (1975) *Partnership in Validation* London

CNAA (1976) *Summary of Comments received on Council's Discussion Paper on 'Partnership in Validation'* Cyclostyled

CNAA (1977) *Planning for Academic Diversification in Higher Education* Cyclostyled

CNAA (1979) *Developments in Partnership in Validation* London

Cantor, L.M. and Roberts, I.F. (1979) *Further Education Today. A Critical Review* London: Routledge and Kegan Paul

Church, C.H. (1976) Not up to par? Some problems in comparing the validation of degree courses *Higher Education Bulletin* VI (1) 39-62

Church, C.H. (1977) Validation systems in CNAA (1977) p.6 et seq.

Church, C.H. (1981) The impossible contract: the pitfalls of validation as accountability *Educational Policy Bulletin* IX (1) 83-117

Council (1977) *Information to be Submitted by Correspondence Colleges applying for Accreditation* London: Council for the Accreditation of Correspondence Colleges, September 1977

Cox, R. *The Development of Evaluation* Paper submitted to HEF/SRHE Consultation on Validation

Crequier, N. (1982) Full marks for Chelsea *Times Higher Educational Supplement* 487, 5 March, p.9

Davis, M. (1980A) *Prelude to Partnership? The CNAA, Validation and the Polytechnics, 1964-74* Unpublished paper submitted to a conference on 'The Polytechnics: an alternative', Polytechnic of Central London, 3 May 1980

Davis, M. (1980B) The CNAA as a validating agency. In Billing D.A. (ed.) *Indicators of Performance* Guildford: SRHE

Geddes, D. (1981) Joseph's axe will fall on student grants *The Times* 5 November pp.3 & 28

Gold, P.J. (1979) An E can be the start *Guardian* 4 September

Houston, H.S. (1976) *Course Accreditation in Australia — the past, present practices, and the future* Cyclostyled

James, E. (1972) *Teacher Education and Training. A report by a Committee of Inquiry .... Under the Chairmanship of Lord James of Rusholme* London: HMSO p. 74

Jones, D.R. (1978) *The English University Tradition. Its establishment, maintenance and future* Cyclostyled paper for 4th International Conference on Higher Education, Lancaster

*Journal of Higher Education* (1979) 50 (2) 115-232. Special number on 'The Accrediting Process'

Lane, D. (1975) *Design for Degrees. New Degree Courses under the CNAA 1964-1974* London: Macmillan.

McTaggart Cowan, I. (1979) Private Communication from the Chairman of the British Columbia Academic Board

NCEA (1975) *Guidelines for the Evaluation of Study Courses* Dublin: National Council for Educational Awards, 1 July

Newcastle (1980) *Draft Agreement between the CNAA and the Academic Board of Newcastle Polytechnic* Unpublished manuscript, p.1

New Zealand UGC (1978) *Report of the Curriculum Committee 1977* Auckland

Niblett, W.R. (1981) *Validation and Objectivity* Cyclostyled paper circulated with the papers of the HEF/SRHE Consultation on Validation

OED (1933) *Oxford English Dictionary* Oxford: Clarendon XII pp.24-5

Perkin, H.J. (1980) Le professioni e il gioco della vita. L'Inghilterra dall'800 a oggi *Quaderni Storici* 48, 956-8

Robbins, L. (1963) *Higher Education. Report of a Committee under the Chairmanship of Lord Robbins* Cmnd 2154, pp.107-25. London: HMSO

Rowntree, D. (1981) *A Dictionary of Education* London: Harper Row p.339

Secrétariat d'Etat (1975) *Arrêté du Secrétaire d'Etat aux Universités* 31 December 1975 and 16 January 1976

State College of Victoria (1978) *Accreditation Procedures and Policies*

Tolley, G. (1974) Accreditation for all *THES* 140, 21 June, p.16

Warren, J. (1976) *Evaluation of the Office of Education Criteria for the Recognition of Accrediting and State Approval Agencies* Cyclostyled, Berkeley, California: Educational Testing Service

White, A. (1979) Private communication from the Assistant Registrar of NCEA

Williams, B. (1978) *Systems of Higher Education: Australia* New York: ICED

David Billing


The structure and organization of the Council for National Academic Awards (CNAA), along with its place in course control in the public sector, are well known and understood today. Its system of committees and subject boards, which have evolved from sketchy beginnings in the Charter, with their membership of academics and some industrial and commercial representatives, now forms a sophisticated and developing organism to carry out its tasks of advancing education through the approval of courses of study and granting the academic awards to which they lead on the basis of standards comparable to those in British universities. This process, of course, follows on the satisfaction of the CNAA's normal administrative and social requirements. All this is common knowledge, even if its future role is uncertain because of the piecemeal emergence of new mechanisms for the management of local authority higher education (Committee of Enquiry 1976; Working Party 1978; Education, Science and Arts 1980; DES 1981a, b). What is less well known are the criteria according to which the process of validation is carried out. In this paper I wish to try and outline some of the crucial issues thrown up by the CNAA modus operandi, by setting the kind of criteria that are intended and imagined against the criteria that seem to emerge in practice. However, it must be remembered that these criteria are not absolute but are the product of continuing development and policy discussion inside the Council as it functions in its other role as a forum for the Public Sector. Hence the views expressed here are those of the author and do not necessarily correspond with those of the CNAA as a whole.

INTENDED CNAA CRITERIA FOR COURSE VALIDATION
The aim of the CNAA process is to subject courses and staff operating them to appraisal by peers and thereby to improve these courses and their teaching. The statutes require the CNAA to ensure that its awards are comparable in standards to those of universities.

"Standards" refers to more than simply the level of performance. The notion of standards implied in Statute 8(5)b includes (Alexander, Billing and Gent 1980):

1 the calibre and potential of the students at admission;
2 the quality of the students' learning experience promoted by the institution;
3 the final level of achievement of the course aims as reflected in the assessment of students' performance.

In maintaining standards, the CNAA is therefore concerned with the quality of the educational process and its environment, as well as its products, and it is important to notice that any estimate of the quality of the process rests largely on the perceptions and judgements of staff, students, examiners, and employers. Thus, course aims, student characteristics and educational processes are all important in relation to standards. I have elsewhere defined standards as follows (Billing 1980a):

'a course is of an acceptable standard if all students to whom its awards are granted achieve all of the course aims and if those aims are appropriate to the level of award'.

This must cover the nature of the educational experience as well as the final level of achievement, but what weight should this factor be given and what are the characteristics of a beneficial educational experience? The CNAA's attitude to probing directly and explicitly the quality of the teaching/learning process has been ambivalent (Tait and Billing 1980). On the one hand, the quality of teaching is thought to be important (CNAA 1974a, CNAA 1979a, CNAA 1979b), but on the other side many Subject Boards have felt that, if they concentrate on determining their level of confidence in the staff, this will subsume the quality of the teaching and therefore of the learning process. Such a view makes assumptions about a number of causal connections, about the nature of the students and the professional preparation of the teachers; further, it seems likely that confidence in the staff should be based upon satisfaction about the quality of educational experiences.

One aspect of the educational process which has caused some debate at the level of principle, has been students' rate of learning. This has been seen as a crucial factor in relation to the standard of the award. Yet in 1979, the CNAA first degree 'Regulations' (CNAA 1979a) embraced credit accumulation and with it the possibility of rather indefinitely extendable periods of study. The question of whether rate of learning was always a crucial factor in determining the level of intellectual and creative demand placed upon students (Billing 1980b) was debated for some time in 1976 within the CNAA but the conclusion 'not necessarily' has not been implemented consistently in the 1979 regulations — there are still constraints on maximum duration of study, and resitting examinations. It should follow that a course team will have to identify what is the nature of the honours level demand which ensures the standard of the final award — is it rate of learning, is it mastery of content (in depth or breadth), is it synthesis of concepts from various areas, is it general abilities like problem solving, is it potential achievement, or is it a hybrid? Both the 'rate' and 'potential' arguments have been seen as leading to an attempt to assess exit velocity from the course rather than to assess achievement over the period up to and including the final assessment.

Finally in relation to standards, since they have been related to course aims the appropriateness of those aims needs to be established. The approach of the CNAA is to require that all first degree and DipHE course aims incorporate its Principle 3 about general educational criteria (CNAA 1979a). This may be summarized briefly as requiring a programme of studies to specify its objectives, while emphasizing that these may range very widely; to include among its aims the development of the student's intellectual and imaginative powers; to stimulate 'an enquiring, analytical and creative approach, encouraging independent judgement and critical self-awareness'; to encourage the skills of clear communication and logical argument as well as the ability to relate learned material to actual situations; and to encourage the student to appreciate the modes of thought of disciplines other than his own.

## IMAGE OF VALIDATION CRITERIA

The perceived criteria of judgement of a course submission have been investigated by Alexander (1979a) on a Nuffield project amongst academc staff in colleges of education/higher education and education departments of polytechnics.

For *CNAA* validation, the perceived criteria were:

1  Staff cohesiveness
2  Performance on the day
3  Ethos of the institution
4  Respect for ideology of conservatism in traditional areas and for radicalism in less traditional areas
5  Course coherence
6  Sympathetic panel
7  Quality of documentation
8  Maximal staff involvement in planning
9  Staff qualifications
10 Innovatory nature of course
11 Student participation
12 Library
13 Chance as to which parts of the course are sampled by validators
14 Vocational relevance
15 Conformity to preconceptions of validation panel
16 Effective course administrative arrangements

Compared with intended criteria, the perceived CNAA critera show the importance of performance on the day, ideology (conservative or radical depending on the nature of the course) and preconceptions. The need for lively and imaginative staff does not come through as strongly as the CNAA intended, and documentation perhaps looms larger than intended; omitted entirely are CNAA perceived criteria concerning course aims (apart from ideology and vocational relevance) and their balance (Principle 3), level, intended students (ie admission requirements) and assessment.

The CNAA has periodically been criticized for the effect on its decisions of the events of one day — the staff performance, the consistency and objectivity of the validation panel views, the composition of the panel, the visit programme, other aspects of chance, or the infrequency of such contacts. While there is some validity in these criticisms, they are not completely borne out by more familiarity with the Council's operation and the histories of particular courses.

Consistency of membership of CNAA panels can be a problem. However, a hypothetical validation in 1976 throws some doubt on the importance of the composition of a validating panel. A fictitious combined studies degree scheme was prepared (Billing 1976) for a conference of the CNAA Combined Studies (Science) Board in Bournemouth in November 1976. The Conference divided into six groups to 'validate' the 'Lincoln Polytechnic' scheme, and perhaps unexpectedly came independently to generally similar conclusions about what were the important issues and the panel's views on these issues. It would be dangerous, of course, to generalize from this one, unreal, example; however, there appears to be little other evidence available on parallel validations.

There may be a danger in too much consistency of membership in the case of course proposals which receive repeated consideration. Although three versions of a proposal and three meetings/visits have been a normal practical limit before the panel is in danger of guiding the staff too much or the staff lose morale and momentum, there have been a few cases with as many as six versions. By that stage the Board members may be over-familiar with the staff and may have influenced the course design so much that it is difficult not to approve their own ideas. In such cases, objectivity is endangered.

The objectivity of the CNAA process has face validity, and is claimed as one of the advantages of external validation over internal validation; it is a reason why 'internal' validating panels need to include outside specialists, the other main reason being availability of subject expertise. This claim is made in the CNAA 1979 DPV document (CNAA 1979b). The views expressed there are based upon an extensive series of consultations with Subject Boards and colleges conducted in regard to the 1975 discussion paper (CNAA 1975a) *Partnership in Validation*; this evidence has been summarised (CNAA 1975b).

However, when the CNAA is criticised for lack of objectivity, what is usually meant is that it has formed a subjective impression based upon lack of evidence and upon preconceptions rather than the merit of a course proposal. The CNAA would not claim that it was possible to form judgements detached from impressions — almost by definition *subjective* — about the course team and its intentions. It is therefore appropriate to define objectivity as does Karl Popper (1972) as inter-subjectivity, ie the accumulation and interactions of the subjective judgements of a number of independent people. This, of course, ignores processes of group dynamics within a validating group whereby one view may come to predominate and to become the expressed consensus view; validating groups do not vote, they debate until a consensus emerges with sufficient support, with any reservations set down as conditions of approval or strong comments and recommendations. While the process should filter out idiosyncracies, it may reinforce them if a member is sufficiently influential, perhaps through being in the chair. In these circumstances, the role of the Council Officer becomes more important in trying to ensure that the college's case is fairly heard.

Preconceptions held by members of validating panels have been mentioned above, and may be seen as tending towards the conservative ideology referred to in the perceptions of staff. A study of the many innovations approved by the CNAA would not support the charge of conservatism. However, the histories of some of these validations has sometimes been prolonged and tortuous (for example a degree in Sports Science and Administration) and sometimes may have distorted the original aims of the staff or have placed many constraints on the operation of the course (for example a degree by Independent Study). Some innovations have not been approved, and it remains possible to debate the justice of such decisions. Davis (1979) finds evidence for conservatism in the operation of the CNAA, and, in view of the origins of the CNAA and its mode of operation through consensus judgements, this is inevitable.

One source of conservatism is the composition of CNAA Subject Boards; since they aim to be peer groups and to reflect the balances in higher education, it is perhaps inevitable that they should have the built-in caution expected of a cross-section of people from established departments committed, under the Council's statutes, to safeguard standards. It is proper that radical ideas should be tested in order to draw out points which may require some refinement or conditions of approval or close monitoring during the operation of the course; this process should ensure that staff are aware of the likely problems and have provided for them as far as possible.

The CNAA does not intend to be conservative. A good illustration is the CNAA response to the DES/SED (1978) discussion document 'Higher Education into the 1990's'. This response (CNAA 1978a) has been circulated to all colleges, and summarised again in the more recent evidence to the Select Committee on Education (CNAA 1980a); it merits detailed analysis by colleges seeking assurances about the Council's openness to innovations. What is less clear is that the CNAA Subject Boards have assimilated the philosophies of the Committee for Academic Policy which generated the response.

While the CNAA has tried to operate through providing validation panels, which are peer groups, to engage in discussion with course teams, there is a tendency for the CNAA to want the balance of any advantage which authoritative advice gives. Thus, if a negative decision has to be taken, the CNAA needs to be able to defend it, and might even have wished to be impregnable by virtue of the authority of the experts it has at its disposal.

Although there have been occasions when colleges have thought that they knew more about a new course area than the CNAA panel, in the main the CNAA has achieved this balance of authority by virtue of its directly appointed university and professional members and its selection of the better of the nominations for membership from the colleges; however, there may be times when the conflicting requirements for different sorts of balance on a Subject Board make it difficult for the Board to be as strong as might be desired. This authoritative stance is difficult to reconcile (Bethal et al. 1980) with the spirit of *Developments in Partnership in Validation* (CNAA 1979b). An equal partnership, if that were intended, should presumably lead to a validating panel and a course team working jointly towards a consensus judgement which is truly that of two peer groups. Validation would then become consultative rather than judgemental. However, on the one hand colleges still are wary of total frankness in discussion and pick on any vulnerability which the validating panel reveals if it does not have the balance of authority or if it also is frank. On the other hand, the Council's Charter requires its Board rather than a joint Board/College group to make decisions. (Course validation, which may be joint, and course approval are therefore distinguished). Neither of these positions is conducive to interactions between two peer groups, which may mean that *equal* partnership will always be impossible.

An important problem may be that the course which is validated is the course as designed rather than the real course as it is implemented and operates. The CNAA has a second-hand contact with the educational experience, through talking to the staff and students involved, but not in an on-going manner. In principle something very different to the course as approved could happen in practice and the CNAA would not know until five years later. In fact this stark picture ignores the basis of course approval, which is confidence in the staff — in their integrity, commitment, ability, experience and corporate thinking and decision-making. Further, there is the institutional context — the Council makes the Academic Board responsible for the maintenance of the course standards, including resource support with the requirement that it sets up means of monitoring the course operation. Thirdly, there is the role of the external examiner. Fourthly, at the course review stage, great reliance is put on the critical analysis (CNAA 1981a) of the course operation. The DPV document (CNAA 1976) might easily have been called 'partnership in the maintenance of standards' as it focusses in the sharing of responsibility not just on the initial validation of courses but on the whole of the system of setting and maintaining standards. Expectations for course monitoring and evaluation as part of this system have therefore become more important, and have been discussed in a paper by Alexander, Billing and Gent (1980), based on their observations of internal processes at a number of institutions. However, such interests of the CNAA in the implementation of a course do not really take account of a further criticism of course designs — that they are planned only for the 'normal' or traditional students (Robinson 1978). To the extent to some common level, ie filling in gaps rather than building on existing assets of students. Robinson goes on to suggest that the progress of many students through their courses will be very different from that assumed by the planners and that many students are getting an educational provision that is unsuitable for them.

The CNAA stresses the cohesiveness of the staff teaching the course, which implies that there must be a course team with a course leader who is accountable to the Academic Board for the standards of the course (and possibly also for the deployment of resources). However, there is no explicit requirement for a formalised Course Committee, although such a course management device turns out to be the norm in practice. While cohesiveness does mean that a consensus should exist about the course aims, balance and structure, it does not mean that a course team has to put up a 'seamless' defence of the proposal; openness is increasingly desired of course teams by CNAA Boards acting as peer groups and wanting lively debates stimulated by valid differences of opinion. The cohesion must come from commitment to an agreement reached by corporate discussion and action, and taking precedence over individual opinions. Such corporate agreements may then be expected to become institutionalised, and this is a most important means of legitimating and supporting innovations which otherwise might be rather vulnerable (Tait and Billing 1980; CNAA 1979c).

## CRITERIA IN PRACTICE IN CNAA COURSE VALIDATION

The purpose of this section is to elicit from experiences with problems confronting CNAA validators, what criteria are in practice being applied. I deal in turn with the parameters of course aims, title, student intake, staffing, course structure and curriculum.

Aims may be described as the teaching goals and are usually expressed in very general terms, particularly for Combined Studies schemes where they are forced to describe the structural framework rather than the content. Objectives on the other hand are often distinguished from aims in being more detailed statements and in describing what the students should achieve. In Combined Studies schemes, they may be very difficult to state except at the level of individual subjects and possibly their combination into specific programmes of study. Often, course submissions do not make either clear, and instead there may be a statement about the origins of the course and the need in this particular subject or profession. Yet, the Council must know the course aims or it cannot judge the proposal in its own terms, and is forced to compare it with its own expectations or those of tradition.

The aims are often buried in a section of the submission about rationale — dealing with needs of students, local industry, professions or society. Some statements of aims are unhelpful because they are tautologous and much discussion would be needed before the validation panel obtained a good idea of intentions. Too often no educational grounds are given for proposing a course, but only administrative reasons or institutional needs to attract students. Sometimes course aims get mixed up with philosophy — ie values held, teaching approaches and emphases. It is difficult to draw a line between philosophy and aims and both need stating. When the course philosophy is not stated, the aims can still lack clear meaning. Thus, it is probably necessary not only to state aims and objectives but to put them in the context of an overarching rationale about the premises on which they are based and the constraints which limit what the aims might have been or the interpretation of those which are given. Alexander (1979b) has suggested that the CNAA approach to aims may underplay the existence of unintended outcomes.

The result of seeing only statements of aims is that it is unclear how the course is intended to look from the students' angle; increasingly, Subject Boards are wanting to see this viewpoint as a most helpful form of clarification. Sometimes, in order to clarify vague statements, Subject Boards will ask about the demand for a course — not because it is within the CNAA remit, but because such discussions reveal the nature of the intended students, which illuminates the aims.

A related problem is with ambivalent statements of aims, which usually arise when a course team has not clearly decided whether or not a course is vocational. Internally, conflicting aims can arise, for example that a course is suitable both for students who already have significant relevant knowledge and for those who do not. A similar type of ambivalence is over depth *vs* breadth —both cannot be achieved in the time available. This leads to consideration of the many examples of over-ambitious aims. The usual problem is a lack of a clear focus, and the remedy is refinement and also a more cohesive course team. A course may be too demanding because the design has not responded adequately to the constraints of a very broad admission requirement which means that prior knowledge in the field cannot be assumed. Further constraints, whose neglect leads to over-ambitious courses, come from the limitations of physical resources and the number and expertise of staff. Finally, it is easy to over-estimate the extent to which a course can develop students' higher level abilities, and the CNAA Principle 3 raises this danger.

The course aims and objectives may not fit the proposed award, possibly because they are too demanding, but more usually because they are at too low a level. This is particularly likely where the discipline is just emerging (perhaps from earlier HND or professional diploma work) or where staff have little degree teaching experience or where entry requirements are too broad and progression of material inadequate or diffused. Thus, a course proposal may fail because it aims merely at skills and knowledge rather than higher level abilities, or because in a broad course no inter-relationships are brought out.

Interdisciplinary and cross-disciplinary courses are particularly difficult to appraise, because it may not be clear to what extent interrelationships between different concept areas are intended. If they are valued, and the course is intended to be truly interdisciplinary, then they must be demonstrated both in the content and in the knowledge and attitudes of the staff and students. Therefore, it is dangerous to allow a validating panel to be misled into believing that a Combined Studies proposal is supposed to encourage cross-disciplinarity; most Boards will accept an honest statement of simple multidisciplinarity, ie subject areas put alongside each other. However, the consequences of this are that the Board will look for considerable coherence *within* rather than between the subject areas.

Within a broad range of a list of aims, which all call upon time in the course, the Subject Board will need to be clear where the emphasis lies. The priorities amongst the aims need to be clear so that the orientation and flavour of the course stands out. Thus, very different courses would emerge from different priorities amongst the following list:

1  Knowledge of the social context of planning, concentrating on processes of policy formulation and decision making in Britain;
2  Knowledge of theories and methods used in planning;
3  Knowledge of urban and regional planning and policy, concentrating on problems and issues and the way in which planners deal with them;
4  Knowledge of natural resource policy and social policy as these relate to urban and regional planning;
5  Practical ability in decision making, policy information and implementation.

However, the orientation of the course should not be so narrow that it does not provide a balanced education satisfying Principle 3 of the CNAA. There may be whole fields of study in which a first degree course would be so narrowly conceived (or *artificially* broadened) that it could not satisfy Principle 3, for example Cartography, Furniture Technology; subjects like Secretarial Studies and Remedial Gymnastics seem to be on the borderline. On the other hand, breadth alone will not satisfy Principle 3, and is likely instead to lead to superficiality. The major requirement here may well be in that (Principle 3.4) which refers to 'an enquiring, analytical and creative approach, encouraging independent judgement and critical self-awareness ....'. This does not require breadth of content so much as breadth of vision. The implication of breadth comes from Principle 3.7 which refers to 'attitudes, modes of thought, practices and disciplines other than those of his or her main studies .... perceive his or her main studies in a broader perspective .... factor influencing the social and physical environment'. This has often been thought to need supplementary studies, which then find it hard also to satisfy Principle 3.4. More recently, CNAA courses in Science are either turning to the conceptual framework of the emerging discipline of 'Science, Technology and Society', or attempting to satisfy Principle 3.7 in the main studies.

The questions of balance and orientation raise the issue of the unity of the course team. All of the staff need to understand the aims, emphasis and philosophy of the course and be committed to it, even if they have individual differences of opinion. If aims are not clearly articulated and debated but rather are assumed by the course team, then such unity is unlikely. This may be particularly difficult to achieve in multidisciplinary and interdisciplinary courses where there are no well developed paradigms, and where the staff are working to one side of a primary discipline which conditions not only their knowledge but also their values and their likely future careers.

Within the spectrum of course aims there seem to emerge three main clusters (Billing 1973) depending on their *sources* in:

a   Needs of students
b   Needs of society/industry
c   The subject

To these may be added a fourth, which emerges from (c) when its mediation and protection by a body of professionals is considered:

d   Interests of staff

Lane (1975) has a similar group of types of objective corresponding to (a), (b), (c) which he puts at the corners of a triangle so that any course can be represented as a point of the figure. His three angles are personal intellectual development, knowledge of a discipline and preparation for employment.

The only requirement of a *Course Title* is that it should be an accurate description of the aims and emphasis of a course for *all* programmes of study which it permits. Thus, an Applied Physics degree which permitted a programme made up entirely of 'pure' physics would be misleading as would an 'Energy Studies' degree entirely concerned with Physics or a Nursing degree which did not lead to professional recognition. Society reads into many titles certain assumptions about professional competence, whether or not this is intended by the staff. Therefore, the CNAA must prevent titles from being misleading in this way. The title, aims, intended students and content of a course all interact and should be congruent. Sometimes they conflict, and the college then has to decide which to change. While it may seem that the title could be the last in a row of decisions about a course and therefore the easiest to change, often it is not. It may be that the title was what originally brought staff together into a course team, or that it has institutional overtones in placing the course in one department or faculty rather than another. It may be difficult to alter if DES approval has already been obtained, or if it is linked to a plan to get professional recognition for the course.

There are many aspects of the *Achievement of Course Aims* which are discussed below, but they may be grouped into four main categories:

1  Who is the course for and will students cope with such aims?
2  Are the staff and physical resources adequate for these aims?
3  Will the course as proposed allow these students and resources to meet the aims?
4  Will the assessments reveal whether the students have met the aims?

There is not room in this chapter to deal with all of these aspects, and I illustrate them here by concentrating upon student intake, staffing resources and course structure/curriculum.

*Student Intake* is determined by the CNAA First Degree and DipHE Regulations (CNAA 1979a), which set down for England and Wales normal entry requirements for a full-time course of 2 GCE 'A' levels plus 3 'O' levels and a minimum age of 18 (and in Scotland 3 Higher Grades and two Ordinary Grades plus age 17) along with the 3 'A' and 1 'O' variant, ONC/OND (or BEC/TEC) routes, provisions for Art and Design, and transfer/exemption arrangements. The course proposal itself will then go on to be more specific about which 'O' and 'A' levels. However, it is clear from this and other documents (CNAA 1978b), 1979d, 1980b) that the Council intends these requirements to be interpreted flexibly so that colleges can use their discretion to admit students likely to succeed who do not fulfil the formal requirements; mature students are a particular case, and many free-standing DipHE courses are fully exploiting this flexibility.

The major difficulty in discussions about entry requirements is in discerning for whom the course is *mainly* designed; the CNAA expects the *normal* entry routes to be set down as requirements. Further, the CNAA would not then expect a very significant proportion to enter in other ways (the acceptable maximum percentage has been variously argued to be 10%-50%).

The entry requirements will list alternative main entry routes and these clearly will not equate exactly or even very approximately in terms of prior knowledge/experience. Some assumption will usually then be adopted about the major route which provides a platform for the course design; other routes will be catered for (together with recurrent special entry patterns) by means of 'levelling' studies in the first year of the course, or sometimes beforehand. CNAA validating panels will explore whether these special needs have been adequately identified and suitably catered for. The means employed might, for example, be a pre-knowledge diagnostic test and counselling for all students plus individualised study materials (CNAA 1979c, 1980c) or special tutorials or readings. Robinson (1980) has attacked the philosophy of a common first year for all students, and indeed the whole notion that courses should be designed to take a diverse intake to a common platform and then through to identical outcomes; he suggests that course design should recognise that students' different needs may require different curricula, content and course objectives.

The diversity of the intake is an even bigger issue for postgraduate and post-experience courses. There is a temptation to widen the net for such courses to achieve viability at the expense of any clear assumptions upon which the course design can build; further, such courses are relatively short and there is little time for any 'levelling'. The aims, entry requirements and duration of such courses are all linked via the necessity to achieve an appropriate level. Therefore a broad intake often has the consequences that the aims of the course are not clearly enough focussed and that the duration is inadequate to achieve the aims.

For example, is a diploma in mathematics for teachers or for industrialists, is it an extension of earlier studies or a reorientation or a refresher/updating, and is it post-experience or purely postgraduate? Often for these courses, prior experience in relevant employment is an essential component of the entry qualifications or is an alternative to formal qualifications for some students. There is a further problem which becomes acute for postgraduate courses, that a content listing is not a sufficient guide to level because such content could also occur in an undergraduate course; more important is the approach and pace of study intended, as this needs to assume that postgraduates can cope quickly with new and difficult concepts, that they can contribute to the course from their experience, that they can work well on their own and in groups, that they are mature in outlook and relationships with teachers and peers, and that they are well motivated. These assumptions point to important characteristics of the expected intake.

Part-time first degree courses also raise questions about maturity, as in even greater measure do the variants of mixed-mode study and distant study (directed private study). The CNAA minimum entry requirements for part-time degrees set down a normal minimum age of 21, although courses may be especially designed for 18-year-olds. Is any specified age (21?, 23?, 25?) a sufficient definition of the maturity which the CNAA believes from experience is needed to enable students to cope with the rigours over several years of studying intensely for part of the week at times when they may be tired and harassed by domestic, financial or occupational pressures and studying in their own time on top of work and developing social, financial and career commitments? Probably not, but then what other definitions could be used?

The nature of the intake also has consequences for multidisciplinary courses. A broad intake with many student choices is part of their philosophy. Again, therefore, 'equalizing' studies may be needed. When the course is modular, then additionally the prerequisites and constraints on student choice will have to be specified at each stage. Interdisciplinary courses have a similar problem about the frequent lack of specifically appropriate entry requirements and hence the likelihood of a diverse intake. Both of these types of course may often be wrongly conceived by potential students, and so attention must be given to making clear statements in any publicity material and ensuring at interviews that these are understood. Thus, a multidisciplinary course may be imagined by students to give rather more single-subject concentration (and recognition by employers) than is in fact possible. Interdisciplinary courses may have names which are not obviously related to school work and therefore need explaining, such as energy studies, hotel management, speech therapy, information systems. Both types of course can also place on students very considerable intellectual demands, either in coping with (say) two disparate disciplines or in synthesizing from various inputs; breadth is not a 'soft option'. Counselling of students is clearly necessary if choices of routes must be made at entry to the course.

Transfer arrangements may raise several issues in relation to admission. How will the students' previous achievement be recognized and how will it qualify for specific exemptions? It becomes more necessary with such arrangements to be able to specify the prerequisites at each stage of a course and to have clear objectives set down which have been achieved in the earlier studies. Obviously, a complete match between these is unlikely, and pre-knowledge tests together with supplementary study materials and adequate tutorial arrangements are likely to be necessary. Statements about exemptions also need to cover industrial experience in the case of sandwich courses, and the means of modifying the assessment scheme to take into account (perhaps) earlier academic performance. Looked at the other way round, ie transfer out, validation panels will often want to know what other 'safety net' courses exist for unsuitable students; this is particuarly necessary in honours-only degrees. The DipHE raises an important policy point, that the CNAA requires outlets into degree courses, at least one of which must provide for honours to be attained without loss of time. The DipHE has led to considerable work on credit transfer, for example the idea of a Credit Transfer Agency emerging from the Toyne (1980) Study, and intended to provide information on transfer arrangements; also transfer arrangements have been negotiated between some institutions (including CNAA and the Open University). The CNAA has a issued number of papers on transfer (CNAA 1977, CNAA 1981b).

A related issue concerns courses which are linked by transfer and exemption arrangements and may be operated alongside each other in the same institution; an example would be a degree and an HND with overlapping content. If the aims are reasonably similar, as implied by the possibility of transfer, then the question arises of whether common teaching of some or even all of the overlapping parts can be considered. There are obvious resource pressures in this direction, which must be guarded against by asking about real differences in aims, in student needs, and in appropriate teaching and learning methods. Usually the balance of the aims is different in that one course may be rather vocationally orientated whereas the other may put greater value on general educational aims. Principle 3 can be an issue here in that (say) an HND has not been designed to meet it, but students transferring to a degree will have a shortened time to achieve these aims and reorientate their former perceptions before the end of the course.

Finally, intake numbers are an interesting aspect of the intended entry of students. Low intake numbers can place the provision of options within a course in doubt either economically or educationally; if a student spends a lot of time in small groups, he or she may not gain all that should come out of interactions with a wide range of other student perspectives, values and experiences. On the other hand, high enrolments can overload staff, accommodation or practical placement arrangements.

*Staffing Resources.* The importance of the factor of confidence in CNAA judgements has been stressed above, and is due to the fact that a validating panel does not have firsthand experience of the course — only the staff and students have that. The staff together with the external examiners (and overseen by the college's internal machinery) are responsible for maintaining the standard of the course as it operates between the points of validation. However, the adequacy of the course team cannot be judged in isolation from the course aims and the target group of students. If the documents are poor, it may delay the time of a crucial interaction between a validating panel and the course team. However, institutions frequently underestimate the importance of the quality of the staff and place their reliance instead on documents. Boards often visit institutions with severe reservations about the course based on the documents, only to come away afterwards with such a strong impression of the quality of the staff that the reservations pale into insignificance; in some cases, it may be that members would be happy for such staff to run virtually any course within their competence. The opposite has also occurred, ie excellent documents (perhaps written by one person or knocked into shape by an internal validation panel) which are overtaken by an impression of low levels of competence, experience, imagination, coherence and commitment gained from a visit. The dangers of placing too much reliance upon one day's performance have been referred to earlier. It is therefore important to gain corroborative evidence, from other meetings, from students' work and quite importantly from meetings with students.

It follows from the importance of the staff factor that approval of a course is not really approval of documents but of a total environment in which a course having those aims for those students can run; therefore the documents are not sacrosanct and can be reinterpreted and modifications easily agreed. However, a definitive course document is expected to be available at all times to the CNAA and within the college, showing the present state of the approved course. From the status of documents it also follows that the details of the points raised about them in discussion are not so important as what the answers reveal about the thinking, experience, imagination and cohesion of the staff. Thus, for example, syllabus material simply forms a vehicle for obtaining impressions from the staff. That is not to say that sloppiness is acceptable, the students must know what is expected of them at all times. In fact, *initial* impressions of staff will be based considerably upon the quality of communication within the documents; unclear aims, inconsistencies, incomprehensibility, platitudinous rhetoric, unnecessary complexity etc., do not help, but a penetrating critical appraisal and a concise and lucid presentation of course rationale and structure certainly will help.

Many factors contribute to a level of confidence in the staff.

1    Staff expertise: The CNAA needs to know enough about each staff member to judge whether he or she is competent to teach the section intended. In the end, this is a subjective decision after discussion, but time can be saved if documents match staff names against syllabuses and list the qualifications, teaching experience, industrial/ commercial experience, research, publications and consultancy. Clearly there needs to be enough depth of expertise in each of the areas of the course to cover it at the level intended. There would be difficulties if an area depended on one member of staff, not only because he or she might fall ill or leave (without replacement) or go on secondment, but because of the need for staff to develop their subject and its teaching through interacting with each other. It may be necessary to employ visiting lecturers, but if dependence on them becomes considerable then they would be expected to become involved in the course design. Courses have been rejected for too little input from the institutions offering them.

2    Quality of staff: This is a vague concept but of the greatest importance. It probably combines liveliness, imagination, understanding, perceptiveness, open-mindedness, vision, anticipation of problems, realism, commitment and enthusiasm plus expertise.

3    Staff cohesion and leadership: The course leader needs to have all of these qualities plus the ability to marshall his/her team, to delegate yet to coordinate and oversee, to focus and to enthuse. A democratic rather than autocratic style is desirable if the course team itself is to be fully involved.

The body of staff need to understand the scheme, its philosophy, focus and structure and their own roles. Whether they are evidently working together may have much to do with the extent to which they have participated in the course design. Alexander (1979b) has criticized the CNAA view of the necessity of consensus amongst the course team.

The course leader must have adequate access to the necessary staffing resources. The course team needs to involve all important areas and the course should draw upon support from obviously relevant departments within the institution. For example, there have been examples of physics courses where electronics components could be taught in a more up-to-date manner by electrical engineering departmental staff. This is not to say that some 'servicing' inputs can not be made by staff appointed to the parent department for that purpose. The opposite problem is that of a course team which is so large as to threaten fragmentation of the teaching. A related issue is the need to ensure that visiting lecturers, and people such as clinical placement supervisors, are suitably involved with the course team.

4   Staff development: In general terms, every member of the teaching team should be professionally active in some way and those who make key course contributions should be developing themselves in ways directly relevant to the course and its development. Many departments have claimed unsuccessfully that a plethora of research in (say) biochemistry or marketing was directly relevant to the support of an honours degree in (say) hotel management.

While there is no direct evidence that research and other forms of professional activity do lead to improvement of teaching, the CNAA believes that these activities are marks of lively staff, and that independent learning can best be promoted by staff who themselves are learning heuristically and tackling conceptual problems in their work.

Further, the CNAA likes to see departments covering in a balanced way the major forms of staff development without undue neglect of (for example) applied research, fundamental research, consultancy, subject updating or reorientation, recent industrial/ commercial experience, or teaching/curriculum development.

5   Turnover and grading of staff: The need for staff development, including secondments, study leave and conferences, becomes particularly acute when staff mobility is low. In such circumstances ideas do not easily move around and interact, nor do staff have contact with problems and solutions developed elsewhere, nor do they get stimulted by contact with the development, application and teaching of their subject. This, together with lack of career prospects, deteriorating resources, and overwork may lead to stagnation and declining morale. Clearly, therefore some degree of staff turnover is healthy.

However, too high a turnover of staff can also be a problem, even if staff are continuously replaced, the cohesion of the course, the stability of the student body, the maintenance and evolution of the course philosophy can suffer.

Further, staff who do not stay long may not have much opportunity to develop professionally and exploit that development within the course. One reason for high staff turnover can be low gradings of staff; this is particularly important at the level of subject leaders and the course leader. A problem is often found in some vocational areas in attracting appropriately qualified and experienced staff to fill vacancies because of high salaries in professional practice, commerce or industry.

6    Total academic staffing: The total number of staff must be adequate to enable the course to be implemented alongside other courses without overloading the staff. Therefore, the CNAA frequently enquires about staff total teaching loads in hours of 'contact' per week, together with details about allowances for administration, research etc. Sometimes, Subject Boards may ask about student/staff ratios, since a course with a high SSR may overload staff unless there are large numbers of students or low student 'contact' hours; a low SSR may mean that staff are not operating an efficient course structure and overloading themselves in this way together with jeopardising the viability of the course. While it can be argued that these are all questions for the institution, trade unions and staff individually, the CNAA's interest in these issues is justified by the difficulty of staff pursuing research, staff development and course development if they are overworked. Subject Boards will never set down a figure for staff workloads because of the danger of being too prescriptive, nor will the CNAA or officers in an offical capacity; personally, I get concerned by workloads which when averaged for staff over the year get as high as 15 hours per week genuine 'contact'.

Because of the present resource difficulties, courses are increasingly having to be staffed by developing some staff, by redeploying vacancies and by phasing out other courses or reducing their intakes.

7    Technical and clerical staffing: The number of techncians needed will depend on the amount of practical work in the course, the number of students on the course and the other teaching done by the department. Thus, at one time a survey of biology departments running honours single-subject degrees showed a norm of about 1:1 for technicians: academic staff. Realistic levels of support staffing may now have fallen below this. Other influences are the arrangements for pooling technicians across a faculty.

Similar pooling arrangements often affect judgements about the adequacy of secretarial and administrative staffing. Perhaps one departmental secretary per fifteen academic staff might be an appropriate norm which avoids staff having to do clerical work which makes incursions on time for preparing for teaching, for assessment and for staff development.

The gradings of technicians and administrative staff can become an issue if sufficiently experienced people cannot be attracted to posts and retained. This is often also an issue, together with total numbers, for librarians and computer centre staff; these matters are frequently dealt with during institutional review visits. Adequate numbers of professionally qualified librarians and of computer program advisory staff are important. In extreme cases, teaching staff have been expected to operate the computer and advisory services; such arrangements are unacceptable.

*Course Structure and Curriculum.* The means of achieving the course aims with given students and resources is the teaching and learning of the content of the programme of studies. Much of the discussion which takes place during CNAA visits derives from the content as described by the syllabuses and booklists; for example these may be too overcrowded or superficial and descriptive, or they may not progress or underpin each other.

A rather neglected area of discussion, as Cox points out below, is that of teaching and learning methods. Mainly, members ask about the proportion of time to be spent on lectures, tutorials, seminars and practical work. Sometimes Subject Boards find that there is inadequate use of case studies, for example, of open-ended approaches to practical work or of remedial work for heterogeneous student groups. Often there is concern about the number of hours of student 'contact' work either on the basis that more is needed to cover (say) clinical work or the digestion of engineering concepts, or that less is essential if students are going to have enough time to study independently, to read, to think, to solve problems and to sound out their own ideas and those of others in discussion. Thus, more than say 20 hours a week in a 'laboratory - based' course or 12 hours a week in a 'library - based' course might be questioned. Unfortunately, 'laboratory - based' courses also need students to write-up their work and to do all the things usual in 'library - based' courses. On the face of it, there seems to be an argument for reducing the student 'contact' hours in science courses so that students are able to use the same time for independent study that humanities students have.

A further aspect of the actual operation of courses is their management arrangements and Subject Boards do explore the administrative arrangements. Not just the size and scope and authority of the course committee are explored, but increasingly the arrangements for monitoring and evaluating the course. I have elaborated elsewhere (Billing 1982) on the issues concerned with course review. It is important to know at the stage of validation, what the process involves and where the responsibility lies at the level above that of the course committee. Further, it is important to ensure that evaluation looks at the large scale issues of whether the course is coherent and meets its aims and whether resources are adequate and staff are developing — rather than just trouble shooting on individual problems which monitoring has detected.

I shall now concentrate in this section on the macroscopic aspects of course design — the structure and curriculum.

1   Firstly, the duration — is it sufficient for the aims to be satisfied with these students? Unfortunately, the duration of full-time under-graduate courses is fixed at three years (four years for honours in Scotland) so that this constrains what aims can be achieved. There is a little flexibility in this in the use of vacations for placements or field-work.

Issues which do arise within a full-time course are whether it can contain enough industrial training or professional placement without expansion to four years (and perhaps designation as sandwich) in order to ensure that academic components are not skimped. Such additions and subtractions, of course, grossly oversimplify the interaction between 'academic' and 'training' elements. At present, for example, the Health and Medical Services Board believes that it is unlikely that a degree course which also includes a licence to practice can be contained in three academic years.

The possibility of two-year full-time degree courses was mooted by the University College at Buckingham, on the basis of four-term years. The CNAA did not believe that there would be enough time, not just to cover the content but to do so in a way which left enough time for independent study and simply for maturation; members were familiar with the difference which a year makes to students (for example 48 weeks away in industrial placement), not just in greater knowledge but greater maturity, confidence, respon-sibility, self-motivation and ability to identify and focus on fundamental concepts and methods. The College was not prepared to negotiate other arrangements.

Courses are designated 'sandwich' by the CNAA if they contain at least 48 weeks of supervised work experience which satisfies certain aims set out in the first degree regulations (1979). The figure of 48 is generally agreed to be arbitrary and the 'sandwich' label might well have ceased to be a useful category.

There is more flexibility with the duration of postgraduate courses, although the norm is one year full-time for a master's course; however, that would be a specialized master's course starting from a relevant honours degree basis. Less relevant or non-honours first degrees might require longer, while a master's course based on a postgraduate diploma would usually be shorter; thus duration is linked to entry level and the type of course (specialized, reorientation etc.).

Part-time courses offer the greatest flexibility in duration and although there are minima set-down (eg five years from 'A' level equivalent to honours), the basic question is how long is needed to enable the aims to be achieved. This depends not only on the entry level but also the attendance pattern: day-release, two evenings or three evenings a week etc. Previously, some Subject Boards have unfortunately counted the number of hours of teaching in the course and compared it with their norms or with full-time courses or with norms understood to be operated by professional bodies. Durations of programmes of study may, of course, be altered when individual students enter with exemptions for previous work or when the course is offered in a mixed-mode pattern. In the latter case students can take parts of the course full-time and parts on a part-time basis; in other cases, part-time study may be accelerated or decelerated by taking more or less modules per year.

Programmes of study have sometimes been criticised for permitting too long a duration. In these cases, the Subject Boards are concerned that attenuation may diminish the level of demand (particularly for honours) and that the material may become out of date. The CNAA regulations limit the maximum duration for individual students to three years more than the planned duration.

2  Means of organizing course components: All courses have components — eg syllabuses or groups of syllabuses collected into subjects or options. However, in some courses these components are more standardized in size and ways of connection; such course structures are called *modular* or *unit based*. The CNAA has no views about the relative preferences for modular or non-modular structures. Where course aims emphasize flexibility in student choices, a modular structure might seem justified; however, these choices can be illusory, as the contraints necessary to ensure coherence or the viability of modules may limit choice in practice.

While the CNAA does not require integration of all course components, Subject Boards will need to be convinced about the coherence of each programme of study, brought about by organizing concepts or themes. A further problem in modular courses is that units are normally designed to be multi-purpose in terms of the programmes into which they can fit; thus the group of students taking each module will be heterogeneous in terms of background and intentions.

While it is not necessary that modular courses espouse the credit principle, many do so and the assessment arrangements may then raise problems in the demonstration of honours ability in meeting over-arching aims, rather than simply accumulating credits. The advantages and disadvantages of modular courses have been summarized elsewhere (Billing 1974; CNAA 1974c).

3  The Curriculum: This is taken here to be the arrangement of
subject areas in the course. In a non-modular course, it will consist
of the list of syllabuses in each year with the time allocations for
each and the options. During discussion, if not in the documents,
the means of linking the syllabuses conceptually within each year
and through progression between years will need to be indicated;
themes and organizing principles will need to be drawn out.

The CNAA will establish whether the right subjects are present in
the right amounts to constitute a core with support so that the course
aims are met; this should include satisfying Council's Principle 3.
Sometimes meeting Principle 3 can be done within the main subjects
and this may be preferable to the alternative of including a specific
course component. There is a danger of the 'core' of such courses
being too slim or of the whole course being so broad as to lack
focus — especially at the final-year level.

The same issues arise for modular courses, but they have then
to be applied to each individual programme of studies. The important
structural questions are then the size of modules, the number to be
taken/passed, the number of levels of module and the rules for
combining them into programmes. Thus, small modules can lead to
fragmentation and inadequate time to tackle the ambitious material
included in each; large modules can cause timetabling problems, can
restrict choice, and can lead to students failing large chunks of the
course. In practice, the size of modules varies from 1/12 to 1/3 of a
year's full-time work. Often there are three levels of module, roughly
corresponding to years of a full-time degree, and perhaps with
additional introductory/remedial modules. There are courses with
only two levels, but there are then problems of ensuring adequate
progression of material to follow intellectual progression. When years
two and three are composed of modules of the same level, the honours
classification scheme frequently weights these years equally — this
again causes problems in properly demonstrating progression. Some
degrees of this type build in prerequisite restrictions which link
modules within the same level and effectively produce an additional
level.

The major means of determining how modules may be combined
is through lists of prerequisites, such that a particular module
needs to be preceded by another specified one. This ensures 'vertical
coherence' but 'lateral coherence' is not so clearly facilitated; in
some schemes, there are no restrictions on the modules of the same
level which may be combined. In other degrees, integration is valued
and non-cognate modules are excluded, or the student has to choose
two or three subject areas first, and then select modules within
each of these areas.

A major issue with the curriculum has been the means of

distinguishing between honours and non-honours degrees. The CNAA has always been under pressure to allow an ordinary degree to be a fifth band below third class honours on a continuous scale. It has resisted this on the basis, initially, that the ordinary degree was different and was for a different type of student who needed segregating in order to ensure special treatment. Resource pressures have decreased the extent of feasible segregation in the programmes of study and the norm is probably now for non-honours students to do less material in the final year or sometimes different material. Subject Boards would then explore the rationale which distinguished the selections of material for honours and non-honours; sometimes this might be depth of study for honours, sometimes higher abilities such as problem solving or independent work, and sometimes synthesis of concepts across a breadth of study. Some course teams laboured under the delusion that breadth was less demanding than depth and sometimes CNAA Boards also apparently saw breadth and depth as opposites.

Structural differences between honours and non-honours programmes are often based on additional numbers of options or modules which honours students take. Unless these additional elements are of a more demanding kind, eg projects or options not accessible to non-honours students, then such structures imply that honours may be just 'more of the same'. Although course teams have argued that covering more work itself is demanding enough for honours, this argument about pace of study is not always convincing and some Boards have in fact suggested that honours students need more time not less to think and read around. If such arguments about pace of study are not sustained then the 'more of the same' structures will not satisfy the (1979) CNAA Principle 4.4 which requires a qualitative difference between honours and non-honours awards.

However, the 1979 first degree Regulations made possible undifferentiated honours/non-honours programmes where the qualitative difference is achieved entirely in the award criteria. Since the CNAA will not accept the fifth band of marks for non-honours on a continuum, these undifferentiated programmes require some clear differences in the assessments. It is probably time that the need for a qualitative distinction was reviewed, since it seems unlikely that students fall clearly into two kinds rather than a single spectrum of abilities; most teachers would see more differences between first and third class honours students than between third class honours and non-honours students.

## CNAA POLICIES AND FUTURE DEVELOPMENT

This discussion of honours and ordinary degrees serves to remind us that the criteria used in CNAA validation are related to ongoing debates. Thus the 1979 Regulations probably mark simply a wayside halt along the road away from the belief that students are rigidly divided into two distinct types. Similarly, there has been both continuing thought over the question of how to liberalise or balance a curriculum which continually edged towards subject specialization, and a halting progress towards full acceptance of the credit principle. Many of these debates have been echoed, of course, at the postgraduate level, an area which is closely connected with the Council's interest in developing both research (CNAA 1974b) in institutions which diversified (CNAA 1976, 1977b) away from the purely teaching role first envisaged for them (DES 1967) and in staff development (Billing 1977, 1982). Indeed the whole question of the future development of higher education (CNAA 1978a) and in particular the possibility of extending access to courses (CNAA 1975b) has been a major concern.

INSTITUTIONAL REVIEWS

Policy has also been evolving in relation to institutional review visits and relationship with institutions. Continuing pressure since the 1973 Procedures paper (CNAA 1973) had led the Council to issue a Discussion Paper (CNAA 1975a) in 1975, and to rethink its proposals when they were fairly generally rejected for either of the conflicting reasons of not going far enough or going too far. An internal paper was referred back in 1977 by Council itself and the special Working Party finally put forward more flexible and realistic proposals which were implemented in the 1979 paper (CNAA 1979b) *Developments in Partnership in Validation.* Ths provides for:

1   Improvement of the procedures for the initial approval of courses.
2   Introduction of indefinite periods of approval, subject to regular progress reviews.
3   Replacement of the process of the renewal of approval of courses by progress review visits.
4   Extension of the limits within which institutions can change approved courses.
4   Provision for institutions to propose variations from the normal validation methods.
5   Improvement of the procedures for linking course validation and institutional reviews.

This has still not gone far enough for some institutions, and proposals for course accreditation, or licenses to grant degrees under conditional charters (incorporating reference to the CNAA) have been considered. At present the Council wishes to make the DPV framework operate fully so that further evolution can then be considered 1 (CNAA 1981c).

The DPV paper also set up the Committee for Institutions, which has been looking at the form of Institutional Reviews (CNAA, 1980d). So far, it has opted for smaller visiting parties where these are feasible, with the implication that it will no longer be feasible to have discussions at departmental levels. Council Visits had built up into complex and major events, yet without a clear remit to form policies or reach conclusions on a number of aspects regularly discussed — such as academic structure and student services. As many as forty people might be involved over one and a half days, and in 1975-77 the Council Visits were in six cases preceded by visits to each Faculty and to some of the central services.The position now is that two aspects of the institutional environment are of greatest concern for course validation — safeguards on resource allocation, and internal processes for the setting and maintenance of course standards. Council Visits now concentrate on the *effectiveness* of these processes rather than on criticising the academic structure in itself. However, in order to probe the effectiveness of policies and processes, it is necessary to test them at all levels in the institution. Therefore, some discussion at the level of course leaders, departments and faculties has been justified and is still justified; smaller visiting parties will need to safeguard such multi-level probing. Institutional Reviews had been criticised sometimes for the composition of the visiting parties. In the case of initial Council Visits, these had been conducted for a while entirely by officers as this was the policy set out by the 1973 Procedures paper. Increasingly, members of Committees and Boards had been added in order to discuss matters more at departmental level, so that the compositions of officers' visits came to resemble those for subsequent Council Visits. Now, the call from institutions is for appraisal by visiting parties which are more clearly peer groups relating to experience of the matters at issue.Therefore, members are now being selected more for their experience of academic and resource management in higher education institutions than for their subject experience. Each Institutional Review visiting party will now contain a core from the Committee for Institutions, and Subject Board members will be selected for their ability to contribute on general institutional matters.

CONCLUSION
The CNAA may in all this be evolving by reacting to events (inside and outside) rather than on the basis of a researched picture of actual strengths and weakness, but it is undeniable that it is adding a new dimension to its operation through 'Partnership in Validation'. And although there is room for much more investigation into the way validation works, enquiries perhaps best carried out through case studies, this enquiry does show that many of the criticisms of CNAA course validation are not justified. There is a form of objectivity, and a degree of radicalism to be seen. And, perhaps more significantly, the process does encourage rigorous internal monitoring. Although there are problems, some of these, like the inevitable inequality between validator and validated, are beginning

to fade, partly due to 'Partnership in Validation'. Moreover, the process itself provides a means of making teachers consider a vast range of issues, principles and questions, the very examination of which surely serves as a guide to the amelioration of the whole educational process.

REFERENCES

Alexander, R.J. (1979a) Personal communication

Alexander, R.J. (1979b) What is a course? Curriculum models and CNAA validation *Journal of Further and Higher Education* 31-45 3

Alexander, R.J., Billing, D.E. and Gent, B. (1980) *Partnership and Standards: Validation and Evaluation, A Discussion Paper* unpublished London: CNAA

Bethel, D., Billing, D., Gent, B., Kerr, E., Oakeshott, M., Webster, H. and Wyatt, J. (1980) Contributions to *Evaluation Newsletter* 4 (1)

Billing, D.E. (1973) Classification of educational objectives. In Billing, D.E. and Furniss, B.S. (Eds) *Aims, Methods and Assessment in Advanced Science Education* London: Heydon and Son

Billing, D.E. (1974) The pros and cons of modular courses *Times Higher Educational Supplement* 8 November

Billing, D.E. (1976) *Proposed Degree and Honours Course in Combined Studies* Conference of the Combined Studies (Science) Board, Bournemouth

Billing, D.E. (1977) Nature and scope of staff development in institutions of higher education. In Elton, L.R.B. and Simmonds, K. (Eds) *Staff Development in Higher Education* Guildford: SRHE

Billing, D.E. (1980a) Maintaining the standards of the Council for National Academic Awards. In Billing, D.E. (Ed.) *Indicators of Performance in Higher Education* Guildford: SRHE

Billing, D.E. (1980b) *Problems with Credit Accumulation* Conference on Modular Courses and Credit Accumulation, Garnett College, London

Billing, D.E. (1982) *Staff Development in Higher Education* SCEDSIP Occasional Publication

Committee of Enquiry on Local Government Finance (Layfield Committee Report) (1976) Cmnd 6453. London: HMSO

CNAA (1973) *Procedure for Validation of Courses of Study* London CNAA

CNAA (1974a) *Interim Statement: Regulations and Conditions for the Award of the Council's First Degrees* London: CNAA

CNAA (1974b) *Report of the Working Party on Resources for Research in Polytechnics and other Colleges* (Rochester Report) London: CNAA

CNAA (1974c) *Reflections on the Design of Modular Courses* London: CNAA

CNAA (1975a) *Partnership in Validation: A Discussion Paper* London: CNAA

CNAA (1975b) *Partnership in Validation: A summary of the comments received on the Council's discussion paper* London: CNAA

CNAA (1976) *Diversification in the Former Colleges of Education* London: CNAA

CNAA (1977a) Agreement on the reciprocal transfer of credit between the CNAA and the Open University

CNAA (1977b) *Report on a Conference on Planning for Academic Diversification in Higher Education* London: CNAA

CNAA (1978a) *Response to the DES/SED Document: Higher Education into the 1990s* London: CNAA

CNAA (1978b) *Opportunities in Higher Education for Mature Students* London: CNAA

CNAA (1979a) *Principles and Regulations for the Award of the Council's First Degrees and Diploma of Higher Education* London: CNAA

CNAA (1979b) *Developments in Partnership in Validation* London: CNAA

CNAA (1979c) *Learning Resources in Relation to Course Design: A Discussion Paper* London: CNAA

CNAA (1979d) *Notes for Guidance on Matters Relating to the Award of the Council's First Degrees and Diploma of Higher Education* London: CNAA

CNAA (1980a) Evidence to the Report of the Education Science and Arts Select Committee of the House of Commons: Funding and Organisation of Courses in Higher Education

CNAA (1980b) *Extension of Access to Higher Education* London: CNAA

CNAA (1980c) Response to the CET Discussion Document: Open Learning Systems

CNAA (1980d) *Institutional Reviews: Notes for Guidance of Institutions* London: CNAA

CNAA (1981a) *Notes for Guidance: The Critical Appraisal of Courses* London: CNAA

CNAA (1981b) *DipHE Transfer Arrangements*

CNAA (1981c) *Developments in Partnership in Validation Report* London: CNAA

Davis, M.C. (1979) *The Development of the CNAA 1964-74; A Study of a Validation Agency* PhD Thesis, Loughborough University of Technology. See also Davis, M.C., The CNAA — the development of a validating agency 1964-74. In Billing, D.E. (Ed.) *Indicators of Performance* Guildford: SRHE

DES (1967) *Research in Polytechnics, DES Administrative Memorandum 8/67*, Appendix B

DES/SED (1978) *Higher Education into the 1990s. A Discussion Document* London: DES/SED

DES (1981a) *Higher Education in England Outside the Universities: Policy, Funding and Management, Consultative Document* London: HMSO

DES (1981b) Press Notice, 23 December

Education, Science and Arts Select Committee of the House of Commons (Price Report) (1980) *Report, Funding and Organization of Courses in the Higher Education* London: HMSO

Lane, M.R. (1975) *Design for Degrees* London: MacMillan, p.69

Popper, K.R. (1972) *The Logic of Scientific Discovery* London: Hutchinson p.44

Robinson, E.E. (1978) Courses for whom? In Billing, D.E. (Ed.) *Course Design and Student Learning* Guildford: SRHE

Tait, J. and Billing, D.E. (1980) The development and provision of learning resources *ACID Journal iii* (2) 34-53

Toyne, P. (1980) *Educational Credit Transfer Feasibility Study*

Working Party (1978) *The Management of Higher Education in the Maintained Sector* (Oakes Report) Cmnd 7130. London: HMSO

Clive H. Church

Validation is a relatively clear cut and well understood matter in the public sector. Within universities the situation is rather different. As a concept the term is not greatly used and can mean no more than simply assuring consistency of standards (Carter 1981). As a practice, although it has been rightly said that 'the curriculum is the essence of any university' (Grant 1975), its management does not seem to attract a good deal of consideration either. Yet it obviously exists, both within universities themselves, and in the public sector colleges for which they are responsible. This lack of familiarity, and the consequent lack of study, is one of a number of obstacles in the way of grasping exactly how British universities do exercise control of their courses.

Obviously the fact that things are not understood in this way in universities has meant that not a great deal of research has been done on the subject at least in this country. The curriculum as such seems to fall outside the remit both of ordinary academics, who stick to the detail of their subjects, and of people who take higher education as their field of study. Thus studies of the way universities work, like that by Moodie and Eustace (1974), have little to say about it and, while a great deal of effort has been put into analysing teaching, studies like Beard's (1979) concern themselves more with method than with either content or management. Clearly there is a very curious gap between the structure of research and the common currency of university conversation and life, which often turns round problems of course management and control. The gap is almost as notable when it comes to outside activities as it is domestically.

However, here the problem is more one of changeability. The situation of university validation has changed very rapidly in recent years and is likely to continue to do so. At the end of the sixties well over thirty universities were involved in this activity and tens of thousands of students were following their courses. Many colleges then opted out of university validation because they found it insufficiently adjusted to the post-James world. Moreover, the general contraction of higher education has also affected both teacher training and university finances very badly, so with the conveniently expanding safety net of the CNAA available, many universities have withdrawn from the field. Those that remain involved are dealing with reduced numbers although there has been a redistribution amongst institutions too. Numbers of students on courses under Liverpool, for example, have declined by a quarter since 1976 alone (Liverpool 1981).

Any assessment of what universities do in this field therefore covers very different periods and situations.

Of course the main problem is that we cannot really talk of what the universities — in generalized terms — do because this suggests they are all alike. Many criticisms of university practices in the area of validation have really been posited on the assumption that they are — or should be — all the same, whether organizationally or academically. In reality, to look for the equivalent of a CNAA cycle of operations and for discrete social entities called 'courses' is to turn one's back on the way universities are. Because the universities are chartered, autonomous bodies they are constructed not round courses but around basic departmental and other units. These can offer a range of degrees. Given their range of options and the possibilities of switching from one degree to another, which now exist, courses are immensely varied and hard to classify. To seek for discrete courses is to separate things like teaching, research, resources and academic policy which are naturally united (Kelly 1981).

Moreover, the precise structure of universities varies a great deal, and the way federal, unitary, faculty or departmental institutions work can vary considerably. Similarly, the relations between universities and public sector colleges can vary enormously, both as between universities and sometimes (Heywood 1981) as between colleges in the orbit of a particular university. So, although it will be argued that there is more similarity than diversity amongst universities in the way they handle external validation, this is only part of the problem.

Any appraisal of course control in the university sector must therefore be provisional and tentative, with as many exceptions to any generalization as there are cases covered by it, whether on the grounds of variation, change over time or fallible information. Nonetheless, given the present state of our knowledge, and the somewhat hostile view of what universities do by way of validation this has encouraged in the outside world, the attempt to set out exactly what they do is worth while. Even if we can only set out the formal structures through which validation is meant to take place this will be an improvement on the current state of affairs, particularly as the very existence of such formal structures is significant. To some extent, the attempt to do this relies on personal experiences of validation in the University of Lancaster and elsewhere, particularly in the field of history (Blyth and Lewin 1979), but the basic source is a questionnaire sent to the registrars of virtually all university institutions in Great Britain, some 87 per cent of whom replied, often in great detail and accompanying their replies with literature on their operations and regulations etc. To them, and the sample of 20 per cent who commented on the factual accuracy of a first draft, the writer is very much obliged. Responsibility for all judgements and errors, however, is solely his.

The aim of the present paper, then, is to set out what exactly happens by way of validation in universities firstly, where internal procedures are concerned and secondly, at a somewhat greater length since this is the more documented and contentious area, by way of what is best called trans-mural validation since it involves collaboration between the universities and the colleges, whereas extra-mural has connotations of imposed authority and especially of continuing education. Obviously, not all aspects of this can be dealt with here, but attention will be paid to organizational structures, academic review, and the process of validation. Thirdly, some attempt is made to sum up the output and effects of course control in the university world, both in institutional and academic terms, and finally to ask how far the criticisms made of it are really justified. It soon becomes quite obvious that the extreme critique of universities which claims that, whereas public sector colleges take great care over their courses, universities take none at all, particularly trans-murally, cannot be substantiated. To deny that university staff think and act seriously about their teaching and degree schemes is to deny the obvious in order to claim a slightly exaggerated distinctiveness.

Furthermore, in recent years there has been something of a convergence between the ways in which the two sectors treat teaching, internally and externally, as common sense suggests was bound to happen. Beneath the appearance of widely varying and often ad hoc arrangements there are common patterns of structures, review and processes of course control, patterns which, though they may vary between institutions, increasingly overlap the internal/external divide. Institutions throughout higher education have been affected by similar trends of late and, with due allowance for their different natures, have reacted in parallel ways. It is, in the last resort, not a question of better or worse but of different ways of doing the same thing. A sad world it would be if all had to conform to one model, no matter how excellent this were thought to be.

## INTERNAL VALIDATION

The way in which universities handle their curriculum has been denounced as elitist (Pedley 1977), as amateurish and managerially diffuse (Dowdeswell and Good 1978) and bereft of clear objectives (Betjemann 1978). As a result, it is sometimes said courses can be launched without due thought, put together any old how and monitored, if at all, by external examiners rather than by proper self-scrutiny (Piper 1981). A quarter of the universities circulated specifically addressed themselves to this problem, and it appears that the norm is for consideration of courses to be handled by the normal channels of academic governance rather than by special bodies. The most common way for consideration of new or revised courses to start is at the level of department or subject group. Thereafter the resultant proposals will be considered by Faculty or School boards before going on to the Senate level, sometimes via a Planning Committee as at Sussex (Ivey 1981), or a Rectorial Policy Committee, as at Imperial College (Mee 1981). Faculty board consideration can be fairly effective and at Aberdeen it is rare for courses not to be modified (Begg 1981). At Reading each Faculty has its own syllabus committee to examine new and revised proposals plus an inter-faculty harmonizing committee for central approvals. And in the case of a federal university like London there is further scrutiny at the university level.

Such scrutiny, many respondents insist, is not to be regarded as merely a rubber stamp. In Surrey visiting members of staff and representatives of industry can be brought in to examine new or radically altered proposals (Haigh 1981) while the Manchester Committee of the Senate Development Committee appoints Faculty Development Committees to receive, evaluate and co-ordinate requests about course development (Hewton 1975). A computerized data base is at their disposal to provide information and bench marks for assessing proposals. Where decisions are favourable conditions of review and amendment are imposed while there is an appeals procedure in case of unfavourable decisions.

One of the most detailed procedures is that laid down by the University of Salford (1976) which requires that a department initiating a proposal first informs the central Academic Policy Committee (APC) of its intentions. If the latter is convinced that there is, prima facie, a place for the new course in the University's plans, then approval in principle has to be sought by the department through the normal channels. Merely to obtain approval in principle requires the submission of much information on likely student demand, career openings, entry requirements, course structure, staffing, research potential, administrative and other forms of support and funding. Then, if the principle is accepted a further submission on the same lines but with the addition of precise detail on teaching programmes, has also to run the gauntlet of department, faculty and APC consideration. The whole process can take at least six months to complete.

In some cases this type of scrutiny is entrusted to machinery which is somewhat apart from the normal channels of decision making. Thus at York while single honours courses are dealt with normally, combined courses have to be referred to a special Combined Courses Committee (Riddell 1981) because of the special burdens imposed by combined degrees. Only if it is satisfied that the proposal does not involve unacceptable student workloads or timetable difficulties does it set up a special Combined Board of Studies to administer the scheme. Brunel University takes the approach further (Chandler 1981) through the working of its First Degrees Sub Committee of Senate, composed of a Chairman and five members of staff who have to see a 'Scheme of Studies and an examination schedule' for all new courses. The documentation is expected to cover the objectives of the course, demand, entry requirements, work placements, teaching hours and assessment plans. Only when the course has cleared this initial hurdle can the proposal go forward through the normal channels of Resource Committees and the like. No major changes can be made in agreed schemes without the approval of the First Degrees

Committee. Similar arrangements are made for higher degree courses as well.

Lancaster also had, for a while, a Senate Courses Committee which vetted all proposals for new or altered courses and also began to undertake some more general review of the whole teaching operations of specific departments in the late seventies, before being wound up once the recession meant that new courses ceased to come through in such large numbers as before. However, the process of scrutiny *per se* has not been abandoned. All new and revised proposals, whether for degree schemes or individual units, have still to be submitted in a standardized and detailed form and considered, either by the full Board of Studies or by a special courses committee in the case of language and area studies on the one hand and humanities and social sciences on the other. The Board of Graduate Studies also operates in much the same manner for Masters degrees.

So while the structures of internal validation may vary with the internal structures of universities, they obviously do exist in many institutions. In certain cases they can involve some kind of external reference whether to representatives of industry as in Surrey, to external examiners as at Lancaster, or to professional bodies as in Aberdeen. And, of course, it is not just academics who are involved in such procedures. The administrations of universities play a part too, notably at UCL (Arterton 1981) while it is not unknown for many of those involved in scrutiny of courses to have experience whether with the CNAA or with trans-mural validation. Finally, in the case of London, the federal nature of the university with its Boards of Studies drawn from many schools and institutes, provides a kind of external appeal of its own (London 1982). While this kind of external reference may be of a limited and intermittent nature, it does exist and the absolute autonomy of the university teacher suggested by Gent (1981) does not really exist. Moreover, the existence of course control at the Faculty level or its equivalent provides some assurance that those who take part in the process are relatively familiar with the areas being considered, so that internal expertise in the subject concerned is not restricted purely and solely to those proposing the course in question.

The scope of course control is not limited merely to the launching of new courses. Amendments to approved schemes have also to be submitted in the same way, often in a systematic manner as with the London Course Unit Degree scheme. Similarly, there are forms of continuing review although this is very largely done on a subject by subject basis mainly through the external examiners. This is certainly the case at Sussex and Kent for instance (Linfoot 1981). It can be supplemented by questions raised in departmental, faculty and senate level bodies. Some universities do, however, operate what might be called a 'market' check, assessing admissions, take up between Part I and Part II of a degree where this is appropriate, and examination results as at Lancaster. At Reading such information can lead the dean to alter student targets accordingly. And at

Newcastle some note is also taken of feed back from Staff Student Consultative Committees, questionnaires to students and even of the *Alternative Prospectus* (Bond 1981). The Newcastle Senate has been known to order reviews of courses when such evidence suggests it is necessary, and some places have formalized this like Manchester and York. The Development Committee in the former has both annual and quinquennial reviews of courses, a practice voluntarily adopted by some departments at Guildford.

Although the case is less compelling here than with initial scrutiny, it remains the case that universities do worry about what happens on their courses and can, and do, take action to remedy the problems, although generally there is a problem of enforcing sanctions inside such autonomous communities. There are managerial controls and care is taken over launching, running and monitoring courses. The informality of the way this is done, moreover, may well allow easier response to needs than would more formal structures. However, this is hard, if not impossible, to prove. The important thing is that although the efficacy of internal validation in universities may legitimately be challenged, as Alexander and Gent do below, its actual existence cannot be, even if every institution may not measure up to the standards described here.

## TRANS-MURAL VALIDATION

If this is so, then it is unlikely that similar practices would not be employed in the colleges whose degrees are run in conjunction with the universities (and often with other colleges as well, hence the use of the term trans-mural), particularly when one of the universities' main fears was of the low academic standards in some of the colleges (Holt 1977). On the other hand criticisms of the way universities treated colleges of education have been even more trenchant than those of internal practices (Church 1976). Universities have been criticized for a lack of concern and provision for the process of validation; their handling of the colleges being allegedly marked by a lack of concern for managerial matters, by a use of untrained and often inexpert conscripts, by a failure to obtain resources for the colleges, and especially by an inability to provide a central location for validation.Their academic controls were, furthermore, said to be conservative, over academic and marked by the legacy of the old London External degrees, so that courses lacked imagination and innovativeness. Finally, the whole process is said to be carried out without rigour. There is no concern for monitoring standards, for adequate resources, for sufficient documentation and for academic quality control in general. All this has recently been said both to have its roots and its outcome in a patronizing disdain for the colleges, denying them autonomy and status, refusing students representation in the validating process, and seeking profit for themselves while denying the colleges the chance to mature (Billing 1981).

Before looking in turn at these three main charges and their effects on institutions we need to remind ourselves of the actual scope of university validation at the moment. Details are somewhat hard to come by, particularly because of the rapid run down of colleges of education already mentioned (Taylor and Gosden 1975). However, it seems that by 1981 no more than twenty universities were still involved, including a number like Bath, London and Sussex who were in the course of phasing out this involvement. There are thus sixteen members of the new Council of Validating Universities. The numbers validating with BEd degrees as opposed to diversified awards is even smaller. Nonetheless, about fifteen thousand students are still registered according to figures circulated at the 1981 meeting of administrators responsible for university validation. The majority of institutions involved are to be found in the north-west, Scotland and West Yorkshire.

There seem to be three basic types of operation amongst universities which seem set to continue validation. The first comprises those universities who validate one local college, whether for general or merely education qualifications. Hence the Southampton College of Higher Education looks to Southampton University, Nene College to Leicester and Rolle College to Exeter. Then there is a second group where validation is offered to a number of colleges in the area, who thereby form a kind of consortium. Thus Kent, Lancaster, Leeds (1980), Liverpool, Manchester, Nottingham, Surrey (which is partly taking over from London) and Wales all have between two and five colleges in their orbit. Finally, in Northern Ireland and Scotland (and to a lesser extent in Loughborough and Birmingham) there are those which teach or recognize a variety of awards in colleges which are very closely associated with the university in question. This is true of Belfast, Coleraine, Dundee, Heriot Watt and Stirling. The difference between these universities and the others is as much the nature of the relationship and the qualification as the number of institutions.

ORGANIZATIONAL STRUCTURES

Although the scope and extent of validation may vary there are some uniformities relevant to the first criticism of university validation, that it lacks structural provision for the operation. In the case of Bath, and to a lesser extent Birmingham, Kent and the Scots and Ulster universities, the ability to validate is specifically written into the Charter. Thus clauses of that of the first (1981) entitle the university to affiliate other institutions to recognize teachers and periods of study, and even to incorporate whole institutions. Moreover some universities have taken this further and laid down very detailed regulations on the operation of such processes, even when this is not actually being undertaken as at Salford (1981) and Strathclyde (1981). The new Delegacy of the University of Surrey (1981) also joins a large number of institutions in providing detailed handbooks and regulations to guide those involved in various aspects of the validation process. Examination regulations can give rise to particularly formidable publications (Nottingham 1980) which obviously serve as a control mechanism so that it is clear that universities can have clear statutory and regulative provision for trans-mural validation.

The operation of validation almost always relies on special mechanisms within the general governance of the University. Only Exeter seems to rely simply on the ordinary Faculty structure to deal with proposals from Rolle (Cannon 1981). Proposals there have to be submitted to the appropriate Faculty board, together with supporting papers, which then creates a joint Panel with a majority of university members which, largely acting through its Chairman, steers the proposal through to the Senate and later monitors progress. The creation of a special Board of Studies in Aberdeen for the BEd at Aberdeen College of Education points somewhat in the same direction (Begg 1981). In some cases talk of special mechanisms is a little misleading, since what happens, notably in London, is that the Institute of Education or its equivalent is charged with all validation-like activities although drawing on wider academic expertise. This was the case in Durham (Saxton 1981), Warwick (Warner 1981) and is probably also so in Stirling. At Bristol there were only education qualifications which helps to explain why this was so (Harvey 1981). Very often educational bodies had college representation, special committees like the College Degrees Committee of Newcastle reporting to it, or provided vital administrative support. In one or two cases, only educational qualifications were handled by Faculties of Education leaving diversified awards to special bodies. Thus in addition to Boards of Education at Leicester and Sussex (1981) we can also find a Committee for Collegiate Studies (Dunkley 1981) and a Senate Validating Committee respectively.

It is perhaps significant that the majority of universities which are continuing to validate have all worked mainly or entirely through a new and special board, which deals with all qualifications, whether educational or general. In other words, rather than relying on established contacts and knowledge, an attempt has been made to create a specific forum for trans-mural validation, usually with the style and status of an internal faculty, albeit with different composition. Thus Keele had its Validating Committee (Hodgkinson 1981), Kent has its Collegiate Board, Lancaster its Board H (for Associated Colleges), Leeds its Board for Collegiate Studies, Surrey its Delegacy and Wales its Validating Board. Since they have the rank of Faculties and report to Senate, in Lancaster, at least, the Colleges have been given their own representative on the Senate. Such Boards are usually chaired by the Vice-Chancellor or his deputy and can be serviced by their own staff, as in Liverpool, or by the School of Education as in Lancaster (1982). This role can, of course, give Schools of Education a very considerable influence.

Although at Leeds Senate membership excludes collegiate representation, the norm is for membership of such Boards to be weighted equally between university and college representatives. In Surrey the latter are represented on the basis of one member per thousand students. In Leeds the colleges make up about a fifth of the sixty members. College members often include the Principals ex officio, as at Kent and Lancaster, together with others elected by College Academic Boards. University representatives can be chosen on a university wide basis, as at Lancaster where the Senate nominates them or, as at Liverpool, by Faculties. There the Arts Faculty has six representatives and the three other Faculties four each. It is not uncommon for members to serve for longish periods of time and to have had experience with the CNAA so that there is a reasonable degree of experience available from the University side. In addition, there can be DES observers, external assessors, whether full members as in Kent or non-voting as in Surrey, and student representatives. Normally student representation is limited to the colleges (and can, as Harrison says in Chapter 7, not be totally excluded) but at Manchester and Sussex internal student representatives are also appointed so as to emphasize the special nature of the body and its operations.

Such Boards have extensive powers to maintain academic standards. The means for doing this can include a share in appointments made in colleges as in Liverpool, representation on course management teams as in Southampton, nomination of external examiners, inspections, a share in internal assessment, sometimes a role in admissions and, in the last resort, the right to withdraw approval of courses. Obviously not all such powers are exercised by the Board as a whole so that it has usually a network of sub-committees, for assessment, examination, course approvals, recognition of teachers, professional teaching matters, in-service courses, graduate studies and often, as in Manchester and Sussex, powerful steering committees. And, of course, a vast amount of validation work goes on informally outside such channels altogether. Both Board and Committees can be serviced by the officers of Schools of Education, by those of central university administration, or, as in Liverpool, by the Board's own deans. Although such bodies can obviously be rather formal, they do provide a forum for discussion not just of the minutiae of course approvals — often as in Lancaster and Leeds referred to small specialized bodies — but for general and policy matters of interest. Thus they can provide a means for colleges to have some voice in the running, not just of their own affairs, but even at times in those of the university as a whole.

ACADEMIC REVIEW

If there is clearly located legal and structural provision for validation within the university what of the second criticism of university validation, that it fails to provide for adequate development and review of the actual stuff of higher education? Generally Collegiate Boards deal with matters of general principle, leaving matters concerned with the disciplines taught to a range of Subject Boards, somewhat like those of the CNAA. Only

Nottingham, Lancaster and Kent do not have such bodies, although the latter's Boards of Examiners fulfil something of the same role (Kent 1982). Boards of studies, subject panels, or subject authorities as they were called at Durham are ubiquitous. Normally, they have joint membership from the two sides, although at Surrey outsiders could be added. Liverpool has as many as twenty such boards and Sussex had fifteen: art, drama, education, English, geography, history, home economics, languages, mathematics, music, physical education, teaching, religious studies, science and social studies. Their membership was three each from Brighton Polytechnic, West Sussex Institute and the University together with three students and three teachers or advisers. Durham's were even bigger. Such bodies are obviously directly aligned on traditional subjects, and in degrees which range across a number of such areas, a problem of co-ordination presents itself. However only London with its joint degree committees and Southampton with its Intermediate Arts, Education, Science and Theology panels seem to have responded to this problem institutionally. On the other hand such bodies could offer a forum to a large number of people actually teaching on courses validated by the universities and, in the cases of Aberdeen, Bath and Dundee (1981) the Boards served as the central mechanism for running the degree scheme as a whole. Obviously this is very different from the position of CNAA subject and interdisciplinary boards.

An even greater divergence from the latter's patterns of academic review is the fact that with the exception of London and, to a lesser extent, of Exeter and Leicester, most universities also designate a specific individual to take responsibility for assisting and overseeing the development of a particular subject. Such people can be known as Advisers as in Manchester, Internal Co-ordinating Advisers in Nottingham, Moderators in Leeds, Wales and Warwick and Visitors at Liverpool. However the most frequently used term is Assessor which appears from Sussex, Surrey and Bath in the south, through Birmingham (1981) and Lancaster, to Heriot Watt (Jamieson 1981) and Queen's, Belfast (Graham 1981). Duties are broadly similar: it falls to the lot of those at Nottingham, for instance, to advise on standards, syllabus and structure, approve examination papers and marks, ratify dissertation topics, and identify candidates likely to fail. Others can actually set examination papers, chair examination meetings, sample essays and examination papers, oversee library policy, and sometimes share in teaching and appointments. At Warwick, therefore, they were regarded as the eyes and the ears of the university, and in Wales (Lewis 1981b) as a major channel for monitoring progress.

Yet at the same time they are also representatives of the colleges vis-à-vis the university, seeking resources, sympathy and curricular changes. When, as in Leeds, they meet together regularly they can also be a force for standardization and change, both inside the university and amongst the colleges. So here again, rather than the problem being one of an inability to discern the university, it might be suggested that the latter can become too identified with one individual in the minds of the college staff. Hence in Lancaster arrangements are being made to move assessors round. Nonetheless, personality clashes do arise, often where relatively young lecturers have to advise senior college staff. The relationship is face to face but like other such relationships needs to be sensitively handled. In Nottingham and Lancaster, perhaps as a consequence of this, efforts have been made to reduce the assessors' role, particularly at Part I level, as the system settles down and the colleges become more self-confident.

The existence of an assessor is, of course, one form of resource provision, as well as seeking the increased assistance from college administrations and funding bodies, a task on which Exeter places great stress. The assessor can teach, although this is more in the way of showing the flag than the common teaching on BEds found before James. However, in cases where colleges have not the requisite expertise universities can help out, as they do in science in Belfast. It is also not wholly unknown for college staff to be invited to teach on university courses because of their close contacts, and some universities have a complicated and somewhat debated system of recognition of individual teachers in colleges.

Obviously all this can vary a good deal between institutions and subjects, but it is a significant and somewhat neglected channel, as Alexander and Wormald testify in Chapter 5, albeit one which is particularly hard to appraise. Certainly, along with the reports of externals the assessoral system — particularly when it involves a share in assessment — provides a continuing check both on standards and progress in general. Many universities, like Loughborough with its DipHE in Library Studies at the Technical College there (Arthur 1981), claim to subject their courses to continuous review. However, there has recently been a trend towards more formal and periodic reviews, just as the CNAA has moved somewhat away from this tactic towards sine die approvals for which universities were once criticized. Bristol carried out such evaluations on a triennial basis, others for five years. Surrey and Strathclyde formally intend to limit all recognition to five years in the first instance.

Reviews of this nature are far from casual. Kent for instance has just completed a process of re-validation, a task taken on by special panels and leading to approvals still limited in time. In Leicester, where a rolling programme of quinquennial reviews beginning in 1980-1 was decided upon in late 1978, some five areas are inspected per term, each one by the whole of the relevant Board of Studies, often aided by the external examiner. Although the process does not use formal visitations and seeks to limit unnecessary and costly documentation, it goes into considerable detail on teaching loads, staff research, course descriptions, cohort progression, resources and modifications. It also demands that the college presents a critical appraisal of the courses' operations. The aim is both to stimulate the college to action and to produce a full statement of the course and its syllabus, even if the latter has not altered over the five years. So there is an element of collaboration as well as of inquisition. This shows itself in pressure on maintaining bodies to increase the resources available and in the attempt to secure parity of treatment for trans-mural and intra-mural students. Taken together with the working of the assessoral system it does seem as though universities do take steps to ensure that the actual content of courses is reviewed and developed.

## THE PROCESS OF VALIDATION
Yet even this does not take us very far towards the nitty gritty of what actually happens on courses and in validation, towards, that is, the third area of criticism, that the process of validation is insufficiently rigorous and not concerned enough with the quality of the academic output of the system. There is one crucial point about an appraisal of the process of validation in the university sector. That is that, although there is a CNAA type cycle of course approvals, modifications, and reviews, this is only part of the story. University validation is built round people and organizations rather than courses.Thus the process of validation includes things like Collegiate Boards discussing changes in regulations, implementation of DES circulars, and reactions to the Cockcroft report for example. It also involves discussions of new approaches and methods in individual subject boards on the one hand and visits, telephone calls and discussions by assessors. All this is not peripheral to the university way. It is its very essence. It is easy to lose sight of and very hard to pin down and appraise, as Alexander and Wormald again show.

Even so, it has to be constantly remembered, alongside the way the courses are actually dealt with. Sometimes, where major degree schemes are concerned, such proposals could emerge from College Academic Boards as part of a general strategy. At other times, and of course where individual units or simple modifications were at issue, things could develop at a lower and more informal level, whether by discussions with assessors or at subject boards. Most major proposals would have to be submitted initially to a body such as the Leeds Standing Committee on courses which would advise the full Collegiate Board on whether the idea was acceptable in principle. Lancaster for some time tended to set up ad hoc committees to look at new degree schemes and, like many other universities, was prepared to approve the general structure of a degree before referring it to subject specialists for confirmation that subject content and resources were both acceptable and appropriate for the degree in a way rarely found under the CNAA. This had the advantage of giving the individual teachers some guarantee that devising new units was a worthwhile exercise. But their recommendations on such matters, as on modifications, are liable to challenge in Courses Committees and Collegiate Boards so that there is no doubt that a serious effort at course control was and is made. The process can be long and the arguments involved, complex and sometimes acrimonious.

To some extent the criteria used in such discussions varied according to the subject concerned. It probably is true that new and inter-disciplinary courses are more difficult than others for universities to handle (Squires 1975) on an institutional and intellectual level (Leftwich 1981). However, it does not follow that university validated courses are by definition less imaginative and innovative and more academic and anti-vocational than others, although in education there may have been a tendency to value cognitive more than professional elements. Such judgements are highly subjective and the CNAA has itself been criticized both for stifling innovation (Davis 1981) and for demanding forms of 'innovation' (Gaskell 1982). Similarly the criticism of universities who did take a chance and agreed to validate subjects they themselves did not teach tends to cancel this out. In fact, if we take the example of history, it soon becomes apparent that exactly the same curriculum models appear inside universities as in polytechnics and university validated colleges, as we should expect in a relatively centralized culture (Church 1979). Moreover, the criteria used by universities in assessing history proposals are very similar to those used by the CNAA History Board: coherence, progression, depth, breadth of coverage, teaching methods which stress student involvement and initiative, staff scholarship, integration and resources. Obviously there are differences. There are fewer modular courses under universities, which is perhaps to their advantage, since they do not fit in with the developmental nature of learning in history and can reinforce tendencies to stereotyping. This should remind us that innovation can be found not only in broad structures but in the basic components of courses as well. It may well be that this is the area which university validation has chiefly stressed.

Whether standards of student performance vary as between the sectors is very hard to say. One analysis of comparative examination results shows that universities do award more higher grades of degrees than public sector colleges (Hindmarch and Bourner 1980) but while this may be due to an imitative rigour in the latter, it is also related to entry levels. College staff in the university orbit can also be reluctant to award first class degrees. Certainly it is the firm conviction of many respondents and others that universities are in fact *more* demanding and rigorous than the CNAA, perhaps too much so. On the other hand it does seem as though the external examiner system has moved more towards the consultant role common in the CNAA, both intra-murally and especially trans-murally (Williams 1979) although opinion in some universities suggests that the CNAA still has insufficient liaison with externals.

University insistence on standards has certainly had one unfortunate and often self-defeating effect. This is in the habit of either refusing to allow colleges to do honours degrees and insisting on ordinary ones (Lewis 1981a) or of creating a new genus of degree which ignored the Honours/Ordinary divide like BA Collegiate or BH the latter being used in London for subjects which the university did not itself teach. On the other hand, outside Wales, and perhaps Southampton, the DipHE has not been taken very seriously. All the London colleges only ever produced one diplomate between them. So, if the extent of Ordinary degree work is perhaps exaggerated by the way in which statistics are recorded, the evidence of universities like Lancaster shows that, where transfer from Ordinary to Honours degrees is possible at the end of the first year, the majority of students will nowadays — the situation was a little different in the seventies, at least where education qualifications were concerned — seek for Honours courses and are capable of obtaining them. Ordinary courses therefore can become an unviable rump as well as calling into question the universities' search for comparability and collaboration.

In this respect then, the universities' claims that validation is a joint and co-operative venture cannot be accepted at face value. Nonetheless, while it is true that universities were slow to appreciate the needs of colleges for self-respect they have increasingly moved in this direction. Some, indeed, have refused to undertake the inquisitorial visitations demanded of them by critics precisely because these were regarded as a threat to autonomy, by too pointedly reminding colleges of the ultimate authority and superiority of the university. Hence they do at least seek to avoid creating a state of dependence. Similarly there are moves to encourage college staffs to take more responsibility for the management and assessment of their courses. A point often overlooked here is that, while in universities with only one college the disparity in size between the university and the college is a problem, where there are more colleges involved, not only is this problem mitigated but the creation of a regional forum means that colleges share in the validation of courses in other colleges in the area through their membership of sub-committees and subject boards. And there their voice is equal, at least in theory, to that of other members. Indeed, as Lewis and others have implied, the existence of such arrangements can actually assist colleges to resist innovation and university policy just as much as it enables the university to have its own way. Nonetheless, Nias has concluded (1976) that these complex negotiations can produce inter-dependence and internalization of political skills and political imperatives more effectively than more obviously 'rational' procedures.

The related charges that universities exclude students from participation in the validation process and make untold profits from the operation are much less convincing. As the CVCP Concordat with the NUS of 1968 would lead one to imagine, students are represented both internally and on trans-mural boards, so that their part, although limited, is at least a continuing one. Moreover, were it true that validation was an immensely profitable business, it is unlikely that so many universities would either have refused to undertake it or have dropped out relatively soon after. Nor would the evidence of the 1978 survey have convinced the DES that its proposed fee reductions were unjustified. Obviously some universities do make money from validation (and such monies can be passed on to the individuals involved) but economies of scale operate very stringently against institutions so that it is by no means all institutions who pay their members. In any case the payment does not always outweigh the losses suffered in other directions by those involved in validation. Hence the somewhat contradictory claims that university validation relies on conscript labour.

So while it may be true that the roots of some of the mistakes which universities have undoubtedly made in their validation operations have sprung from a feeling that the colleges are essentially inferior — a view which no doubt still exists in some places — things seem to have changed. There is certainly a commitment to partnership. Whether this is a reality is something which can be decided only by much more detailed research, if a decision is indeed possible. It would be interesting, for instance, to know how far universities have required rigorous internal validation in colleges. One straw in the wind is the conclusion of the Ross and MacNamara (1982) report on the BEd that the universities and the colleges have settled down into closer and mutually acceptable relationships.

CONCLUSIONS
To sum up, not all the extreme criticisms of university validation are substantiated by the evidence. If the existence of separate structures for validation is a sign of taking the matter seriously then the matter is indeed taken seriously. And the structures function in two directions. There is also a concern for the development of what is being taught, and the means to achieve such development are there. While the processes may be different form those elsewhere, they are well established and do have their own forms of rigour. These forms, it must be insisted, do vary considerably, not merely between institutions — whether of similar or varying types — but even inside them. It is not always the case that the same tactics are adopted by a university to deal with different colleges (Heywood 1981). The basic organizational model moreover, is not that adopted by the University of London, although this has been one which has determined most of the criticisms of university practice.How effective the model is, is another matter. It is not the intention to suggest that all is for the best in the best of all possible university worlds. There is strength and weakness inside universities as well as in the CNAA system. The important thing is to stress that this is the case and that there is no simple black and white polarity between the two systems.

In assessing the university style of validation we need to stress not merely its differences but also its similarities to practices elsewhere. Thus although the basic model has often been described as being face to face and informal, in fact it relies to a considerable extent on formal regulations and structures, centrally arrived at, although these are interwoven with the

74    CHURCH

personal actions. There is no doubt that it is not as ad hoc as has been suggested. Documentation and regulations have thus become fuller and more complex with the passage of time, and to some extent this is due to the convergence already noted. So while it may be true that the university style of validation 'has the casual informality of a family housekeeping budget rather than the procedural rigour of a company audit' (Becher, Embling and Kogan 1977) it seems to be the case that the normative element has developed more than the operational one in recent times. One authority with experience of both systems believes that, while — for political reasons — many university validated colleges' courses would not get through the CNAA — the nature and standard of the experience they offer their students is no different (Gaskell 1982). It may well be that universities have yet to stress sufficiently the need for internal evaluation by their colleges.

It is probably the case that the element of informality is greater where internal validation is concerned. There separate structures have been much slower to emerge and procedures are less well defined. Hence one can find skeletons in the cupboard such as the withdrawal of support from the MSc in Town Planning at Heriot Watt in 1976 (Morrison 1978) not to mention the more recent problems involving social work at Brunel and chemical engineering at Sheffield. The general movement towards more systematic course control still has some way to go inside universities, though here too there has been significant change in recent years, and the value of its informality can be variously assessed.

Nonetheless, there has been movement and people are now much less likely to regard validation as a neologism (Chapman 1979) or as something to do with programmed learning (Rowntree 1981). There is more awareness that evaluation and programme review can be a source of strength to institutions in difficult times (Shattock 1979). In Leeds the validating exercise had led to a tightening up of extra-mural provision. We need more discussion of how the educational offerings of higher education are managed and controlled, and more awareness of the precise forms which such discussion and control can and does take. There is no one flawless system, and little virtue in seeking a monopolistic panacea. Validation and course control are tools, not ends. Indeed taken to excess they can become stultifying and self-defeating (Becher 1981). It would be ironic if the informality, adaptability and diversity of University course control procedures were to give way to normative centralism just at the time that the polemic has died away and the rigidities of the bureaucratic distance system are proving something of a handicap in devising flexible responses to the threatening situation of higher education.

REFERENCES
Alexander, R. (1979) What is a course? *Journal of Further and Higher Education* III (1) 31-45

Arterton, J.W. (1981) Communication from the Registrar, University College London

Arthur, D.A. (1981) Communication from the Academic Registrar, Loughborough University of Technology

Bath (1981) *Charter, Statutes and Ordinances*

Beard, R. (1979) *Teaching and Learning in Higher Education* Harmondsworth: Penguin

Becher, R., Embling, J. and Kogan, M. (1981) *Systems of Higher Education: United Kingdom* New York: ICED

Becher, T. Eraut, M. and Knight, J. (1981) *Policies for Educational Accountability* London: Heinemann

Begg, N.R.D. (1981) Communication from the Clerk to the Senatus, University of Aberdeen

Betjemann, A. (1978) Evaluating University Courses: Problems and Proposals *Higher Education Bulletin* VI (1) 13-21

Billing, D. with West, R. (1981) *External Academic Validation.* Paper circulated for the HEF/SRHE Consultation

Birmingham (1981) *Relationships with affiliated and other colleges* Cyclostyled. The University

Blyth, J. and Lewin, J. (Eds) (1979) *The Teaching of History in Further and Higher Education* Cyclostyled. London: NATFE

Bond, M.A.H. (1981) Communication from the Senior Assistant Registrar, University of Newcastle

Cannon, A.G. (1981) Communication from the Senior Assistant Registrar, University of Exeter

Carter, C.F. (1980) *Higher Education for the Future* Oxford: Blackwell

Chandler, E.R. (1981) Communication from the Academic Registrar, Brunel University

Chapman, G. (1979) *Course Validation in a Federal University* Talk given to a MUPAL Conference, London, March 1979

Church, C.H. (1976) Not up to Par? Some problems in comparing the validation of degree courses *Higher Education Bulletin* VI (1) 39-62

Church, C.H. (1979) Structures and syllabi. In Le Guillou, M. (Ed.) *History in the Polytechnics. A Conference Report* Cyclostyled. London: DES pp.34-50

Cox, R. (Ed.) (1979) *Co-operation and Choice in Higher Education* London: UMTU pp.29-30

Davis, M. (1980) The CNAA as a validating agency. In Billing, D.A. (Ed.) *Indicators of Performance* Guildford: SRHE pp.31-42

Dowdeswell, W. and Good, H. (1978) Adaptive change in university teaching *Impetus* 9, 8-14

Dundee (1980) *Faculty of Environmental Studies: Degrees in Architecture etc.* Dundee: The University

Dunkley, C.M. (1981) Communication from the Deputy Registrar, University of Leicester

Gaskell, S.M. (1982) *The University Validated Degree: Present and Future Imperfect* Revised unpublished paper originally presented to the March 1982 meeting of the Conference of Secretaries of Schools, Institutes and Faculties of Education, Lancaster

Gent, B. (1981) *Internal Validation* Communication circulated for the HEF/SRHE Consultation

Gosden, P.H.J.H. and Taylor, A.J. (1975) *Studies in the History of a University: Leeds 1874-1974* Leeds: Arnold

Graham, A.H. (1981) Communication from the Secretary to Academic Council, Queen's University, Belfast

Grant, M. (1975) In Niblett, W.R. (Ed.) *The Sciences, the Humanities and the Technological Threat* London: University of London Press

Haigh, G. (1981) Communication from the Academic Registrar, University of Surrey

Hajnal, J. (1972) *The Student Trap* Penguin: Harmondsworth p. 94

Harvey, C.W. (1981) Communication from the Secretary, School of Education, University of Bristol

Heriot-Watt (1980) Ordinance 28/9: *Validation of Courses*

Hewton, E. et al (1975) *Supporting Teaching for a Change* London: Nuffield Foundation

Heywood, J.H. (1981) *A Note on the Validation of Courses in Teacher Education by an Irish University* Cyclostyled

Hindmarch, A. and Bourner, T. (1980) CNAA degrees in the Social Sciences *Studies in Higher Education* V (1) 17-31

Hodgkinson, J.F. (1981) Communication from the Registrar, University of Keele

Holt, J.C. (1977) *The University of Reading — the first fifty years* Reading UP

Howell, D.A. (1979) Academic decision making — the BEd degree in British universities *Higher Education Review* XI (2) 17-42

Ivey, G.M. (1981) Communication from the Secretary, Education Area, University of Sussex

Jamieson, J.G. (1981) Communication from the Senior Administrative Officer, Heriot-Watt University

Kelly, T. with Whelan R.F. (1981) *For the Advancement of Learning. The University of Liverpool 1881-1981* Liverpool: University Press

Kent (1982) *Collegiate Board: Examination Arrangements, Regulations and Conventions for Christ Church and Nonington Colleges* Cyclostyled

Lewis, D.G. (1981a) *The University and Colleges of Education in Wales 1925-1978* Cardiff: University of Wales Press

Lewis, D.G. (1981b) Communication from the Senior Assistant Registrar, University of Wales

Lancaster (1982) *Handbook of Degree Courses in Associated Colleges* 3rd ed. School of Education

Leeds (1980) *Validation: A Co-operative Venture* The University

Leftwich, A. The politics of case study *Higher Education Review* XIII (2) 38-64

Linfoot, A.D. (1981) Communication from the Registrar and Finance Officer, University of Kent at Canterbury

Liverpool (1981) *The Board of College Studies and its Committees* The University

London (1982) *Background Note on the Organizational Structure of the University* Cyclostyled

Manchester (1981) *Working Together: The University of Manchester and its affiliated Colleges* Cyclostyled. The University

Mee, P.E. (1981) Communication from the Registrar, Imperial College

Moodie, G. and Eustace, R. (1974) *Power and Authority in British Universities* Montreal: McGill UP

Morris, D.C. (1979) Validation of diversified awards in colleges of higher education *CUA Proceedings Edinburgh* Conference of University Administrators

Morrison, J. (1978) How planners fell foul of the RTPI *THES* 362 (20 x 78) 8

Nias, J. (1976) Colleges of education. External pressures and the negotiation of internal power. In Flood Page, C. and Yates, M. (Eds) *Power and Authority in Higher Education* Guildford: SRHE pp. 20-31

Niblett, W.R. (1974) *Universities Between Two Worlds* London: University of London Press

Niblett, W.R. et al. (1975) *The University Connection* London: NFER

Nokes, A.G. (1973) Diversified degree courses: A commentary Cyclostyled. London: CNAA

Nottingham (1980) *Faculty and School of Education: Examinations and Assessment for the Bachelor of Education: Procedural Document*

Parkin, C. Across the binary line: establishing a joint postgraduate diploma in a polytechnic and two universities. in Cox, *Co-operation and Choice* pp.79-92

Pedley, R. (1977) *Towards the Comprehensive University* London: Macmillan pp.58-68

Piper, D.W. (1981) Contribution to Oxtoby, R. (Ed.) *Higher Education at the Crossroads* Guildford: SRHE pp.179-80

Ramsden, P. The department as an environment for learning. In Billing, D.E. (Ed.) *Indicators of Performance* pp.139-42

Riddell, A. (1981) Communication from the Academic Registrar, University of York

Ross, A.M. and MacNamara, D. (1982) *The BEd Concurrent Degree. Report of the Initial Teacher Programme* Lancaster

Rowntree, D. (1981) *Developing Courses for Students* London: McGraw-Hill pp.252-3

Salford (1976) *Approval of New Undergraduate Programmes of Study* Cyclostyled. The University

Salford (1981) *Arrangements for Approval of New Degree Programmes at Affiliated Institutions* Cyclostyled. The University

Saville, M.V. (1981) Communication from the Registrar, Queen Mary College

Saxton, W.E. (1981) Communication from the Deputy Registrar, University of Durham

Shattock, M.L. (1979) Retrenchment in U.S. higher education *Educational Policy Bulletin* VII (2) 149-68

Squires, G. et al, (1975) *Interdisciplinarity* London: Nuffield Foundation pp.13-15

Stone, I.R. (1982) Communication from the Administrative Assistant, University of Kent at Canterbury

Strathclyde (1981) *Report of the Working Party on Validation* Cyclostyled. The University

Surrey (1981) *The Delegacy: Guidelines and Procedures* Cyclostyled. Guildford

Sussex (1980) *School of Education: Committee Members Handbook*

Williams, W.F. (1979) The role of the external examiner in first degrees *Studies in Higher Education* IV (2) 161-8

John Heywood

Traditionally the term 'profession' was applied to the Church, the Army, and the Law. Very often official forms such as application for passports required that the witness be from one of these professions. Thus clergymen were in great demand for this service. But the term 'profession' is now used by a wide variety of persons and organizations. Thus actors commonly speak of the 'acting profession', engineers of the 'engineering profession' and so on (Lees 1966). We also speak of professional civil servants. Some also make a further distinction between professions and sub- or semi-professions (Carr-Saunders 1933).

A striking feature of social change in the twentieth century has been the rise of a number of occupations into the ranks of the 'professions'. This has not been without controversy, for what are the characteristics definitive of a profession?

The occupations which concern us here are ones based on extensive knowledge and/or social skills in virtue of which they generate a special mystique of their own. The clients of these occupations constitute a very varied and heterogeneous population who offer considerable potential for exploitation by members of the occupations. As a result these practitioners tend to establish formal associations to create and protect a monopoly and to control entry; the occupational associations build up a system of education and training and define the standards of acceptance; and in order to establish a position as responsible guarantors of the public interest they adopt a code of practice or professional ethic (Johnson 1977; see also Schein 1972; Houle 1980). Taken together, all this serves to provide the professional person with status, and society clearly acquiesces in the hierarchy which has evolved. For example, most 'doctors' do not have doctorates. Nevertheless we all accept that they should be called 'doctor'.

The selection process also enables a profession to restrict entry and so create a scarcity value for the services which it offers. Education and training are *used* as the prime means of selection. This discriminatory role would seem to be as important as their use in the provision of knowledge, for it seems that sometimes an education is provided which is not necessarily suited to the work task (Youngman et al 1978; Clements and Roberts 1980).

A high scarcity value usually enhances the prestige of a profession. The large numbers in the teaching and engineering professions contribute to the low esteem with which they are held. Their scarcity value is low. A high scarcity value coupled with other factors for services may enhance the renumeration of those fortunate enough to be licensed if society accords them high status. Doctors and lawyers are well paid because of the contribution they can make to personal well-being. For this reason doctors can earn significantly more than dentists. There is therefore a potential for conflict between public and professional interests. Public support for restrictive practices may depend in some measure on public perceptions of the extent and nature of the harm which might arise from professional malpractice. Nevertheless, it is often difficult to sue practitioners for incompetence. Professional groups which exhibit all the above characteristics and in particular are registered by statute are solicitors (Acts of 1729, 1888, 1919, 1957 and 1959), pharmacists (1852, 1933, 1954), medical practitioners (1858, 1956), dental surgeons (1878, 1956), veterinary surgeons (1881, 1900, 1948), patent agents (1888, 1949), architects (1931) and opticians (1958).

The internal organization of the professions is also complicated. In the case of medicine the General Medical Council is the statutory committee which controls professional conduct. It also regulates medical education which itself relies on an association between the health service and universities. But there are also learned societies within medicine, membership of which is attained by educational work of high standing after graduation. These are the Royal Colleges (eg general practitioners, medicine, obstetrics, psychiatry, surgeons). Possession of their diplomas and fellowships is important in the search for standing as an academic teacher of medicine, or consultant. The majority of medical practitioners are in the British Medical Association. Consultants also have an association which they can join.

The education of medical practitioners, together with dental and veterinary surgeons, is confined to the university sector, or to chartered colleges regarded as having university status. Otherwise all of the professions and sub-professions listed above may utilise courses provided in either the university or the public sector. The complications of their administration within the public sector are many and various as will be seen.

Self-regulation is possible without legislation provided that competing organisations are not generally recognized by society, or clients or employers. The major example of this is the Bar, which controls the entry of barristers to the courts. It is a closed profession and finds support for its activities in common law. And the codes of conduct suggested for many groups could bring individual members of their profession into conflict with their employers (Moon 1966) as might be the case with engineers (IEEE 1982).

This situation is equally problematic in management, where the British Institute of Management has recommended a code of conduct for managers (BIM 1981) and is also involved in education. The problems for the Institute in becoming a profession arise from the fact that it caters for all levels, and most areas, of management (see below), and that, within these levels, there are a variety of routes to the top not all of which depend on qualification or, for that matter, success. Recognition must be given to successful enterpreneurship, however it occurs. The penalty for failure at the top may not be serious. Even if it ends in bankruptcy it is not regarded by society as a serious matter when compared with the loss of life, limb or personal freedom. Thus a 'true' management profession cannot be created although a strong managerial organization could in certain circumstances be an influence on Government if the recent history of the British Institute of Management is anything to go by. In many respects the professions do not differ from Trade Unions in the operation of restrictive practices, particularly in respect of the right to control entry as for example the Print Unions over apprenticeship.

Certain jobs require by statute (or statutory instrument) that the personnel in them shall be certified as competent. The Merchant Shipping Acts of 1850 and 1854 require that Merchant Navy Officers (engineers and deck) shall be certified by the Board of Trade (now Department of Trade and Industry). Radio Officers also have to be certified and certain ships are required to carry a Radio Officer. Airline pilots have to be certificated. Under the Coal Miners Regulations Acts (1872, 1877 and 1887) mine managers are also certificated. The certificates which are awarded by the Board of Trade contrast with those awarded by many institutions after the successful completion of an examination. They are certificates of competence which state that this person can do ... Beyond such competence there are no codes of professional conduct except those pertaining to the movement of shipping in the Acts and International Conventions.

In so far as teachers are concerned statutory instruments require that they should possess a university degree, or its equivalent, together with a teacher's certificate equivalent to one year's full-time training. Although the British set up a Registration Council for a certain class of secondary school teacher in Ireland, which is still in operation, the scheme proposed for England in the 1889 Act was repealed in 1906. However, the Irish council does not regulate professional conduct. It only controls admissions. The British statutory instrument has the same effect. Like the medical profession it is relatively easy for a Local Authority to sack a teacher for immoral behaviour but almost impossible to sack him or her for imcompetence. Statutory and related controls are therefore less significant than educational ones. And recently these have greatly changed. The changes are complex and often divergent. Moreover, they do not seem greatly to have improved innovation, cost effectiveness or flexibility. It is in the field of individual retraining in such things as systems approaches that the best hope of progress would seem to lie.

## THE CHANGING PATTERN OF CONTROL OVER QUALIFICATIONS

Control over admission to a profession then is clearly an important step in the achievement of professional status. The more specialized and complex the requirements for knowledge and skill are, the greater the chance those who use that knowledge have of creating a profession. Control over the education and training requirements is therefore important. The knowledge explosion, specialization and the meritocracy together provide structural and value systems which encourage the search for professional status by newly established professional groups. Sometimes this leads to conflicts among these groups. At other time professional bodies have preferred to hand over this role to others. These points can best be illustrated by examples such as that of *engineering*.

The distinguishing feature of the British Engineering Institutions was the fact that they were the main sponsors with the Department of Education of the National Certificate system created in 1919 (Payne 1960). This enabled persons to obtain professional membership via part-time study. After the Second World War it was argued, particularly by the electrical engineers, that engineers for industry required an education more thoroughly based on the application of science. In this they were supported by the recommendations of the Percy Committee (Percy 1945) which recommended that technologists for industry and especially manufacturing industry should be trained on sandwich (co-operative) courses of four years duration.

Spurred on by fears of Soviet advances in technology a National Council for Technological Awards was created in 1955 to award a Diploma in Technology (Cotgrove 1958). This was to be equivalent to a degree. It was to be different to a degree in that the courses in ten colleges of advanced technology would be designed to produce technologists for manufacturing industry. It was the National Council for Technological Awards which began the practice of vetting detailed course submissions and visiting colleges to check on the quality of staff and the resources available.

The Diploma in Technology's prime backers were the electrical and mechanical engineers (Heywood and Mash 1968). There were only two small courses in production engineering. For a short period of time, around 1962, the old established engineering institutions were able to prevent the Institution of Production Engineers from gaining a Royal Charter. At the same time the British Institution of Radio Engineers, whose president was Lord Louis Mountbatten, gained such a charter. This illustrates the low esteem in which production and manufacturing technology is held by professional people in industry (Burns and Stalker 1961). Most of them were not trained as graduates. To improve therefore the status of manufacturing engineering the University Grants Committee has, within the last five years, sponsored four-year courses in manufacturing technology in eight universities with a view to creating an elite in this area.

But, as if to parallel this attempt to upgrade engineering, from the time of the creation of the Diploma in Technology, the Department of Education and Science, with the support of educationalists and the professional institutions, sought to separate the existing national certificates from any professional qualifying role. The report of the Crowther Committee (Crowther 1959) had shown high wastage from these courses. The committee recommended better selection and a broader education for technicians which should be sandwich or block release structured. These ideas were taken up in the 1961 White Paper (Cmnd 1254) which indicated that in future National Certificates would be for technicians. Block release (as opposed to day release) structures would be encouraged. The engineering institutions proposed changes in their regulations which would exclude those with the new national certificates from membership and this caused a furore among their members who wished to retain the existing system. The Engineering Institutions Joint Council, the forerunner of the Council of Engineering Institutions, issued a list of technician institutions which included the Society of Engineers and the Junior Institution of Engineers. But these societies were not prepared at that time to undertake a role merely as technician institutions (Heywood 1969).

Neither was there great support from industry for these changes which, when the Engineering Industries Training Board (EITB) was established as a result of legislation in 1964, reinforced these ideas through the levy which it was able to impose on employers. Throughout these developments there was continuing conflict, between those who supported the EITB and industrialists, who felt that practical experience was on the whole more important than theoretical knowledge. This tension between practice and theory in engineering remains to this day. The failure of the Institutions to create their own organisation for technicians at that time led eventually to the creation of the Technician Education Council in 1973 and subsequently the Business Education Council. From this structure a new group of semi-professional technician persons were to emerge in the second half of the nineteen-seventies.

Where *biology and chemistry* were concerned, the problem was that, despite strong support from the Royal Institute of Chemistry, the science side of the Diploma in Technology was weak. This Institute had also supported the National Certificate Scheme almost from its inception at ordinary, higher national and higher diploma levels (ONC, HNC, HND). When the Institute of Biology was founded in 1950 it also supported the National Certificate scheme which it greatly esteemed. This was because the Institute was founded to obtain professional recognition for biologists working in agricultural, biomedical, environmental and educational fields, whose work emphasised applications. The two main grades of membership of this institute relate to educational qualifications thus:

*Member*  1st or 2nd class honours degree or the Institute Part II Examination, plus three years appropriate experience
*Graduate* As above but without the appropriate experience
*Associate* Pass degree or the Institute Part I examination, or HND/HNC or Teacher's Certificate of Education with appropriate experience

The recognition given to National Certificate qualifications is clear. Provision is made for transfer from the higher technician level if the candidate can pass the Part II examination. Twenty-three colleges provide courses for this examination, which have to be recognized by the Institute. The Part I is a combination of internal and external examination while the Part II is internal subject to external moderation. Candidates with five years' experience at the associate level may also obtain membership by thesis or dissertation.

## THE COUNCIL FOR NATIONAL ACADEMIC AWARDS AND ITS EFFECTS

On the other hand, during the last ten years numerous societies have preferred to develop educational programmes within the public sector, a possibility which came about by the creation of a Council for National Academic Awards. It is appropriate therefore at this stage to give brief consideration to its development. The recommendations of the Committee on Higher Education (Robbins 1963) led to the creation of the CNAA. At the same time the National Council for Technological Awards was wound up, its officers becoming the first officers of the CNAA. Unlike the National Council the charter of the CNAA allowed it to offer the degrees across the spectrum of subjects. Apart from the fact that this solved the problem of diploma status it allowed the newly created polytechnics to develop degree level work in many new areas. The scale of the operation made the CNAA much more influential than the NCTA. Like its predecessor the CNAA required substantial submissions for course proposals although much more was required in their presentations. Also the CNAA greatly helped those polytechnics offering its degrees to improve the quality of their staff and both the quality and quantity of their resources. To a limited extent the Technician and Business Education Councils followed in the same path but with less concern for, and effect on, the resources in the colleges.

The creation of these institutions led to substantial rethinking among the professional societies. It enabled some institutions to bring their qualifications up to degree level. For other specialisms it posed the question 'what constitutes a degree in my subject?' and beyond that 'is there a role for a professional organization in a subject such as for example, home economics?' (Matthews and Golightly 1981). In the two sections which follow we look at some of these developments. There was for instance the case of *accountancy, commerce and management.*

Although accountancy is regarded as a well established profession qualifications like those in engineering were obtained mainly by part-time study. But recently new institutions have emerged, in the Chartered Institute of Public Finance and Accountancy for example. Others seem to have gained in status, sometimes with an accompanying change in name as with the Institute of Cost and Management Accountants. These six accountancy institutions have found it difficult to arrive at a common policy. Traditionally, like solicitors and architects, accountants were articled to a firm and progressed through part-time education more often than not in the evenings.

A Joint Board of Accreditation of colleges and courses has been established by The Chartered Accountants of England and Wales. The Board approves foundation courses in colleges. Professional external examinations are set by the institutions and certain CNAA degrees provide exemptions. In the area of business the Institutes of Marketing and Personnel Management provide examinations and offer exemptions by recognition of courses. The British Institute of Management, while having a considerable involvement in the Diploma in Management Studies, does not rely primarily on qualifications as a means of entry.

The growth of *para-medical services* and *social work professions* and the need for their control was recognised by an Act of 1960 (The Professions Supplementary to Medicine Act). This established a Council for professions supplementary to medicine. Separate Boards were established for chiropody, psysiotherapy, dietetics, medical laboratory technology, occupational therapy, remedial gymnastics and radiography. In the area of social work the Health Visiting and Social Work (training) Act of 1962 established the Central Council for Education and Training in Social Work as the statutory authority with power of certification to promote education and training for social work and for certain other kinds of work in the personal social services. The Council describes its functions thus: it

'Promotes education and training including preliminary, in-service, qualifying and post-qualifying studies.

Recognises courses leading to its awards and gives statements of attendance.

Develops educational objectives, content, methods and organization of courses.

Advises upon and undertakes research into training matters.

Assesses individual qualifications in social work obtained overseas and issues letters of comparability to its own awards (in repect of overseas qualifications only).

Issues certificates of qualification or statements of attendance and keeps a record of students who have satisfactorily completed courses or programmes of the following types:

— courses leading to the basic qualification in social work — the Certificate of Qualification in Social Work.
— schemes of study and supervised practice leading to the certificate in Social Service, the basic qualification for a range of jobs in the social services.
— qualifying courses for teachers or instructors of mentally handicapped adults — Diploma in the Training and Further Education of Mentally

Handicapped Adults.
— qualifying courses for workers in residential homes for children —
Certificate in the Residential Care of Children and Young People (last
intake in 1979) and the Senior Certificate in the Residential Care of
Children and Young People (last intake in September 1977).
— qualifying courses for social workers in residential homes for adults —
the Certificate in Residential Social Work (last intake in 1979).
— post-qualifying programmes for those with social work and social
service qualifications.
— a post-qualifying course for managers of centres for the education and
training of mentally handicapped adults — Diploma in the Management of Establishments for the Training of Mentally Handicapped
Adults.
— non-qualifying courses combining further education and some
elements of vocational study for 16-18 year olds — Preliminary
Residential Care Courses.
— non-qualifying day-release study courses for unqualified staff working
in residential homes or day services — In-Service Study Courses.'

When the Council was established in 1971, it assumed the responsibility
of several training bodies. In 1974 its duties were further extended to include
those of the Training Council for Teachers of the Mentally Handicapped.
The para-medical and social work subjects now provide large numbers of
students in the polytechnics and constitute an area of continuing growth.

## DEVELOPMENTS IN THE NATIONAL STRUCTURE OF SUB-PROFESSIONS

Although consideration of scientific and technological education dominates
the higher education scene, there has nevertheless been a considerable shift
in resources to other areas and this has been accompanied by a considerable
growth in professionalism. As the previous discussion shows, the sub-professions have been as marked by it as the higher professions. Nothing illustrates
the rise of the meritocracy more than the growth of sub-professional
(technician) qualifications. The creation of the Technican and Business
Education Councils was a landmark in British education. It will be some
years before the educational and social structure adjusts to their role and
before a satisfactory evaluation of their qualifications can be made.

They were not introduced without opposition. Many teachers and
industrialists continued to think that the national certificate schemes were
the most appropriate means of study for practical work in industry. In
the case of TEC it was argued that the unit structure of the courses
would not lead tc a coherent technical education. Thus the Royal Institute
of Chemistry (now the Royal Society of Chemistry after a merger with the
Chemical Society), which in opposition to several other professional bodies
continued to support the National Certificate, was faced with a major

problem of adaptation after it became clear that National Certificates and Diplomas would be phased out. (See Russell, Coley and Roberts (1977) for a discussion of the Institute's contribution to education.) Their role had been to provide an educational ladder for able chemists which ensured that they had an adequate general scientific education.

Faced with a bewildering number of units the Institute has moved towards the blanket approval of TEC awards which have a prima facie breadth of ancillary courses. They no longer look at the details of the content of courses. At the lower level ten Standard TEC units are accepted as giving an appropriate background in maths, physics and chemistry. Any TEC award which includes these units is acceptable.

This simplifies recognition procedures, for they can then be analysed by administrators. Thus applications for approval have to contain

1    the names of the units/modules etc. that comprise the TEC programme as a whole and of any further units etc. to be taken outside the programme for RSC purposes.
2    details of the unit content, except in respect of TEC standard units or Committee of Heads of Polytechnic Chemistry Departments 'illustrative syllabuses'.
3    details of the moderation/assessment proposals in respect of each unit.
4    proposals for external assessment of any units not covered by TEC moderating/assessment arrangements.
5    proposals for exemption from any part of the course on the basis of other qualifications (eg HNC in Chemistry or a TEC Higher Certificate obtained elsewhere).

The Institute is much more concerned with its higher levels (licentiateship and graduateship). To establish standards it negotiated the right to provide the names of members to join the relevant TEC validating panels for higher awards and/or to undertake a role in the moderation of the programmes and in the assessment of certain subjects. The TEC units do not permit total exemption from the graduateship. One year's further study beyond the Higher TEC award is required. The graduateship examination is being retained as it is believed to provide a useful route for the upgrading of industrial chemists.

Under the national certificate scheme, responsibility for the award of certificates was vested in each separate joint committee, which was set up and staffed mainly by the professional institution concerned. It controlled standards primarily by controlling the examinations, which were proposed by the colleges, but vetted by the joint committee. Thus professional bodies such as the RIC gained considerable expertise in examining. There is, however, no place for the professional institutions in the control of TEC and BEC examinations, since award of the certificates is vested in these bodies. They rely on external assessors appointed by themselves to monitor standards and on prior validation of the courses. There was, therefore, no direct way in which, for example, the RIC's accumulated experience could be transferred to TEC, although in practice many RIC members, in an individual capacity, were appointed as TEC assessors.

As has been noted above, the RSC does not possess the resources to validate separately each individual TEC course and it can therefore only award a blanket recognition to all such courses satisfying a few broad criteria. There is thus now no way in which the RSC can influence directly the content and standards of chemistry technician courses. It does, however, maintain very close links with the TEC panels. The responsibility for validation shifted therefore to the statutorily approved CNAA and TEC. All the professional societies have inevitably had to face the same problem, for the qualifications of the Councils have charter status and DES approval. While it is too early to obtain a clear picture of the overall response to TEC and BEC some clear features of the response to CNAA are emerging.

THE CHANGING ROLES OF THE PROFESSIONAL INSTITUTIONS

During the life of the Council for National Academic Awards (from 1966) validation has become part of the educational scene. Because of this, many professional institutions in addition to CNAA, TEC and BEC, conduct validations, a few of which extend beyond the public sector to the universities. Apart from the potential for conflict between parallel validations in the public sector and apart from the work load created, this raises the major questions of how and who should control the curricula.

The case study of the Royal Society of Chemistry indicates the directions likely to be taken by the professional societies in the future in this regard. The promotion of academic qualifying institutions like the CNAA with the power to award degrees can make further validation by professional bodies of the academic components of courses unnecessary provided that members of the course validating committees are also members of the professional institutions. It behoves professional bodies to seek formal or informal links with validating organizations. These may be at the formal level of membership of Council. Davis (1980) notes that 'there was a very fine distinction between membership of the CNAA's Committee structure as part of the process of course approval, and at the Council's invitation, and the assertion of professional interest in shaping Council policy, and thereby advancing the influence of a profession. This area of contact with professional associations was always one of considerable delicacy.'

He notes that generally the professional institutions were less concerned with the affairs of the Council than with those of the NCTA. There is no evidence, it seems, that there was any attempt on subject committees of the NCTA to express a professional point of view. This is supported by information from industrialists which suggests that the professional point of view is associated with industrial practice and thus with industrial training.

Academic courses were seen to be the responsibility of the colleges (Heywood 1969).

In respect of the CNAA Davis writes that 'where qualifications were linked to statutory requirements, for example pharmacy, navigation and mining engineering, it was agreed that representatives of appropriate professional associates should accompany visiting parties. It was also agreed that the Council of Engineering Institutions (CEI) should nominate members of each relevant subject board as an official link between subject boards and the CEI Education and Training Committees. In relation to industry generally there were a number of links with Industrial Training Boards. Despite occasional difficulties the overall impression is one of a relatively harmonious relationship, with the associations giving the Council useful support in relevant areas of validation whilst not in general seeking to dominate its policy or degree courses from a narrowly professional point of view'.

It is self-evident that if by and large the members of subject boards have professional qualifications then there is a 'hidden', probably unconscious, promotion of professional values. Validating organizations are inevitably influenced by these hidden relationships even though they are able to make use of non-professional member but distinguished colleagues in the university sector. The importance of the CNAA lies first in the national credibility which its awards have gained and second, in the development of validation as opposed to examining procedures. The responsibility for examining is delegated to external examiners.

Although there are regular reviews the validation procedures are propter-hoc. That is, they relate to the planning of the course in respect of the quality of staff, available resources and syllabus. They predict that the course will be successful. Once approved by the Council they go ahead. No detailed attention is given to the process which follows apart from the collection of reports by external examiners. The preparation exercise is substantial and substantial fees are charged by the CNAA. In these terms the professional institutions cannot hope to compete. There is, therefore, a pressure on them to accept the judgements of the CNAA panels in regard to the academic quality of the courses submitted to them for accreditation.

At the same time the importance of validation as a means of confirming status has not escaped the notice of the professional institutions and they now seek not only to recognize college courses in the public sector but courses in the universities as well. Thus the application form to the Royal Society of Chemistry is titled Application Form for the Use of Universities and Institutions Seeking Approval of Courses and Degrees for the Purposes of Exemption from all or part of the RIC Examinations. The professional institutions are increasingly visiting university and college departments as part of their own accrediting process. Costs prevent some institutions from undertaking more visits than they do. The emphasis seems in general to be more on the professional components of education and training than on the practical. Given a network of close informal relationships the academic components of courses can be left to the validating body (CNAA or university). Nevertheless, the work of both the validating bodies and the professional institutions depends on the willing acquiescence of academics whose representatives by and large make up the numbers in the educational and subject committees which are the focus of this dual network. Whether they are sufficiently prepared for their tasks is a very real question. A case can be made for saying that their operations would be enhanced by the use of objectives or systems approaches.

## THE ADOPTION OF A SYSTEMS APPROACH

There is much debate about the value of the objectives approach to the design and evaluation of the curricula at both the secondary (Cohen and Mannion 1977; Eisner 1979) and tertiary levels of education (Heywood 1977). Talking to those involved in the preparation of technologist and technician courses suggests that the full implications of a systems approach have not been understood. A statement of aims and objectives by themselves is of no better value than a list of syllabus headings. The purpose of a systems approach to the design of curricula is to relate the methods of assessment, teaching/learning strategies, materials and evaluation procedures to significant objectives which have been carefully screened for their applicability within courses. (Screening is a technique which brings together the philosophy and sociology of education with the psychology of learning in the evaluation of significant and consistent aims and objectives (Furst 1958; Heywood 1981).) In such a system considerable changes in teaching style and learning management are to be expected.

Screening aims is a complex activity and the available evidence suggests that in so far as TEC courses are concerned this has not been done properly. Clements and Roberts (1980) for example argue that there is too much attention to theoretical study and too little attention to practical aspects of technician employment including management. Criticisms of standards could be overcome if there were national components of assessment as for example in multiple choice tests (Carter and Lee 1975). Similarly careful screening of aims and objectives would lead to a more coherent understanding of course structures and provide answers or respond by change to the criticism that TEC courses are too detailed, narrow and fragmented within watertight compartments so that no overview is possible. But screening is a complex activity for which substantial training is required. As it is while aims and objectives may be declared there is little evidence to suggest that they influence teaching or assessment. Teachers it seems revert to traditional styles of teaching, a view which is supported by at least one report to the Further Education Curriculum Review Unit (Dodd, Lovell and Oxtoby 1982).

This is not surprising for by and large teachers have not been trained in the system design of curricula and there are few illustrations of how such screening is accomplished. The evidence is that substantial training is required if this idea of curriculum design is to be internalised and acted upon (Murphy 1976). Such training, which can be in-service and problem oriented, has to be substantial. Moreover, the theory suggests that assessment procedures and teaching strategies should be determined by the objectives to be obtained and not by any pre-conceived and naïve notion of the value of continuous assessment when compared with examinations. Such training should extend to external assessors.

AN INCREASED WORK LOAD
As it stands this training has not yet happened. And a further problem moreover is the extra strain imposed by validation in professional education. The professional institutions vary in their requirements for submissions. Some forms of application would seem to require as much as the CNAA. Exhibit I shows the requirements of the Institute of Biology. Most of the heads of department in the polytechnics with whom I talked were happy with the system they had helped to create. Applications to the CNAA required so much detail that the points likely to be asked by the professional institutions would be covered in those documents.

*Exhibit I*
Information required by the Institute of Biology to begin the recognition procedure for M.I. Biol. (Institute of Biology 1979).
    'In order to be recognised as a centre for the provision of an M.I.Biol. course, the college will be required to provide the detailed information indicated below.
    General information about the course including its title and duration, its objectives, and how it is proposed to achieve them; the relationship of the course with the present work of the department.
    Course structure and organization including details of formal periods spent out of the college in the case of full-time courses.
    Course syllabuses including the deployment of staff.
    Examination schedule including details of the proposed method of course work assessment.
    Staff support giving details of the present departmental teaching staff (full-time and part-time) and of technical and clerical staff together with the expected future establishment.
    A list of names of the academic staff concerned with the course giving their qualifications in detail, their experience in industry, teaching and research, and their membership of professional or learned societies.
    Research and/or advanced study being undertaken in the Department.
    Accommodation including specialist and research facilities.
    Equipment for teaching and research.

Library facilities.
Financial support for the course in terms of capital support and the provision of on-going expenses.'

Sometimes the same application documents were used. There is much less duplication of effort than might be imagined and the visitations of the professional institutions have the advantage, as was indicated above, of focussing attention on matters of professional education and training.

Compared with the situation prior to the CNAA staff involved in courses have undoubtedly to do more preparation work. By and large this procedure was, in retrospect, welcomed for the 'rethink' which it provided. How adequate this thinking was is a matter not only of conjecture but for research. At the technician level there seems to be more of a change of emphasis. Once the CNAA has accepted the submission it leaves the college to get on with the job. TEC and BEC, however, do not require so much forward planning but they keep a much closer watch on the ongoing teaching and examining process. There is some evidence to suggest that they are moving toward the CNAA model in respect of visitations. At Luton College of Higher Education staff felt that the continuous assessment associated with technician courses had increased their administrative load by between twenty and forty per cent. These Councils have given considerable thought to the role of external moderators (Midgley 1981; TEC 1975)

When courses are subject to periodic validation a big and cyclic work load is placed on staff. Lecturers involved in courses which require validation will do much more work than those engaged in teaching for external examinations. Similarly those who have to provide continuous assessment information will do more than their colleagues. There seems to be a tendency to recruit senior and therefore older members of staff to plan for and organize the new technician courses. In general it seems that technician courses have created much more work for staff involved in their design and implementation, which is confirmed by other studies for the Further Education Curriculum Review Unit (Dodd, Lovell and Oxtoby 1981) and the Society for Research into Higher Education (Heywood 1981).

At the collegiate level institutions like Luton College of Higher Education and Leeds Polytechnic have to undertake a huge administrative exercise in connection with validation visits. The former deals with more than forty examining and validating bodies. Because of all this considerable changes in attitude have been required of staff. The question which has to be answered is whether or not this huge endeavour has been worthwhile.

BROADER ISSUES
Two major issues arise from the changes in the structures and style of validation in the professional field. The first relates to *the costs of the accreditation of professional courses*. The second to innovation in higher education generally.

When most of education for industry was part-time, courses were validated by the professional institutions through the examination system in the public sector. University courses were accepted in their own right and their graduates obtained recognition without difficulty. For one reason and another — among them the inability to raise fees — the Institutions did not conduct extensive appraisals of the kind conducted by the CNAA. It is probable of course that such appraisals would not have been acceptable and that the work of the NCTA was a necessary step in the direction taken by the CNAA. It is not without significance that many of those working in professional subject areas in universities now accept accrediting parties from the professional institutions as necessary. The demands made on manpower in the public sector for degree level validation by the CNAA are considerable when compared with the demands made by universities on associated colleges or by university departments on themselves. The Institutions did not make comparable demands on the public sector when they operated the national certificate system.

There seems to have been less demand from staff operating degree courses in public sector colleges for their institutions to become universities than the experience of the development of the colleges of advanced technology might have led one to expect. This seems to be in part due to the fact that many staff believe that they are protected from inadequate funding by the CNAA. In contrast many colleges in the public sector used to operate London internal and external degrees without such fears. Little is known about the effect of resources on the quality of performance of either staff or students and in this respect a system of validation which develops resource criteria that are but notional must be open to criticism.

All these lead to the view that the system and the problems associated with it are relatively complex. Among the questions which may be asked are, 'Is CNAA any more efficient or credible than the professional institutions or universities?' and 'Why should the degree-granting power not simply be given to the professional institutions?' Answers to these questions relate in part to the effectiveness of appraisals and in part to the likely response of the professional institutions to change in the patterns of knowledge (ie innovation).

*Innovation* takes place at a number of different levels and relates not only to curriculum and teaching but to course and degree structures and thus to the wider society. Little attention has been paid to the sociology of the curriculum in higher education despite all the work on the school curriculum (Eggleston 1977). Much restructuring takes place in the seminar room but generally curriculum change in higher education takes place within a received perspective. There has been little response to the bold ideas presented at the 1974 inter-government conference on *The Future Structures of Higher Education* (OECD 1974).

The problem of innovation has no simple solution. CNAA could have an important role to play in facilitating major innovations, in making aims and objectives explicit and in serving to emphasize the development of higher order cognitive skills rather than the mere accumulation of information. But to state aims and objectives is not enough: in the last resort the assessment system is the predominant influence on teaching and learning and therefore on the attainment of goals (Heywood 1977). CNAA is inevitably subject centred but a judicious extension of the membership of subject committees might make a useful contribution to the development both of curricula suited to the kinds of problems which have to be solved in life (Jones 1970) and of assessment techniques.

The case against the professional institutions is that they may be reinforcing curricula and examination structures which are inhibitive not only of educational innovation but also of social mobility (Jones 1970). T.H. Marshall (1939) wrote:

It is important to notice the effects of these changes in social mobility. An organized profession admits recruits by means of an impartial test of their knowledge and ability. In theory they are selected on merit, but it is a merit of a particular kind which usually must be developed and displayed in a particular way. A narrow road leads into the profession through certain educational institutions. How far this favours social mobility depends on whether those institutions are open to the masses, so that merit can win recognition in all classes. Granted the broadening of the educational ladder typical of modern democracies, the system of the official examination is more favourable to mobility than one of arbitrary appointment or casual promotion. But the chance to move comes early, during school days. Once it has been missed and a career has been started at a non-professional level the whole system of formal qualifications makes movement at a later stage well-nigh impossible ... there is another point. In the church or the army, in law or medicine a man at the head of his profession is on top of the world. He admits no superiors. But many of these new semi-professions are really subordinate grades placed in the hierarchy of modern business organization. The educational ladder leads into them but there is no ladder leading out.

Immediately it can be seen that CNAA, TEC and BEC have an important conjunctive role in creating structures which allow for greater mobility. In terms of work expectations such mobility is essential, as are educational programmes which help people become flexible and adaptable. Such courses have been developed for degree programmes at all levels (DES 1980). Present structures, however, do not seem to be suited to this purpose.

The Bosworth Committee (1966) on education and training for the electrical industry suggested that the equivalent of a Schools Council for Higher Education would better ensure a response to change. Whatever one's view of the Schools Council is, it certainly caused many valuable ideas to be generated, particularly in the area of interdisciplinary study. Yet the evidence suggests that, without substantial training of individual teachers, such ideas are unlikely to be fully or successfully applied, as the example of systems approaches shows. To some extent this may be the result of cultural conditioning (McClelland 1969, Mant 1979).

It is therefore difficult to believe that any advantage would accrue to higher education if all university courses were simply to be validated by the CNAA, as has been proposed, even though it seems clear that the CNAA system has been of immense value. Similarly any reversion to the old system of validation purely by professional examinations would equally run up against inhibitive effects on socio-technical evolution. Structural changes of themselves are not enough. They need to be accompanied by changes in the attitudes of teachers and others working in the structures.

If all teachers in higher education were required to consider these issues within the framework of a teacher training programme, some progress might be made in developing more flexible attitudes. The need for a politically motivated forum through which to conduct a national debate on these issues is great. Equally there is need for a substantial evaluation, by independent investigators, of the different processes of validation currently in use and their effects on policy on the one hand and student learning on the other.

## ACKNOWLEDGEMENTS

As a result of the original presentation the working group asked me to discuss practical issues of professional validation with teaching staff concerned. To facilitate this Dr B.B. Gent, Deputy Director of Leeds Polytechnic, enabled me to spend some considerable time with his heads of department. Another member of the working group, Mr R.D. Harrison of the Open University, volunteered to visit Luton College of Higher Education where Dr R. Oxtoby, the Deputy Director, arranged discussions with various members of staff. Mr Harrison also discussed these issues with the representatives of several professional institutions. In addition I was able to consult Dr D. Webb of Leicester University. I am grateful to all of them for this help.

Although the responsibility for the preparation of this final report and the opinions expressed therein are mine, I have been greatly helped by Gerald Collier and Roger Harrison in its revision.

## REFERENCES

Alverno College Faculty (1979) *Assessment at Alverno College USA* and *Liberal Learning at Alverno College USA* Milwaukee: Alverno College

BIM (1982) Code of conduct and supporting guides to good management practice *Management Review and Digest* 8 (4) 31

Bosworth, G.S. (1966) (Chairman of a Committee) *The Education and Training Requirements for the Electrical and Manufacturing Industries* London: HMSO

Carr-Saunders, A. and Wilson P.A. (1933) *The Professions* London: Frank Cass

Burns, T. and Stalker, G. (1961) *The Management of Innovation* London: Tavistock

Carter, C.F. and Lee, L.S. (1975) University first year electrical engineering examinations *International Journal of Electrical Engineering Education* 11, 149

Clements, I. and Roberts, I. (1980) Practitioner views of industrial needs and course unit content. In Heywood, J. (Ed.) *The New Technician Education* Guildford: Society for Research into Higher Education

Cmnd 1254 (1961) *Better Opportunities in Technical Education* London: HMSO

Cohen, L. and Mannion, L. (1977) *A Guide to Teaching Practice* London: Methuen

Cotgrove, S. (1958) *Technical Education and Social Change* London: Allen and Unwin

Crowther, Lord. (1959) (Chairman of a Committee) *15 to 18* (two volumes) London: HMSO

Davis, M. (1980) *The Development of the CNAA* PhD thesis. Loughborough University of Technology

Dodd, S., Lovell, R.B. and Oxtoby, R. (1980) *The Impact of TEC on the Day to Day Work Activity of Teachers* Interim Report of a project sponsored by the Further Education Curriculum Review Unit. London: FEU

Eggleston, S.J. (1977) *The Sociology of the School Curriculum* London: Routledge and Kegan Paul

Eisner, E.W. (1979) *The Educational Imagination* London: Collier-MacMillan

Furst, E.J. (1958) *Constructing Evaluation Instruments* New York: David McKay

Further Education Curriculum Review and Development Unit (1980) (1) *Experience Reflection Learning* (2) *Developing Social and Life Skills* London: Department of Education and Science

Heywood, J. (1969) *An Evaluation of Certain Post-War Developments in Higher Technological Education* (two volumes) Thesis. Lancaster: University of Lancaster Library

Heywood, J. (1981) The academic versus practical debate: a case study in screening *IEE Proceedings* A. 128 (7) 511

Heywood, J. (1981) (Editor) *The New Technician Education* Guildford: Society for Research into Higher Education

Heywood, J. and Mash, V. (1968) Secondary education and occupational choice of students on undergraduate sandwich courses (DipTech) *International Journal of Electrical Engineering Education* 6, 109

Houle, C.O. (1980) *Continuing Learning in the Professions* San Francisco: Jossey-Bass

IEEE (1982) Ethics code proposed for all technical professionals *The Institute* (IEEE) 6 (3) 5

Institute of Biology (1979) *Notes for Guidance of Colleges* London

Johnson, T. (1972) *Professions and Power* London: Macmillan

Jones, C.J. (1970) Professions as inhibitors of socio-technical evolution *Futures* March p.24

Lees, D.S. (1966) *Economic Consequences of the Professions* London: Institute of Economic Affairs

Mant, A. (1979) *The Rise and Fall of the British Manager* London: Pan

McClelland, D.C. (1969) The role of the achievement orientation in the transfer of technology. In Gruber, W.H. and Marquis, D.G. (Editors) *Factors in the Transfer of Technology* Cambridge, Mass: MIT Press

Marshall, T.H. (1939) *Reprinted in Sociology at the Crossroads* London: Heinemann

Matthews, W. and Golightly, L. (1981) *The Core of Knowledge Necessary to the Developing Role of the Home Economist* An interim report on the research investigation undertaken by the Association of Home Economists *The home economist* 1, 15

Midgley, K. (1981) A moderating influence *Times Higher Education Supplement* 9 September (about the Business Education Council)

Moon, J. (1968). *The Ethical Attitudes of Chartered Mechanical Engineers and their relationship to formal Education.* Thesis. University of Lancaster

Murphy, D.E. (1976) *Problems Associated with the Implementation of a New National System of Assessment in Ireland* Thesis, University of Dublin

Payne, G.L. (1969) *Britain's Scientific and Technological Manpower* Oxford: Oxford University Press

Percy, Lord (1945) (Chairman of a Committee) *Higher Technological Education* London: HMSO

Robbins, Lord (1963) (Chairman of a Committee) *Higher Education* Cmnd 2154. London: HMSO

Russell et al. (1977) *Chemists by Profession* Oxford: OUP

Schein, E.H. (1969) *Process Consultation: its Role in Organization Development* Reading, Massachusetts: Addison-Wesley

TEC (1975) *The Maintenance of Standards of TEC Awards* London: Technician Educator Council

Youngman, M.B., Oxtoby, R., Monk, J.D. and Heywood, J. (1978) *Analysing Jobs* Aldershot: Gower Press

# 5 VALIDATION IN TEACHER EDUCATION

Robin Alexander and Eileen Wormald

The education of teachers has always been subject to external validation. Apart from postgraduate certificate (PGCE) courses in universities nearly all teacher training courses have been carried out in non-autonomous institutions and control over the years has been exercised variously by HMIs, the Board of Education, local authorities and the universities.

The Robbins *Report* (1963) took the view that further absorption into the university system was desirable and recommended the establishment of university schools of education which would incorporate the colleges as autonomous bodies financed through the University Grants Committee. The opposition of both central government and LEAs prevented the adoption of this scheme but some significant gains were made, including the right of colleges to offer students a degree course in conjunction with the universities to which they were affiliated. The universities responded rapidly, though with varying degrees of willingness, and the first BEds were awarded in 1968. Following the recommendations of the James Committee (DES 1972a) that colleges capable of doing so should be allowed to offer higher education courses other than teacher training, colleges began to weigh up the political possibilities of such developments under university auspices. Some felt that such development would not be endorsed; or that colleges' progress to full partnership in the public sector of the binary system of higher education would be stultified by continual subordination to the other sector: these turned their attention to the possibility of validation by the Council for National Academic Awards (CNAA).

However, events following the James *Report* concentrated debate and for many institutions resolved it. The 1972 White Paper *Education: a Framework for Expansion* (DES 1972b) was followed by Circular 7/73 (DES 1973) which indicated reductions in teacher training numbers required to meet the falling birthrate, together with a basis for 'rationalization' of the colleges of education. This in turn was followed by a series of documents giving an increasingly gloomy prognosis for the colleges. Of those which were to remain open, some were to join with universities and others with polytechnics; for both of these the form of validation was implicit in the amalgamation. The remaining monotechnics and the diversified but free-standing colleges of higher education, on the other hand, had a choice to make and it often involved difficult and protracted decision-making for the academic boards of these institutions (Newton, Shaw and Wormald, 1975). Whichever validation brief was chosen, or imposed, the validation process was to absorb considerable energy and resources from that point onwards, often concurrently with reorganization, reduction in student numbers and contraction of staff.

By the start of the enquiry from which this paper stems (1978), CNAA was validating nearly half the initial BEd courses in England and a smaller proportion of the PGCEs, and the colleges, both CNAA and university-validated, had been through probably the most concentrated and frenetic period of course renewal in their history. It was our intention to analyse the nature of the validator-validated relationships engendered during this unique period and to assess its impact on the shape and character of the new courses, the staff who planned and taught them, and the colleges.

In the first part of the enquiry, sixty responses were elicited, by means of a detailed schedule of open-ended questions, from staff in twenty-nine institutions, of which sixteen were validated by CNAA, and thirteen by nine universities. Most of these responses were individual and came from staff at all levels of college hierarchies. However, several were from named pairs or small groups of individuals, a number were individual responses presented 'after consultations with colleagues' and there were also systematic collations of the responses of faculty and college staff undertaken on our behalf by individual 'agents'. The number of individual voices represented in the sixty responses is thus, we estimate, about one hundred and fifty. With a few exceptions the responses are very full indeed. In the second half of the enquiry we undertook interviews with a sample of staff from five institutions, each having a very different experience of both validation and institutional reorganization, and with representatives of their validating bodies. These will form the basis of case studies to be reported elsewhere.

We are conscious that the responses do not in any way represent a strict sample of either institutions or personnel and that we are recording perceptions held (a) by the validated and not the validators and (b) by particular college staff whose perceptions reflect their personal experience and fortunes during involvement in validation. Our use of views from one side only is valid, we feel, in so far as we do not present them as objective descriptions of actual processes but rather as perceptions, which we take to reveal as much about the validated as about the validating body. So throughout this research we hypothesize that what is revealed as of central significance is not only how different validating bodies operate but how colleges and individuals choose to respond to what they see as the explicit and implicit demands of the validation process.

All types of academic validation have something in common: none is totally 'open' in the sense that an institution can put forward its proposals confident that they will be appraised purely on the basis of criteria intrinsic to the proposals themselves: all validating bodies have their own extrinsic requirements and expectations, sometimes formalized into regulations, sometimes existing in unwritten form, to which colleges have to conform, or at least respond. It is important to establish what these requirements and expectations are, and the influence which they have on the course proposals and the way they are planned.

However, for our respondents the matter was rarely as straightforward as this, for the expectations of validating bodies had firstly to be communicated and secondly to be received and interpreted. At least as important as the validators' 'message' itself was how and by whom it was conveyed and what happened to it during this process. Communication of validation matters within a college was as significant as communication between the college and the validator. In this paper, therefore, we shall consider first how staff became aware of 'what the validating body expects' before summarising variations in the 'expectations' themselves. Throughout, the tenuousness of the communication process referred to above should be borne in mind: the 'expectations' received by rank and file staff as a basis for planning at the level of individual course components might or might not be the same as those actually conveyed by the validators.

VALIDATION BY CNAA: 'WHAT THE VALIDATING BODY EXPECTS'
For a centralized validating body based in London and dealing with institutions as far away as Scotland communication of validation require-ments is a major challenge. As might be expected, CNAA relies to a greater extent on explicit written statements than do many universities whose relationships are with a relatively small number of local colleges where there may be also well-established personal links. The key document is 'Principles and Regulations for the award of the Council's First Degrees and the Diploma of Higher Education', recently (1979) revised, though our respondents, experience related to the earlier (1974) version. This latter document set out in some detail the statutory functions and responsibilities of CNAA together with 'regulations and conditions' for the award of their degrees. The character of degree courses and the broad validation criteria were discussed in some detail: the latter relate particularly to the institutional context, the staff, and the course documentation. In addition there were numerous other documents available to the colleges — directories, reports, a newsletter ('CNAA Commentary'). CNAA 'guidelines' on specific courses were presented as discussion documents, though the boundary between guidelines and directives was recognized in the colleges as a shadowy one (Alexander 1979a).

Those who commented on this relative wealth of explicit material seemed to find it both useful and non-constraining. 'Regulations were explicit within a general permissive framework.' 'In general it (the CNAA information) allowed an open approach that was generally welcomed.' 'You can, within the regulations, set out what you want to do provided you can justify it.' These were fairly typical comments, though one or two mentioned the confusion which the language of such documents could sometimes cause.

So far, then, at this formal, explicit level, 'what CNAA expects' was relatively non-problematic. But most colleges found or felt that it was not enough to rely on documents alone and that some form of direct contact was needed between them and CNAA, particularly first time round. So the usual pattern, repeated in many colleges, was for personal contact to be established between key individuals in the college and the appropriate CNAA officers — in this case the Registrar or one of the Assistant Registrars for Education.

Here two problems emerge very clearly. The first is that, as our respondents point out, the officers had to emphasize that they could suggest and even speculate but, not being the validating panel, they could make no firm judgments about the viability of particular draft proposals other than in relation to points specified in CNAA regulations. However, there does seem to have been a tendency for some college members to give officers' statements, caveats notwithstanding, a formal force they were not intended to have, either because they were grasping for straws or for reasons discussed below. The second, more serious, problem is that direct college-CNAA contact was restricted to a small number of key individuals, and several respondents compare this CNAA experience unfavourably with their earlier relationship with local universities, where a far greater proportion of teaching staff may have had direct contact with the relevant validating/ moderating academic staff members.

These key individuals came to fulfil a vital strategic function for their colleges in relation to the success of a proposal: they emerged as a more potent source of knowledge about 'what CNAA expects' than any CNAA document, and when in due course of time they became members of CNAA panels they acquired additional and valuable 'information' concerning the foibles, prejudices and preferences of validating panel members. They became 'gatekeepers' of information (Barnes 1979) about CNAA which was important for the institution as a whole and essential to preserving their own position within it. But just how reliable was this information? One respondent pointed out that 'these statements (about what CNAA will want) were made with different levels of authority' yet in the event 'virtually all the wise men were proved wrong'. Confusion appears to have abounded over the capacity or willingness of CNAA to validate innovative proposals. Several respondents remarked that 'it was generally believed that the expectations of CNAA were conservative' while conversely others talk of the pressure to be radical:

'We were led to believe that CNAA must have something radically different from the existing course ... we could no longer impose the four disciplines of educational studies on our students.'

Or, as one respondent said:

'Cries .. of "You must say this" or "Never say that" have been heard a great deal. However, since the advice is frequently contradictory

I doubt if it is really as significant as colleagues like to claim.'

With hindsight several respondents used words like 'folklore', 'mythology' and 'rumour' in characterizing the information transmitted by college intermediaries about 'what CNAA expects'. Moreover, the purveyors of such 'information' come in for somewhat derisive epithets —the 'wise men', the 'mystical orders', the 'literati', the 'mandarins', and respondents who themselves fulfilled this intermediary role were quick to acknowledge both its usefulness and the possibility of abuse.

The suspect nature of the information, and the resentment that the manner of its transmission could arouse, were well illustrated by the not atypical remark (referring to the return of a senior college staff member from a visit to CNAA) that 'when Moses came down with the tablets we were not sure whether they came from God or from Moses'.

What these responses reveal is a deeper unease about the impact of this style of communication between colleges and CNAA on college power structures: intermediaries came in several institutions to provide excellent illustrations of the 'knowledge is power' dictum. As one respondent said succinctly, such 'oracular consultations ... did not influence course content so much as course management'. Others saw the process as less academic than 'political' and indeed the essentially politicizing function of the CNAA experience is a recurrent theme in both our questionnaire and interview data.

As a strategy for putting staff in a position to prepare course proposals for CNAA validation, the reliance on a single person to bridge the considerable psychological and often geographical gap between rank and file staff and CNAA officers and panels is thus very questionable. In general our respondents, while conceding that it was invaluable to have a member of staff with inside knowledge of CNAA, responded with varying degrees of resignation, cynicism and antagonism to the intermediary approach. Further, their own lack of meaningful contact with the validators could produce confusion and alienation, a sense of being manipulated, of being kept in the dark. It has to be asked why this style of college — Council communication is still so common if it also appears to be so counterproductive (except possibly in terms of the personal ambitions of the intermediaries —and therein lies much of the answer, perhaps).

By now it must be clear that the task of establishing the nature and impact of the validators' expectations is a difficult one: how do we separate out, from questionnaire data which by definition presents only what college staff *think* CNAA want, the reliable from the unreliable, and reality from the myth? Our answer has to be to stick to the data, since whatever the truth of the matter, the influence of fact and myth were perceived by the validated as having comparable impact on the process of course planning.

Taking the three broad criteria actually specified by CNAA (1974, 1979a) under the headings of 'the college, the staff and the documented proposal', we found that the bulk of respondents' reservations were about the documentation. On CNAA's expectations about academic decision-making, institutional and staff development, and their views on academic climate and community our respondents had less to say. On expectations about staff most attention was given to CNAA's real or supposed emphasis on staff cohesiveness; for example: 'we were told that great importance was laid on staff cohesiveness and that dissent expressed in a meeting with the panel could wreck hopes of approval. We had to support one another. We had not even to indicate that there might have been differences of opinion in reaching conclusions'. That comment, it is clear, says probably as much about the apparent power of the 'wise men' in one college as about the expectations themselves, but the point was repeated, though not always in such strong terms, by many. The other 'expectation' about staff most frequently noted was that 'the staff who will do the teaching must be involved in the planning'. By and large, while the 'cohesiveness' condition sometimes provoked a sense of healthy debate being stifled in the interests of making an outward show of unanimity, the 'involvement' condition seemed universally acceptable.

However, the matter of documentation produced responses which are both strong and diverse. These responses dealt predominantly with three issues: the quantity of documentary evidence required or perceived to be required; the nature of the information included; and the status of the documentation in relation to the course as actually taught. The quantitative aspect seems straightforward. Staff generally saw a value in expressing intentions with clarity and detail in advance, in that to do this required that they engaged collectively in fundamental debate about the rationale and structure of a new course: 'Council's demand for written justification has been most valuable to us and has made us think far more carefully about what we wish to do and how we shall do it.'

However, there was considerable anxiety about the amount of documentation apparently required. Some saw this as reasonable, but most perceived it as a burden, often producing an excessive amount of paper. Some respondents quantified this burden and reported BEd submissions of 'five volumes of 100 to 200 pages each'; of '18 inches in height'; and of 'eleven substantial volumes'. Staff wrote feelingly about the 'frightening weight of paperwork' and the sense of being on a constant 'treadmill' of planning, writing and replanning to the extent that teaching the present generation of students becomes less important than preparing to teach the next generation. We need to observe at this point that the teacher educators' experience here over the past five or six years has been unprecedentedly gruelling: the 'treadmill' of planning has not of course been solely a direct response to CNAA requirements but has necessarily been undertaken to ensure staff and institutional survival. Moreover, our study related mainly to first generation CNAA teacher education courses, and the scale of subsequent documentation was usually more modest.

Yet there was nevertheless a prevading sense that CNAA itself made excessive demands in this regard: some felt that a week by week curriculum breakdown was inappropriate; others reported frustration at being told by CNAA that 'we could be briefer' while the same voice has also asked for more detail.

What did staff feel obliged to include in this documentation? Respondents reproduced the list, or parts of it, contained in CNAA regulations (staffing, institutional background, course rationale, structure, organization, content, assessment requirements, admission procedures etc.) but their main concern was with particular elements in it, notably the emphasis on prespecified objectives which several found difficult to write and not always appropriate to their fields of study.

## VALIDATION BY CNAA: THE DAY OF JUDGEMENT

When the expectations, real or imagined, had been operationalized, the documentation submitted and the course team prepared, the 'day of judgement' arrived. It is in this area that the experience of the process of validation by universities and CNAA most clearly diverged. With one exception in the colleges responding to this enquiry, university teams did not descend in large numbers for a one or two day visit: negotiations went on over a period of time with different parts of the degree going through the appropriate committees at different times. With CNAA there was always a 'visitation': a team of up to forty representatives of CNAA drawn from universities, polytechnics and, more rarely, in the early days, colleges of education, accompanied by teacher representatives and two or three officers of the Council, visited the submitting institution. A pattern emerges which might be termed an 'ideal type' against which deviations can be judged: all members of the visiting group would have received copies of all the final submitted documents and it was expected that these would have been read and understood in advance; on the first day there were initial discussions between chairman, CNAA officers and a core group of the validating panel, and the institution's planning team, to discuss and clarify the structure of the degree; sometimes this was followed by a larger meeting when questions on, for example, interrelations of parts of the course were put to the planning team together with some others of the staff involved in planning specific parts of the course. On the second day subject specialists arrived who, after consultation with the rest of the validators, discussed component parts of the degree with those who were going to teach them. At the end of the day a decision was announced as to acceptance of the degree in whole or in part. The details of the 'validation' and any conditions or recommendations attached were contained in a written report often received some weeks, or occasionally even months, later. If re-submission was required this might lead to another visit, or alternatively small teams from the submitting institution might visit council offices to meet a panel of validators.

It does not appear to matter how these arrangements varied or how they were intended to work by the validators; the validated always perceived them as a confrontation, a contest in which one side could not lose and the other did not know the rules of the game. Even in what might seem relatively trivial details unequivocal guidelines were lacking; it appears to have been uniformly agreed that a good lunch should be provided and that this should be a joint festivity between validators and validated. But what sort of occasion was it to be? Was it a continuation of the vetting procedure or a half-time relaxation? Two comments reflect the uncertainty about this occasion: 'We were warned to be especially cautious in conversation at lunchtime' and 'Many of us felt that we'd got it unless we got drunk at lunch'. Another view was that validators were mellowed by this social occasion and 'the likelihood of getting a submission through has been enormously increased by having a panel in the college, not only because they were influenced by the food and wine'.

In other areas there were matters of more serious concern; should one defend a proposal uncompromisingly or accept some of the comments of the validators as advisory comments rather than provocative, testing, statements? It was the ability to steer a straight course between these two hazards that often distinguished the 'new men or women' of the next stage who followed the original 'gatekeepers' into the inner circle of CNAA 'cognoscenti'. Taking the feel of the meeting was a skill which became highly prized. Those who did stick to their guns had to do so unemotionally and we admired the nerve and verve of the team who, having reshaped a section of a submission in response to criticism from one 'expert', met a new specialist who 'could not understand why we had abandoned the original excellent scheme. Fortunately the staff really had thought through their plan and argued it very eloquently and the panel member accepted their sincerity and conviction (even though he still mourned the lost course).'

But in such a situation staff could misjudge the likely reactions of the 'opposing team' and much depended on the preconceptions and the open-mindedness or flexibility of the validating panel; there were few comments as bitter as the one which attributed failure to 'a complete lack of knowledge as to what the particular validating team would stomach. The course was designed for future teachers of the 75 per cent of children who are unlikely to see a unversity. It was scrutinized by a group solely concerned with the 25 per cent who do', but others expressed uncertainty about how far success could result from sticking to one's guns. Whatever the validity of the belief or myth that a conviction that one was right would win the day, in practice for this or other reasons it did not always work and modifications had to be made to accommodate panels' views which some years later may still be felt to have been inappropriate. 'He (a validating panel member) was out of touch and has since been made to look foolish, but there was no appeal.' Obviously a great deal depended on individuals and 'some personalities and panels appeared to have much greater influence on final decisions than others'.

Throughout these responses there was agreement on the important part played in the process by the idiosyncratic views of individuals. This was inevitable where there were no detailed explicit criteria by which submissions were to be judged. However, it was perceived that a strong panel chairman exercised a controlling, consensus-directed influence. This was particularly true where there were changes of panel membership, a cause of a complaint voiced by the majority of our respondents. 'A good chairman is vital to an efficient discussion if policy is not to swing wildly with changes in panel membership' and happily the chairmen were almost universally praised.

However, chairmen could not completely control the membership of the panels since availability as well as suitability was a criterion for membership. Nor could they override the whims of the members, particularly when these changed either during the visit or for subsequent re-submission: 'wildly contingent arrangements on the day, plus postponement of an earlier date tested patience unjustifiably' while 'the balance of the panel was distorted by unexplained absences' and 'where we have put in a submission more than once the panel has changed and with this demands have changed'. The relationship of individual ideas to general policy was one which interested a number of participants: they wondered to what extent 'all members of a validating panel are aware of a general set of requirements, ie how is the individual approach of a particular member reconciled with the general approach'. It was felt that the policy of having a core group to examine the overall rationale and structure of the degree together with additional members for specialist areas led to discrepancy and indeed contradiction, and that particular subject specialists were inclined to ride hobby horses or staff might be expected to implement 'the gospel according to Prof. X'.

Most of the validated combined a respect for the expertise, open-mindedness and fairness of the chairmen and panel with irritation at the waywardness of individuals. The perceived position might be summarized by this description: 'Some individuals raised odd, not to say bizarre, issues and one, on an inter-site trip, insisted on a detour to do some shopping, got lost, missed part of the next meeting and then downed the proposal', nevertheless this same respondent wrote 'it is interesting that only on two occasions out of twenty one were course teams dissatisfied with their treatment and mostly staff accepted decisions as being not unfair even when adverse'.

In responding to a question about 'external considerations' in the validation process staff from only one institution felt that there might have been an attempt at local authority pressure on CNAA at a time of mergers and closures but a few were worried about the presence of members from competing institutions. Only one offered direct evidence of the effect when 'one member announced that he was opposed in principle to us running a course that might take his students' but others were suspicious and 'questions were asked about the propriety of having panel members whose own home institutions could be said to be in competition with the courses under consideration'. Our evidence in general, however, suggests that these fears were unfounded.

In some rare cases a whole degree was given five years' approval on the day of the panel visit 'subject to minor revisions', in the main concerned with assessment criteria and procedures on which the panel required more details. More usually some revision of structure and/or content, some new appointments or upgrading of current staff qualifications were required for some parts of the degree and usually these were accepted. 'We have, I think, always met the conditions but sometimes one feels that those who wrote them had not really studied the documents.' One of the more disconcerting aspects of the process to some participants was the 'discrepancy between verbal observations of individuals and panels at meetings and the written minutes and records which appeared many weeks later, and which formed the basis for the next stage of validation'. Given the customary method of the many individual panel members submitting written comments which are then collated and ordered by the officers and chairman this does not seem surprising, but it appeared that the printed word was the one with power and we did not hear of anyone who ignored the formal report and acted on the oral judgements.

Appeals against validation judgements do not appear to have been common although panel changes were made, it was believed, as a result of protest: 'the conduct of this panel at this validation meeting and a subsequent one was the subject of letters of protest by disgusted colleagues'. Changes of panels between submissions might therefore be a help as well as a hindrance, though the latter seems to be the majority view. Not all embraced the difficulties this caused but some accepted it as a challenge: 'Although the change of panel created a difficult situation, it prompted a reappraisal of the course which has influenced the planning and preparation of the next submission, beneficially we hope'. Others accepted grudgingly and made changes which 'altered the nature of the course, but we were obliged to accept CNAA recommendations' while those who would not or could not accept the conditions faced, for example, 'a year of slightly frosty and weary dialogue with no evidence given to us of success'.

VALIDATION BY CNAA: AFTER THE EVENT
In looking back on the success or failure of the validation of their course, respondents chose a number of criteria which they felt had influenced the process. None of them helps to penetrate the mystery of what constitutes a degree for teachers, what is degree-worthy and so on. But like the expectations the perceived criteria became part of the mythology of course planning and, whether accurate or not, an implicit part of the concept of what constituted an acceptable model of a BEd for re-validation purposes. The only CNAA criterion for success which appeared to have almost unanimous support was 'staff cohesiveness', which perhaps deserves more

examination as a quality of successful course development than it has so far received. Playing together as a team is an art which can be learned and many felt they improved at second and third attempt; no one tried to define it or explain its relevance to their aims and objectives. Of the other eighteen criteria of success suggested by our respondents some were related to the 'game' of validation: 'change in parts of the course sampled', 'sympathetic validating panel', 'performance on the day', 'conformity to panel's preconceptions'. Others relate to expectations, presumably fulfilled, about CNAA 'requirements'; 'ethos of the institution, more important than capacity of individuals', 'quality of the documentation', 'all staff teaching on the course to have been involved in planning', 'staff qualifications — not as important as performance on the day', 'student participation', 'library', 'effective administration arrangements'. The final category related to the quality of the course itself: 'the course had cohesion and progression', 'innovatory nature of the course', 'conservation in traditional areas, radicalism in less traditional', 'vocational relevance' and 'connections between different parts of the course'.

These were sufficiently diverse to offset any suggestion that CNAA applied the same criteria to all proposals. It is true, if we consider initial teacher education courses, that CNAA has 'Guidelines' for both the BEd and the PGCE, but these are fairly general and in any case the actual criteria to be applied to specific course proposals only become apparent on the validation day, the 'day of judgement'. They are in the hands of the particular panel convened on that day and they reflect a combination of individual and group interpretations, preferences and expectations rather than CNAA policy. In this sense CNAA might reasonably claim, as it does, that it 'lays down no detailed prerequisites for the structure and content of the course ... and expects to judge each course on its merits ...' 'there is ... no prescribed model for a course leading to a council award' (CNAA 1974, 1979a). Hence the sometimes traumatic character of the validation visit, when the specific and perhaps unexpected criteria became apparent, and hence the exhaustive process of 'informal guesswork', of intermediary consultation, of the growth of the power of the 'mandarins' and 'wise men' as a response to colleges' felt need to know in advance what these criteria might be.

And hence the wide variety of ex post facto perceived criteria: with the single exception, as has been shown, of the interesting concept of staff cohesiveness. Where there was a uniform response, and thus confirmation of Alexander's (1979a) thesis about a prevailing CNAA 'model', was at the macro level of overall views about priorities, procedures, and outcomes of course planning, and institutional mechanisms for course implementation, control and renewal, rather than at the micro level of detailed criteria for judging the content of course components. The critical question is the extent to which such a macro-level 'model' constrains the character and quality of teaching and learning. See, for instance, the discussion below on the role of submission documents.

The stringency of the initial validation is often justified on the grounds that once approval was given CNAA had little, other than formal, continuing involvement with an institution: yet CNAA remained the guarantor of a course's academic standard. There was a varied response to this position in relation to the continuing role of the submitted documents during the five year term of validation; were they to be a binding contract or an agreed base on which the institution might build as its students progressed through the course? Whatever the view of the purpose of the documentation or its virtues the majority perceived it as a constraint but not as a strait-jacket.

Several respondents used the term 'blueprint' — some as a term of approval — the document 'provided a blueprint not only for the validation process itself but has since proved immensely valuable'. Others (a greter proportion) had reservations about the blueprint idea: 'we feel, increasingly, that it is almost impossible to be precise, in advance, about content and method in a new course. We place great stress on rationale, philosophy and structure, and on the ability of the course team to fulfil their self-determined aims. We stress this and use syllabuses and booklists to establish standards and areas rather than as revealed truths'.

Others saw this approach as representing 'a rather closed model of curriculum development' and 'at best it is a sort of educational technology style', which can 'encourage a view of curriculum development as implementing plans'. Moreover, several made the point that there could be a considerable time-lag between writing a submission and teaching even the first generation of students in their final year: 'A potential weakness in the CNAA validation model is the way one can plan, write down and then publish — all in fair detail — a course component that may not be taught for another three, four or even five years'. On one course this time-lag was seven years.

Then there is the matter of the usefulness of the documentary style. Naturally, the main function of the documentation is to provide information to enable CNAA to make a validation judgement, but several respondents made the point that it would be better if the documents were also useful to the staff who have invested so much time in producing them. However there was 'some disjunction between documentation for validation and the suitability of the documents for the implementation of the course', and elsewhere: 'Our planning processes were geared as much to the production of documents which would fit CNAA expectations as they were to generating suitable courses for future students'.

Yet, while many respondents commented on the excessive importance of what they termed (theologically?) 'the book', and on the undesirability of having a living course 'cut and dried' in advance, it is also clear that this is one of the several areas where CNAA's actual intentions and expectations were not clearly understood by rank and file staff labouring over the writing of units. One commented 'There remains ... considerable ambiguity in most staff's minds concerning how far syllabi put to CNAA are to be regarded as more or less fixed', and another that 'the mandarins never made it (ie the degree of permitted flexibility) clear either because they thought there was little freedom or because they suspected that units might be prepared less conscientiously if they were not likely to be a strait-jacket'. By and large we find (as might be expected) that senior staff closest to the process and in contact with CNAA tended to take a more relaxed view of this issue, arguing that of course there could be changes. One respondent pointed out what must be an abiding truth in this approach to planning and validation that it is 'the staff, as individuals in a teaching situation, who really determine whether the proposals are implemented as intended ... or do not', and another commented that regardless of innovation and validated proposals 'some colleagues give the same lectures as ten years ago'.

A general impression of the status given to the documents can be inferred from the fact that course structure was not altered except where limitations on student choice were dictated by declining numbers of staff; course content, on the other hand, was modified in discussion with external examiners. A reasonable summary of the way validation of a course has been interpreted is 'gradually, with confidence given to a certain extent by external examiners, the published course has been interpreted more liberally. The legality of not teaching exactly what we said we would teach has not been questioned and only in really marked, fundamental changes has a new version of a component unit been re-submitted for approval to CNAA'. While this suggests on both sides a realistic understanding of the evolutionary process involved in teaching a course it inevitably calls into question what has been called the 'nit-picking' aspects of validation — the changes required of detailed content, of book lists, of sequences, of balance between lecture and tutorial.

VALIDATION BY UNIVERSITIES: EXPECTATIONS
When we turn to the universities as validating bodies it is inevitably more difficult to present a composite picture of either expectations and process or implementation. It might seem more appropriate to discuss each university validation experience recorded by our respondents in turn in that each relates to an autonomous institution. However, we find a practice that there were some marked similarities in the approaches to validation of the various universities involved and that, moreover, the differences between these universities were less significant than the differences between universities in general and CNAA. When we look at the issue of what staff perceived as the expectations and assumptions of the validating body which particularly influenced their course planning style and its outcomes — we find that, firstly, there was a wholly different character of the contact. Colleges related to their local university, whereas CNAA was local only for those in the London area; and with the universities contact was frequently

spread across a greater proportion of college staff and tended to be more personal.

Secondly, validation by universities was a less once-and-for-all, a more continuous process; one of negotiation rather than confrontation, as Church implies in Chapter 3, albeit a negotiation with the cards stacked disproportionately on one side, and the negotiation continued throughout the life of the course after its formal approval, through the universities' extensive system of examiners, moderators and assessors: 'My experience of validation is of an unremitting process with occasional peaks but no discontinuities and which is going on just as much now as ever'. Both these points of difference had consequences with which staff might not necessarily be happy and indeed it was against a sense of over-interference and over-constraint that many colleges were reacting when they transferred to CNAA.

Thirdly, and perhaps critically, although CNAA made known in advance its general approval criteria, the criteria specific to particular proposals had essentially to be anticipated since they only became apparent on the 'day of judgement'. With universities, although the process was ostensibly one of continuous negotiation, it was usually the case that a fairly clear notion of what constituted an acceptable structure for a BEd validated by a particular university already existed, and it was from this basis, albeit of sometimes considerable constraint, that 'negotiation' proceeded. So that although, where universities were concerned, the element of guessing was reduced (and with it the consequent need for the colleges to depend on intermediaries to try by close college/validator contact to anticipate accurately the likely validation criteria), the room for manoeuvre could sometimes be far less and the actual negotiation might be over far less fundamental curriculum issues. In these circumstances a university could not, and probably would not, claim, as CNAA consistently does, to judge proposals on their merits, or to offer anything more than a one-sided negotiation with most of the 'give' on the college side.

At the same time, university validation criteria in respect of a given course at other than the broad structural level were never 'fixed' to the extent that they were with CNAA. With CNAA the 'day of judgement' might be traumatic but at least it led to a clear decision one way or another. With universities the continuous character of the process, coupled with its tendency to involve personal and informal as well as corporate and formal contacts between validators and validated, meant that as personalities changed so in effect criteria could change too. Even basic criteria for validation, therefore, were much more difficult to pin down where universities were concerned. This will be apparent in what follows: we cannot offer, on the basis of our data, the same explications of criteria as we have attempted with CNAA and indeed the overall process of validation by universities is much more elusive.

As with CNAA, the style of the communication between a college and its validating university was significant, though as might be surmised from the analysis so far, staff made somewhat less reference to the role of designated intermediaries. They did appear, however, and frequently much of the hard negotiation went on at senior staff level only. But this was usually offset by at least some direct contact at lower levels between individual staff and their opposite numbers in the university, and at best this could be informal and productive: 'Some good personal contacts ... Many staff were former MEd students of significant individuals in the faculty...'. Or: 'Planning was a dialogue: college expectations and assumptions were at least as dominant as those of the university ... mutual confidence ... led to a relatively painless process.'

What was also important was the longer history of particular college-university relationships, which could ease the planning process, though it could also make real change much more difficult to achieve. In general, however, once a university decided the terms on which it would validate BEd degrees our respondents saw the process as one of negotiation with a flexible institution: 'The group were fair, open-minded and co-operative, often suggesting possible solutions to particular problems'. The validators were known and had usually worked previously with those submitting the degree; where there were representatives from other colleges on the validating team this was not seen as competitive but rather as supportive, indeed in one instance it was described as 'incestuous': 'We were all validating each others' submissions tempered by professional prejudice'. Even where there was considerable disagreement between the two sides this did not lead to rejection but to further negotiation and compromise.

But with whom in universities were college staff dealing? Where CNAA is concerned this much is clear — the contact prior to validation was with the Council's permanent officers. College-university contact was much more diffuse and less predictable: some colleges related to committees convened for the purpose, others to individuals scattered across various faculties, others to non-academic administrative staff — what one of our respondents termed, disparagingly, 'registry validation'. Diffuseness of contact seemed fairly common and made the job of co-ordinating planning in colleges extremely difficult. More than that it implied and to some extent enforced a concept of a course which is the exact opposite of what CNAA values and operates through its system of producing validation panels tailor-made to match particular proposals. For a fragmented validation style makes course coherence much more difficult to achieve.

## VALIDATION BY UNIVERSITIES: PROCEDURES

As we have already emphasized, the 'typical' university validation procedure is hard to find. However, we can isolate from the universities two rather different approaches which seem to represent 'ideal types' to which the others, albeit with variations, conform to a greater or lesser extent.

Firstly there is the relatively unified approach, where a university maintained a coherent view of the proposal by establishing a special body to deal with it. Rather more common, however, was the fragmented approach where although a single body might have oversight of the proposal and of course one body, usually Senate, would eventually ratify it, the proposal's contituent parts were subject to scrutiny by a number (sometimes a large number) of unrelated bodies or individuals, each operating its own criteria, having no inter-validator communication. In its extreme form this procedure produced considerable complexity, exacerbated by the university's desire to achieve uniformity across colleges, despite the very different traditions in teacher education which each might represent.

The consequences of such fragmentation were not only, as we have suggested, the possible loss of a course's coherence and with it a clear rationale in terms of educational and professional goals, but also a considerable expense of time and money: a constant in the university responses was the length of time the process could take, especially when everything had eventually to be ratified by Senate. 'Had we waited for Senate to make up its mind' remarked one respondent whose college transferred to CNAA validation 'the college would be closed by now'.

Three further points need to be made on the matter of who in the universities did the validating. The first is that the validation function might not necessarily be voluntary. Many university validators were conscripts, some of them, apparently, reluctant conscripts who 'displayed a barely concealed irritation with the "extra burden" of examining brought by the BEd'. CNAA validators are, by contrast, volunteers, and membership of a CNAA board, committee or panel is seen by many as a considerable prize even though, while many universities pay their staff for validation work, CNAA does not.

The second point concerns expertise. In the cross-faculty approach to validation operated in many universities the validators might have little knowledge of or interest in teacher education courses yet were expected to judge a component in their subject which aimed to contribute towards a teacher's professional preparation. This cuts both ways — it could produce a refreshingly different perspective: 'There were real debates about the academic validity of professional studies work and there was a determination on their part that the degree should be as cohesive as possible. Naturally, some of these debates were tough ...'

Or it could lead to a sense in a college that university staff were making vital judgements in areas that they were not competent to judge, particularly professional studies and especially in respect of primary schools. Thus: 'I don't want to sound patronizing, but it was the best panel they could produce', and 'When they come down on academic subjects they are the experts. In primary education we are the experts.' Or more strongly: 'The university has nothing to do with professional studies. How can they look at our documents and say something won't work when they have less experience (of schools) than we do'. Considering that professional studies are what makes a BEd uniquely and distinctively a degree for intending teachers, this seems a serious deficiency.

Even with 'academic' elements, where one would have expected communication to have been relatively straightforward since all parties were operating in established domains of discourse, unencumbered by 'professional' requirements, there might be notable differences of perspective. The following comment is of particular interest in that it encapsulates the much more overt student-centredness of the college of education tradition:

> (The university required) 'a different approach to the concept of English ... Thus "study of a book" was preferred to the concept implied by our references to "the experience of a book"'. 'English was seen as an essentially cognitive activity as opposed to the college's concept of its effect on the student's development. For example, the university comment on a poetry course: "Revise aims to focus on course material to be covered — and less on students' response".'

The same respondent compared the college's emphasis on students' collectively shared 'experience' of literature with the university's apparently more aggressively individualistic and competitive notion of academic 'study', the former being seen as essential to the students' future role as a teacher: 'The student should experience fully, so sensitively, so effectively, that he/she is primed to share his insights with others and thereby deepen his/her own'.

The final point here is that we had several references to the possiblity of concern among university staff, 'that they are being involved in validating courses which conflict with their own best interests — particularly by drawing off students from their own potential recruitment pool': a possibility likely to be exacerbated in the present economic climate, if indeed it is anything more than a suspicion on the part of members of colleges who themselves feel under threat.

VALIDATION BY UNIVERSITIES: PERCEIVED CRITERIA

The actual broad criteria for university validation were usually made more explicit in advance than were CNAA's. They fell into four groups: those relating to colleges and their staff; those relating to documentation; those relating to course structure in general; and those relating to the particular content of teacher education courses. The first of these areas can be dealt with quickly. Universities expected the courses they validated to be taught by adequately and appropriately qualified staff, though any 'vetting' might be undertaken when a member of staff was appointed rather than, as with CNAA, in relation to a particular proposal. The meaning of 'appropriately qualified' was not always clear to staff, and for some the personal contact may have been double-edged: 'Individual courses tended to be judged according to the merits and reputations of the staff presenting them ... staff reputations in a place as small as ... tend to count for a great deal'.

Staff 'cohesiveness', perceived as so important by staff associated with CNAA, did not emerge as an issue in university validation: 'I do not think this was ever mentioned or considered. It was just assumed, and in the major university meetings the Principal or his representatives were seen as speaking for the staff as a whole'. This highlights an important difference in emphasis between CNAA and several universities: by and large, the evidence suggests, universities did not give much attention to the institutional context of course proposals and certainly not to committee structure, decision-making, development plans and the like. Their concern seems to have been restricted to the proposal, its formally assessed outcomes, and the staff who taught it; but this is not to suggest that course validation by a university did not affect institutional structures and procedures in other ways.

Expectations about the amount and character of the documentation were various. Some universities required very little (ten pages was the briefest we came across) others a more substantial amount (eg two fairly weighty volumes) and one or two appeared to want as detailed and comprehensive a statement as CNAA. In general universities appeared to place less emphasis on documentation and sometimes this was 'of an ad hoc nature' — being produced cumulatively to meet the needs of particular individuals and committees rather than all in one go. Where fairly full documentation was provided it tended to follow a similar format to CNAA's - eg in one case 'rationale, syllabus, expanded content, time allocation, teaching methods, assessment, resources, staffing, select bibliography'. Sometimes documentation was undertaken in stages with an outline being followed by a fuller statement which may have been reduced after validation to 'calendar entries stating conditions of entry, course content and the mode of assessment' — something akin in fact to the standard university internal course outline which is notable for its parsimony and therefore flexibility, except where examination regulations are concerned. Some cynicism was expressed about the force of these statements: 'inadequate as an exercise in curriculum planning and, in many cases, represented no planning, simply a restatement of existing courses in new terminology or format'. And 'The section on aims was probably written last and perhaps constitutes window-dressing'. Yet another respondent commented on the apparent lack of interest in aims and rationale by comparison with the considerable details required about content.

Expectations about general structure tended to be concerned, where they were expressed or perceived, with the broadest of issues like the proportion of time to be allocated to the main subject, the relative weighting of examinations and course work. Those universities which demanded detail tended to express a similar concern to that of CNAA with course coherence and progression, though as we have pointed out this was usually tied to a validation procedure which was itself coherent (ie it involved specially convened bodies which looked at course proposals as wholes rather than farmed out their components to faculties).

A recurrent theme in the area of expectations specific to BEds was that of 'degreeworthiness', clearly and necessarily an issue in any university validating degrees taught by other than its own internal staff. But just what constitutes a 'degreeworthy' BEd either in universities or at CNAA is one of life's great mysteries. As one university-validated respondent put it: 'We all have deep preconceptions about what a degree should look like. Of course there was a certain amount of under-informed growling from the backwoodsmen, but they are as common in the colleges as in the university: indeed we are all backwoodsmen on some days ...' Another respondent confessed to finding the concept 'somewhat metaphysical'. Several perceived or suspected a concept which in their terms was exclusively academic. One suggested that the university 'required a degree of balance or interrelation between courses not even contemplated for their own'. In all these cases there could be several practical consequences. One was that the degreeworthiness was seen to reside in the main subject, which might be expected to be given a disproportionate time and to be protected from invasions of its continuity and dominance from professional studies and teaching practice. Another was that attempts to integrate main subject study with professional elements might be resisted. Most serious was the fairly widely reported tendency for university validators simply to ignore professional studies and teaching practice, or at the most 'there were elements of distrust and distaste for the more vocational aspects' ... 'combined in this case with pressure to reduce the time given to such work, resulting it was felt from a lack of university experience and expertise in the area of professional studies for teachers.'

If there is something which several universities had in common it was this lack of preparedness to see the professional and practical elements as integral to BEd courses, at least for the purposes of maintaining 'academic standards' and 'degreeworthiness'. Some colleges welcomed the freedom this gave them to organize these areas as they wished, and especially to appoint external examiners whose commitment and interest they could be sure of. But for others the non-recognition of professional studies and teaching practice (more commonly the former) could exacerbate the problems of low status and power and academic marginality experienced by staff in those areas and increase the tension, experienced by most teacher educators, resulting from having to reconcile the generally practical and instrumental demands from the teaching profession with the academic expectations of validators (Alexander et al 1979, Foss 1975). However, when, as with some colleges we received comments from, universities did take a positive interest in professional studies and subject them to a level of scrutiny comparable to that normally reserved for 'academic' elements, colleges were not necessarily gratified to receive such attention. Professional studies staff might be pleased with the validators' recognition of the importance of their work, but uneasy at having to give their courses a rigour of justification and content perhaps lacking previously, while the attention could be equally disturbing to the positions of relative security and privilege enjoyed by some main subject departments. (On this question it should be noted that professional studies could also be problematic in CNAA BEd course validation.)

Because the validation process in the university domain rarely centred on an identifiable 'day of judgement', negotiation proceeded over a period of time with the possibility that the validators' requirements as well as the colleges' proposals might be modified. There were often recommendations made about staff and course content and these were usually met although in one case it was reported: 'some subject panels made remarks about staffing and library resources but such recommendations were generally ignored ... where panels had reservations they still gave validation anyway'.

The continuing dialogue which university vlaidation afforded appeared to allow modification in the light of experience and no respondent referred to any necessity to teach exactly what was laid down in the documents: in any event, as we have noted, these were likely to be rather less detailed than for CNAA. To the CNAA-validated this must seem very appealing but it has to be balanced against the continual control by the university through some or all of the work of assessors, selection of papers for submission to external examiners, involvement in setting examination questions, participation in appointment of new staff, and oversight by a galaxy of university committees. This may appear to the validated as a continuous set of hurdles to be jumped (unlike the CNAA one-off water-jump) or as a relatively flat course: 'Implementation of the degree was the concern of the College. The university was only concerned about standards and assessment' though it is difficult to understand how the one can be separated from the other. Perhaps it means as with another university that 'In practice the final structure plays no part in the actual pedagogic implementation of the degree and only comes into existence, significantly, at examination time'.

## VALIDATION STYLES: CNAA AND UNIVERSITIES

Although we have tried to avoid presenting a polarity of validation styles, with universities at one end and CNAA at the other, there were certain recurrent tendencies which we can legitimately summarize.

1 Validation by CNAA had clear-cut stages of planning, validation and implementation with the process pivoting on the validation visit or meeting, the 'day of judgement'. University validation tended to be more a continuous process of negotiation, though within a sometimes fairly rigid framework, wherein the continuing job of moderation of

assessment arrangements and results was but an extension of the earlier task of vetting proposals, often with the same people maintaining a constant relationship throughout.

2    There was a much more overt element of confrontation, of 'them and us' in a CNAA validation. With universities the boundaries tended to be defined and redefined according to the character of the individual relationships engendered by the process between college and university opposite numbers.

3    For CNAA, course coherence was seen as a major criterion for approval. In many universities it appeared to be not only of little concern but the very validation style (where it was cross-faculty) might militate against coherence, or at least against the university itself, as validator, being in a position to judge such coherence. Moreover, while CNAA always validated the whole course, universities sometimes limited their attention to the parts which in their view provided the 'degreeworthiness'. Almost invariably this approach resulted in a neglect of that element which is the most uniquely professional of a BEd for teachers, namely professional studies.

4    While college staff made similar comments about university and CNAA 'expertise', it is clear that most universities had a more limited range of expertise to draw on and might be unable to provide competence in certain areas, notably professional studies and courses for primary teachers. A university too could become locked into its own local perspectives both on teacher education and validation ('it is all very parochial at x... Mother hen and her three chicks') while CNAA is of course a national body which sees it as part of its function to promote debate about both teacher education and the validation process itself.

5    Documentation was of critical importance in CNAA validation: it had to be because of the geographical separation of college and validator. Universities varied considerably in how much importance they attached to documentation but generally it tended to be less extensive and as often as not emphasized syllabus content and examination arrangements rather than rationale and structure. On the other hand, the CNAA document tended to be perceived as a 'blueprint' by comparison with the looser university 'syllabus'.

6    CNAA was much more concerned with college climate, structure and decision-making, with the institutional context of a course, than, apparently, were most of the universities. All validating bodies were concerned that staff teaching their degrees should be adequately qualified but CNAA's view of staffing 'adequacy' tended to be more comprehensive. In essence, our evidence suggests that a university validates a course's structure and syllabuses and maintains a fairly tight control over assessment and the final award. CNAA validates a

full course proposal — rationale, goals, structure, syllabuses, teaching methods, assessment etc. — together with a college's entire way of orgnaizing itself to implement the proposal. However it is still only a proposal which CNAA validates, not a course in action (Alexander 1979a) and it might be argued that universities come nearer to validating a *course* in that their overview of intentions, processes and outcomes is more constant.

7    This last point of difference brings us to an important divergence in the CNAA and university responses in our enquiry. The former tended to be both fuller and more comprehensive than the latter. This could be because the schedule was in some way slanted towards the CNAA approach and some of its headings proved inappropriate to university-validated respondents. Or it may be that validation was less of an issue in university-validated colleges and certainly the evidence suggests it was less of a performance. This could be beneficial in that college staff might have more time to get on with the job of teaching, or alternatively something of a deficiency in that courses could ossify, there might be insufficient attention to course appraisal and renewal, and to the sort of collective debate about the quality of courses, teaching and learning which CNAA encourages. As one respondent, whose college transferred from university to CNAA validation, said '(University x) was a doddle as far as the process is concerned ... Everyone would prefer (x), it was so easy — but not so good for the institution.'

8    Perhaps the most pronounced difference was that respondents from the CNAA-validated colleges seemed to display a more prominent concern with the politics of course renewal. For all the staff concerned, intensive course planning was, and was generally perceived to be, an educative process; but the politicizing function of course planning, both in respect of the internal politics of colleges and the local and national higher education scene was much more strongly evident in the CNAA responses.

We would not wish to say whether this politicization is desirable or whether the lost innocence of the old colleges of education is to be deplored, but the tougher culture of the polytechnics and the professional challenge of a rigorous planning and validation process may well be essential to institutional survival in the present national climate.

## COST AND BENEFITS

The more tangible costs of validation, as seen by our respondents, were: personal, in terms of stress and career blockage; economic, in terms of the drain on college resources; and academic, in terms of the loss of a certain degree of individual autonomy through the standardization of course requirements and submission formats. The perceived benefits were largely what any validator must hope for: academic improvement, with better courses and higher standards; increased resources, with additional library and other facilities including ancillary staff; and institutional change, with a greater emphasis on staff cohesion and development and democratization, but also, more problematically, on new management structures, which, depending on the extent to which they affected individual autonomy, could be perceived as a benefit or a very heavy cost.

In weighing these costs and benefits one against another certain questions must be asked. Do academic qualifications and research improve the quality of teaching of intending teachers? How can we evaluate whether stated aims and objectives are being achieved? Are we in fact producing better teachers as a result of the validation processes? Do we now need above all 'a period of consolidation when the balance is reoriented away from course preparation, in favour of well-prepared teaching and tutoring'? And more immediately it may be pertinent to ask 'who validates the validators?' In analysing their own successful or unsuccessful validation our respondents tended to see the result as dependent on particular skills in both validated and validators which were not on either side always related to an understanding of the ability effectively to educate teachers. Those seeking validation had to deploy their paper credentials but the validators might be unknown and whilst the process of their selection can be investigated, the criteria for inclusion or exclusion perplexed both the accepted and rejected among the nominated. Or as one of our interviewees riposted to a comment that 'They are only us': 'Well they may be you but they certainly aren't me.'

Finally, we must re-emphasize a central theme in our own interpretation of the data. We asked respondents to tell us about validation and especially about the validating bodies — their expectations, their requirements, their practices. But 'what the validating body expected' became to a considerable extent 'what respondents thought the validating body expected'. Validation is about colleges as well as validating bodies; about colleges making things happen in a variety of ways in order to achieve validation. It is too easy to portray the colleges as passive victims of incompetent or malevolent validating bodies. Some colleges did adopt a passive stance, but it was their decision. Others refused to be dictated to and achieved success — or at least made their mark — by adopting an aggressive stance on the whole process: 'Some colleges work on the basis of "what CNAA wants",' said a respondent from a college having a high validation success-rate, '... but we do not follow CNAA, we lead it'.

Another point of interest in this somewhat rhetorical claim lies in the assumption of collective involvement in the 'we': our data suggests that 'we' were often a very small number of highly skilled, articulate and energetic individuals, chief among whom were the intermediaries, or 'gatekeepers'. The accelerated careers of these people is one of the more obvious manifestations of the sometimes dramatic shifts in colleges' organization and balance of power which the validation imperative has engendered during the post-James era in teacher education. It seems appropriate to suggest that while, for the individuals concerned, inside knowledge of the validators' processes and intentions is power, the lack of it by their rank and file colleagues is probably counterproductive in terms of their progressive alienation, the consequent embittering of professional relationships and their less extensive engagement with the new courses. We would suggest that validating bodies, especially CNAA, need to pay more attention to engendering dialogue, not just with senior staff, but with the teachers who actually plan and implement the nuts and bolts of the course proposals and on whose conviction about what they are doing the quality of the students' learning experience vitally depends.

## NOTE
This paper draws on data collected as the first part of a research project based at Leeds University School of Education and co-directed by the authors. The project ('Perceptions of the Validation Process in Teacher Education') was financed by the Nuffield Foundation. We acknowledge the considerable contribution of Elizabeth Alexander, as project assistant, to data collation and transcription and to the development of some of the ideas presented here. We are also deeply indebted to our colleagues in the colleges whose detailed responses to the questionnaire have provided our raw material. The paper was presented in an earlier version at the joint Higher Education Foundation/Society for Research into Higher Education Conference on Validation, July 1981, and published in that version in *Collected Original Resources in Education*, Vo. 5, No. 3, 1981.

## REFERENCES
Alexander, R.J. (1979a) What is a course? Curriculum models and CNAA validation *Journal of Further and Higher Education* III (1) 31-45
Alexander, R.J., Chambers, P., Hirst, P.H., McCulloch, M., McNamara, D. and Desforges, C., Webster, H. and Biott, C. (1979) Chapters 1-5 and 15 in Alexander, R.J. and Wormald, E. (Eds) *Professional Studies for Teaching* Guildford: Teacher Education Study Group, SRHE
Barnes, J.A. (1979) *Who shall know what?* Harmondsworth: Penguin
Committee on Higher Education (1963) *Higher Education* (The Robbins Report) London: HMSO
Council for National Academic Awards (1974) *Regulations and Conditions for the Award of the Council's First Degrees* London: CNAA
Council for National Academic Awards (1979a) *Principles and Regulations for the Award of the Council's First Degrees and Diploma of Higher Education* London: CNAA
Council for National Academic Awards (1979b) *Developments in Partnership in Validation* London. CNAA

Department of Education and Science (1972a) *Teacher Education and Training* (The James Report) London: HMSO

Department of Education and Science (1972b) *Education: a Framework for Expansion* London: HMSO

Department of Education and Science (1973) *Circular 7/73* London: HMSO

Foss, K. (1975) *The Status of Professional Studies in Teacher Education* University of Sussex: Education Area (Occasional Paper No. 4)

Newton, D., Shaw, K., Wormald, E. (Eds) (1975) *Change in the Colleges* Occasional Papers in Sociology and Education 2: ATCDE

PERSPECTIVE

## 6   A CASE FOR INTERNAL VALIDATION

Robin Alexander and Brian Gent

This paper, though not empirical, draws on practical experience and some degree of deliberate sampling of the processes it discusses. It is offered because no discussion of validation can now afford to ignore internal validation as an increasingly significant variant on the validation theme — especially since the publication of CNAA's *Partnership in Validation* proposals; and partly because neither external nor internal validation per se is adequately explored without an acknowledgement of the extent to which each is dependent upon and influenced by the other. This reciprocity of internal and external, and an increasing blurring of some of the distinctions between them, likewise gains added point and complexity from the CNAA 'Partnership' proposals.

VALIDATION AND EVALUATION
Common to most definitions of 'validation' are three main elements: firstly a *judgement* as to the adequacy of an educational proposal; secondly a *decision* to sanction the translation of proposal into action — the formal declaration of validity; and thirdly the invocation and application of *authority* to legitimate both judgement and decision.

In this respect 'validation' is not synonymous with 'evaluation', despite an occasional tendency in higher education discourse to confuse them. At its simplest the distinction resides in the decision-making aspect. Evaluation is the making of a judgement of the worth or effectiveness of an (educational) venture, while validation in addition bases upon that judgement a decision: go/no-go. But it is worth unpacking the relationship a little further. For validation encompasses evaluations, and thereby also incorporates the central elements of all evaluations in addition to its own unique characteristics: these are, in the process of making the judgement, the use of *criteria* for judgement, the application of such criteria to sought or presented *evidence*, and the enmeshing of both at least as strongly with questions of *value* as with questions of fact.

There are two other important distinctions here. The first is that the addition to the evaluation/judgemental process of a decision backed by authority gives validation a power dimension which of itself evaluation does not necessarily have. Anyone can evaluate, but only certain people are authorised to validate; and while the practical force of evaluation depends on what action it promotes, validation always and inevitably has practical, institutional and personal consequences.

The other distinction is one of focus. There is no good reason, conceptually, why the objects of validation should not include the full range of an institution's educational ventures. However, it must be acknowledged that, in operational terms, validation, in British higher education at least, has a relatively restricted focus. While people evaluate a wide range of educational ideas and activities, the focus for validation tends to be confined to educational proposals rather than operations; to claimed intentions and aspirations rather than demonstrated actions; to words rather than deeds (or at the most to oral or documented accounts of deeds — see Alexander 1979). In contrast, the focus of evaluation can and frequently does include educational processes and outcomes, as they occur, as well as educational prespecifications and/or post-hoc outcome analyses.

## INTERNAL VALIDATION: THE PROBLEM OF IDENTIFYING THE REAL PROCESSES

Thus, in our view of validation we have a web of conceptual complexities — judgements, values, evidence, criteria — rendered vastly more problematic in operation by their power and authority ramifications. An adequate study of validation would explore all these elements and the relationship between them. This would be challenging enough where external validation is concerned, but with internal validation — our concern — it would be almost impossible. For while in studying external validation one is greatly aided by the relatively small number of validating bodies, and by, in the case of the major higher education validator, CNAA, the relative openness, explicitness and visibility of its procedures, where internal validation is concerned we are dealing with the idiosyncracies of particular institutions, about which generalization is fairly hazardous, and whose practices are in any case considerably less open to scrutiny. Validation which is internal has formal procedures which are usually accessible, but if we wish to identify other elements listed above — criteria, evidence, value-basis, power relations — the task is more difficult.

In company with David Billing we observed and recorded some of these formal procedures in public sector institutions. We encountered a variety of arrangements: at department, faculty and whole institution levels; having terms of reference and styles of operation ranging from tightly circumscribed to fairly loose; most to a greater or lesser extent administratively complex and expensive in time and material resources; some wholly internal, others including the use of external perspectives and expertise; many reflecting salient characteristics of the external validation arrangements to which they were geared — the focus on claims/aspirations, the importance as evidence of documentation, the premium on presenting and arguing one's case in across-the-table confrontation (Alexander, Billing and Gent 1980).

However, these formal arrangements were undoubtedly only the tip of the validation iceberg. The evaluations which informed the validation decisions were as likely to be implicit and unique as explicit and shared; without doubt they rested to a substantial extent not only on formalized processes and evidence such as minutes of committee decisions, course statistics and student feedback analyses, but on staff-room chat, behind-the-scenes negotiation, rationalized prejudice and so on. The making of judgements about educational processes is a fairly constant and ubiquitous element in institutional life and it is naive to imagine that it can be possible for staff to compartmentalize their ideas and motivations when engaging in formal evaluation/validation procedures, notwithstanding the rhetoric of academic disinterest, value-consensus and methodological objectivity.

## ACCOUNTABILITY, AUTHORITY AND AUTONOMY IN VALIDATION JUDGEMENTS

The elaborate character of these formal procedures in some public sector higher education institutions points up an important aspect of validation not so far mentioned in this paper: accountability. Internal validation procedures differ between institutions in ways suggestive not only of administrative style and notions of efficiency, but also of accountability relationships between individuals and groups. In some institutions a strict top-down control in validation is exercised, reflecting an upwards only view of accountability, while in others a greater engagement of staff at various levels and a greater degree of procedural openness may reflect a prevailing sense of mutuality of professional relationships. In addition, or course, to such internal accountability which internal validation procedures may reflect, they also take much of their character — and indeed possibly their existence — from public sector institutions' obligation to account to external validation bodies for the standard of their courses and awards.

The lack of such direct external pressures for accountability in British universities (except in respect of certain vocational courses) permits both a distinctly lower profile in internal validation matters and a markedly different internal accountability relationship. Here it is generally accepted that the authority for making academic judgements on a given course is confined to the proponents of that course. Their authority is conferred by appointment to the university and derives normally from some form of academic certification, with the added benefit of references and interview. The Masters and doctoral degrees of the medieval universities served this purpose. In cases where staff serve for a probationary period, this authority may be seen as confirmed in the light of their teaching and research within the institution. Such autonomy over the planning of the course having been sanctioned, responsibility for its standards also rests entirely with the group of staff teaching it; and responsibility for each component of the course rests with the individual teacher. In this country such standards are to some extent underwritten by the external examiner. The academic relationship between staff in these circumstances will vary from place to place. There may be intensive consultation and reflection; or there may be a tacit discouragement of such dialogue. Such internal 'validation' of proposals as takes place may range from (by public sector standards) the moderately thorough to the nominal, some of the more thorough examples being documented by Church in Chapter 3.

This convention of autonomy is not observed by the Council for Naitonal Academic Awards and similar agencies. The CNAA requires academic judgements made by staff to be confirmed by their peers in a process of external validation. From the point of view of a university, such a safeguard might seem redundant. It may equally be argued that the older university tradition is inadequate. It is certainly a common experience that the design of an extensive learning experience for students is considered the more rigorously when it is to be challenged by one's peers. In this way, a wider range of expertise and experience is brought to bear on the task in hand. Before such external validation is allowed to happen, it is common for some form of internal validation to take place, to test the proposal against the institution's own standards, and to forestall any humiliation in public. Further, the influence of the university traditions has led some colleges working with the CNAA to embark on forms of internal validation which may seem to pre-empt the need for external validation. And this leads immediately into problems of authority. If, as is commonly the case, the proper authority for the academic judgement of a course is to be found largely in the course's proponents, the tendency must be for internal validation to concentrate on those aspects of a course for which external authority is available: that is, on administrative judgements.

Questions about resources and the administrative framework for admissions and assessment must bulk large and academic judgements may be neglected. Constraints such as accommodation and student-staff ratios (related perhaps to job preservation) begin to be accepted as ersatz values. Attempting to redress the balance, an institution may then bring in consultants from elsewhere, who will be asked to supply the academic appraisal which is lacking. This is not an easy task. Some of the judgements needed will be entirely noetic, having to do with syllabus content; some will be pedagogic, relating to the teaching of the subject; some may even be professional, depending on experience of the applications of knowledge. And some judgements will connect with two or more of these. Further, these aspects may be not only related, but in tension with each other. Rigorous development of subject matter may stand at odds with the psychology of the learning process; the demands of professional practice may require radical shifts in the presentation of long-standing disciplines. Such judgements are always difficult and to expect them of a lone visitor may be to expect too much. In the case of external validation, CNAA teams have at least the benefit of shared and prolonged experience of academic validation.

If this view of the situation suggests the strengths of external validation, it must be said that it also has its weaknesses. One danger of external validation is that the values entailed are not necessarily internalized by an institution's members. Course designers may sometimes be tempted to follow precedents without a full understanding of the reasons for them. Authority is from without; the prime task may be seen as satisfying that authority, rather than probing the basis of its judgement. So, a process of external validation which developed historically as a response to a need for apprenticeship could well end by stunting the sense of professional responsibility it was designed to foster.

Perhaps the best way of combining the best of both internal and external validation my lie in a process of joint validation; in this the professional competence of the proponents is properly recognized, the internal contribution to administrative validation is maintained and the academic validation is strengthened by an experienced team drawn from the national network of higher education. This sort of arrangement is now greatly facilitated in public sector higher education by the CNAA 'Partnership' proposals. As yet (1981) there are few working examples of such an approach.

## VALIDATION AND ACADEMIC VALUES

But this is to digress. A major concern of this book is with the values on which the validation of courses depends. But, as we have argued, perhaps the most striking characteristics of such values is their elusiveness and inconspicuousness. Yet the judgements which are made and the authority which sanctions them are both heavily laden with values; and the decision which follows the validation judgment may be informed by other values — political as well as academic and administrative.

Different educational institutions see their purposes in different ways. Some may intend a single-minded cultivation of intellect; some may offer a broader response to society's needs. Varying degrees of altruism and self-interest are also to be found; and institutions vary in the image they try to present, both internally and to the public. Compounding these variations is the variety of sectional interests within any one institution. This complex — and shifting — set of purposes helps to define what is seen as good; and this evidently directs the judgements which are made and actions which are taken.

A course proposed in engineering, for example, may include a range of learning objectives ranging from the mastery of highly abstract mathematical concepts to the ability to perform basic manual skills. Any validation of such a course must depend on a relative valuation of these elements. If, then, the judgement is made from a perspective which is alien to that of the course designers (by a mathematician, say) a collision is likely. This will have arisen from a discrepancy of institutional or professional values; but it may well not be recognized as such.

Closely related to these institutional purposes are variations in managerial style and accountability. The professional autonomy described above in relation to universities is only one possible role which may be cast for a teacher. At other times, in other places, he may be seen as directly accountable for the content and quality of his teaching to some overseeing manager. Elsewhere, he may find himself part of a collaborative team bent on consensus, or at least cooperation, in which he will be expected to respond to his colleagues' views of both their own and his professional work. The source of authority for the teaching process is therefore variable; and this clearly influences the authority by which internal validation judgements are made.

What is expected (and permitted) of the proponents of a course and those undertaking its internal validation will depend on the systems of accountability which are extant in the institution. This will affect the way a course is presented, the character of any challenge or enquiry, and the style of responses. It may be presented in outline or detail; it may be received with deference or resentment; the response may be laconic or scrupulous, placatory or retaliatory. Again, such phenomena may be interpreted as springing solely from personality or academic calibre while the managerial circumstances go unnoticed. To embark on internal validation without some feeling for such factors is rash. It is also necessary to bear in mind the differing valuations individuals may put on knowledge itself. The nature of knowledge may of course be discussed in philosophical terms; but its personal and social meanings are often more potent in influencing behaviour.

Knowledge may be viewed either as an absolute good in itself or as a good in relation to some more extensive (or practical) benefit to society. In either case, any particular quantum of knowledge may be seen as absolute truth, or as a conditional statement awaiting further exploration. Presumably the latter view will prevail in more sophisticated circles. These issues profoundly influence the common sense of communities, but the problems of validation within a community will more often arise from more idiosyncratic attachments to knowledge.

Knowledge, for instance, may give a sense of security. We may be reassured by the imposition of some order on an unruly world; and it may enhance our security by appearing to provide us with status among our fellows. And one of the benefits of any badge or trophy is that it reassures us of our own capability and therefore worth. Extending beyond these narcissistic aspects, knowledge also means power. Like any other power, it may be used for many purposes: it may enable us to build better bridges, write better books; or it may be used as a mere tool for personal advancement within the academic community. Rising above these uses of knowledge as machismo, is the possibility of knowledge as pure love-object. A life-time's work wedded to a discipline is likely to forge firm attachments which may range from an adolescent fixation to a maturing devotion.

Clearly these attitudes do not exist in isolation. An academic's attitude to his work must be influenced by his general values in regard to people, property, purposes and self. And these in turn will reflect those of the cultures which he shares. (See Becher 1981 for a recent empirical discussion of these issues.) It is hardly surprising, then, if academic debate in the process of internal validation should sometimes trigger unexpected reactions. Those proposing a course and those validating it are unlikely to share the same set of private values; and all are ikely to be affected by one or more of the perversities mentioned above — we are none of us free of them. Further, the public values of the institution itself may be vague and differently perceived by different individuals.

Further — and more significantly — these factors must have an important bearing on the question of academic standards. Whatever the care taken in establishing aims and objectives for a course, and in assessing students' performance in the light of these, the quality of the learning experience is a subjective judgement, based on personal values, and therefore subject to all these many perturbations. The conclusion to be drawn from these reflections is that we should, at least, give more attention to the influence of values in internal validation. Open discussion of such matters within an institution is felt often to be unbecoming. Religion and politics are taboo in the mess; debate on values may be felt to be dangerous in the common room. These matters may be potentially disruptive to a community — but they may also be avoided merely because we feel inept in broaching them. In any case, it is always dangerous to assume that when a subject is buried, it is therefore dead.

Modern institutions of higher education, it has been said, demonstrate the way culture has become bureaucratized. It may be that the opening up of enquiry into the bases of their ways of achieving consensus may have an invigorating effect; it may counter their tendency to decline from being academic communities to being assemblies of specialists held together only by a common system of remuneration. Internal validation is an important way for an institution to become more conscious of itself. Those responsible should be keenly aware that what is being appraised includes not only individuals — as persons, academics, managers — but also the network of relationships between people which welds the community together.

## HOW TO VALIDATE THE SELF-VALIDATING INSTITUTION?
In the post 'Partnership' era CNAA has attached increasing significance to 'Institutional Review', and in that review process to evidence of the institution's capacity for generating such collective self-consciousness as we commend above. Despite recent criticisms (Ball 1981) that, while external *course* validation is feasible, external *institutional* validation is 'impractical, unreal, impertinent, unprofessional', it needs at least to be acknowledged that CNAA's shift of focus from courses to context represents — for whatever reasons it came about — an important acknowledgement of the extent to which the former are influenced by the latter.

But how to 'validate' whole institutions? By what criteria, by reference to what value system, on the basis of what evidence? Put thus baldly the question justifies Ball's sense of the hubris of the undertaking. For CNAA the problem, writ larger than heretofore, is pre-eminently the practical one of all external validation: the invisibility or inaccessibility of just those areas of institutional life which are the best indicators of institutional health. So, just as course validation has concentrated to excess on documents, prepackaging and performance (Alexander 1979, together with Alexander and Wormald in this volume), so institutional review seems set to concentrate on the most readily available manifestations of institutional adequacy: committee, faculty and departmental structures, resource allocation, channels of control and communication, and, pivotally and pre-eminently, formal procedures for internal course planning, validation, evaluation and review. 'Evidence' of the latter, predictably, and probably inevitably, will tend to consist of the externals of the validation/review process — structures, documents, procedures, statistics of admission, programme choice, examination results — rather than the internals of the debate about values and processes which ought to be central to educational discourse. How can the latter be represented for evidential purposes? Can it be 'validated'?

All this shifts the burden of proof, and the implied culpability, on to those who provide, or who feature most prominently in, such tangible 'evidence' of institutional health. Where pre-Partnership validation made culpability local — individual course lecturers and leaders felt particularly exposed — post-Partnership institutional review implies a more evenly-spread allocation and acceptance of culpability, and in practice, since an institution cannot be blamed, shifts culpability from course teachers to institutional managers. Small wonder then that most of the protest about institutional review has come from principals and directors whereas in earlier years adverse correspondence on CNAA (eg in the *THES*) was supplied mainly by the disgruntled junior staff. Is the protest justified? Is there not at least some basis for examining the extent to which institutional health is a function of institutional management? Or is the problem not one of judgemental criteria but of the inappropriateness of what is deemed valid evidence for making such judgements?

(As a not wholly facetious test of the process it is worth asking which comes nearer to presenting a 'valid' view of those features in institutional life which are most conducive to institutional health, the review document of course logistics, or the portrayal of a Bradbury, Snow, McCarthy, Amis or even a Sharpe.)

CONCLUSION

Finally, to return to university and public sector comparisons, we have suggested that at least one virtue of maintaining an external validation presence is that it sharpens up, or even generates de novo, internal processes of collective self-appraisal in general, and course appraisal in particular. Most university departments have no such external stimulus, and — even in matters like course planning where a collective, cooperative approach seems essential in the interests of producing a coherent educational experience for the student — the dominant and strenuously defended ethic of privatization contrasts markedly with the public sector approach.

One of the most familiar trans-binary gibes of recent years has been that many university courses would fail to survive the rigours of CNAA validation (a process designed, according to that body's Charter, to ensure in public sector institutions standards comparable to those in universities). By the same token, now that CNAA's emphasis is shifting from courses to institutions, how would many university departments fare in institutional review? Would their procedures for ongoing critique of courses, teaching and learning, for the generation and application of new ideas and practices, and for the internal validation of course proposals stand scrutiny? Would their internal decision-making procedures be deemed sufficiently responsive to changing external needs? Would they be considered capable of allowing plurality, scepticism, critique and dissent — supposedly hallmarks of academic discourse — to be used to institutional advantage?

These are questions which public sector instititions are increasingly obliged to answer. Are such questions 'impractical, unreal, impertinent, unprofessional' or are they a basic prerequisite for educational progress?

REFERENCES

Alexander, R.J. (1979) What is a course? Curriculum models and CNAA validation *Journal of Further and Higher Education*. III (1) 31-45

Alexander, R.J., Billing, D.E., Gent, B.B. (1980) *Partnership and Standards: Validation and Evaluation* Cyclostyled. CNAA

Ball, C.J.E. (1980) *The Advancement of Education, Learning and the Arts* Cyclostyled. Thames Polytechnic Annual Lecture, June 1981

Becher, A.R. (1981) Towards a definition of disciplinary cultures *Studies in Higher Education*. VI (2) 109-22

Council for National Academic Awards (1979) *Developments in Partnership in Validation*

# 7 STUDENTS AND VALIDATION

Roger Harrison


After some discussion, Anne Evans of Manchester Polytechnic and I identified four questions which seem to be relevant to this section of the inquiry. Unfortunately pressure of work forced her to abandon the project at an early stage. However, I am grateful to her for encouragement and help in this early stage. The four questions we felt should be asked were: How aware are students of the validation processes carried out on their courses and what is their attitude to these? How does validation affect the impact of the courses on the students? How does validation affect the degree to which students are consulted during their course? To what extent are students consulted during the initial validation process and during the revalidation of a course?

This chapter is an attempt to answer these questions. I did not attempt to enquire to what extent, and how, the validating bodies attempt to assess the likely impact of course proposals on students, or their suitability for the students who will actually take the course, or the likely quality of the teaching/learning interaction which will be generated. Nor did I enquire about the criteria which the validating bodies employ, which may affect the impact on the students. I confined my attention to the effects which past validations appear to have had on students. These prior questions could, however, well be the subject of a separate enquiry.

## METHOD OF ENQUIRY
After some preliminary enquiries, two questionnaires were prepared to guide discussion of validation issues with staff and students respectively. I then visited nine polytechnics and colleges (and received reports from two or three more) offering courses in arts, social sciences, law, education, business studies, management, computing, natural sciences and engineering, validated by the CNAA, universities, BEC, TEC, various professional bodies and several learned institutions. It was thus possible to sample opinions of students and staff across a fairly broad spectrum of validated courses. Altogether, I talked to some forty staff and eighty students.

It soon became clear that the questionnaires were not capable of providing quantitative data on the range of opinions put to me. This was partly because I did not have the resources to cover a sufficiently large sample, but mainly because predetermined questions are much too blunt an instrument to investigate the nuances of a highly complex and variable field. Such insight as I have been able to generate comes mainly from chance remarks and personal narratives.

A wide variety of different approaches and styles of validation are experienced in the different colleges, and even in different departments within the same college, relating to the different demands and practices of the various discipline areas, institutions and professional bodies. Without a far more rigorous longitudinal study of the complex interactions involved it would be misleading to put forward any definitive analysis with a claim to universal validity. Indeed, universally valid generalizations may be impossible in this field: there will always be exceptions which work well.

I can, therefore, only describe impressions and raise questions about trends and practice which struck me as being worth consideration. They are certainly not the only points which could be raised, although I am reasonably confident that I have lighted on most of the more significant ones, since the number of new ideas being put to me fell off quite noticeably during my last interviews. All the statements made in this chapter have their basis in points made by someone — usually by several people in more than one institution. It is therefore reasonable to claim that all the opinions and feelings and attitudes described really do exist. I am not able, however, to judge how widespread they may be and, of course, the fact that an opinion is held is no guarantee that it is reasonable or justifiable. In at least some cases it may be a rationalization or projection of something more deep-seated, on which I do not speculate.

I am only too aware that somebody, somewhere, can justifiably object to almost everything I say. Quite apart from any mistakes, misunderstandings, and omissions I may have made in entering a new domain of inquiry, there are just too many exceptions to the rules to be able to satisfy all points of view all the time. It is also only too easy to stray from the objective to the normative — from describing what appears to happen to discussing what ought to happen. I hope my prejudices will not obtrude too obviously. Inevitably questions about students and validation impinge on other areas of the inquiry — particularly on course development, monitoring, evaluation, course review and accountability. I ask forgiveness if I have trespassed too far from my appointed domain.

So far as I am aware, this is almost a virgin field of enquiry. Perusal of eighteen articles on validation which have appeared over the last six years showed that only seven even mentioned students and none of these really addressed themselves to any of my four questions. Hence the paucity of references.

## STUDENTS AND THE VALIDATION PROCESS
My first question was prompted by a sneaking suspicion that students might not even be aware that their courses were validated by a body outside their own institution. I am pleased to report that this is not so: almost all the students I spoke to (some accosted at random in their unions) could at least name the body which would grant their award, apart from three higher diploma students who had not heard of TEC. The majority approved

validation, obviously feeling it enhanced the value of the certificate in the outside world: some even expressed doubts that the validation was sufficiently rigorous.

External validation is, potentially, a selling point for the course. One polytechnic head of department emphasized that he goes to great pains to explain just what is involved in CNAA validation when he speaks to local schools, since he feels the realization that the standards of the courses are vouched for by a national body impresses would-be students — and their parents and teachers. He also believes that students ought to understand the processes involved in validation and attempts to inform them. I was not able to check how far he succeeds in this, but it was only too obvious that the majority of students in other departments, apart from those who have been personally involved in a validation exercise, have only the haziest idea of the complex mechanism by which their course gained approval, maintains standards and is open to review, or of who actually set and mark the examinations and decide the ultimate outcome. The CNAA has also noted the lack of awareness of some students of these matters (Ridler 1980). A 1978 quinquennial report remarks of one department: 'Students seemed surprisingly ill-informed on (and indifferent to) course management structure'. Some, also, were in doubt about their right of appeal against the decisions of the examiners (though, to be fair, this is a matter which is likely to affect only a very small minority of students). Even when an attempt had been made to inform them, for example during an induction course, I suspect that they had not really taken it in, having many other, and to them more important, matters to think about at the time.

Nevertheless, there may be some merit in attempting to explain these things to students more systematically, preferably in print as well as orally, in the hope that this will encourage some of them to play a more active and better informed role in the continual improvement and renewal of their courses. The National Union of Students (NUS), to whom I sent a first draft of this chapter, inform me that they are intending to take an initiative to produce a suitable handbook in collaboration with the validating bodies. Institutions might usefully expand on this, in prospectuses or in induction courses, to show how the general principles apply in their particular courses.

Although the majority of students I consulted approved of validation, two groups of students on in-service courses for teachers (INSET) felt that the requirements of the CNAA had directed the focus of attention away from the practical topics which where their greatest concern towards more theoretical considerations and one group of business studies students deplored the fact that BEC had removed the practical element from their course. One or two other individual students also said they thought validating bodies tend to overvalue theory at the expense of practice: a tendency which may be aided and abetted by some course committees. One student officer remarked 'Courses in polys should be job oriented, but there's a tendency to go for academic subjects'. I discuss this again in the next section.

There was some difference in student attitudes to different validating bodies: this is a reflection both of the different preoccupations of the bodies and of the different kinds of students attracted to their courses. On the whole, the attitude to the CNAA seems to be the most positive. Quite a few of the CNAA students I spoke to had either been involved in the consultations which take place during validation and revalidation or knew students who had been so involved. They appreciated the efforts made on their behalf to make sure the course is not only academically sound but can also be taught effectively without excessive workload. Student representatives and union officials are also aware of the efforts CNAA makes to improve facilities available to students.

By contrast, the other validating bodies were felt to be much more remote from the students and there was some criticism that they do not always consider students' interests sufficiently: in two cases it was even alleged that validating bodies had forbidden developments proposed by the college which would have improved the students' lot. In particular, one university had refused to countenance students' representatives on the course committee or to allow certain widely desired course combinations. (It is interesting to note that staff in the same college thought the university developed a closer, sustained relationship with their students than did the CNAA.) Students for whom professional recognition is important seem to accept fairly passively the right of the professional bodies to make arbitrary rules without any court of appeal, while students on TEC and to a less extent BEC courses seem more concerned with getting on with their studies than with their rights and desires (although most of them seem satisfied that there are adequate informal channels of communication if they should encounter difficulties or something goes wrong with the presentation of the course).

## THE IMPACT OF VALIDATION ON STUDENTS
A validating body can affect the direct impact of a course on the students in four ways: through the content of the course, through the assessment arrangements and standards, through the course structure and through the administrative arrangements approved for dealing with difficulties as they arise. It can also affect students indirectly: positively by insisting on adequate facilities, staffing and leadership; negatively by the demands it makes on the time of both staff and students and by the matters it chooses not to consider.

To a large extent, students are forced to accept the course content prescribed for them on trust, since they lack the experience to know what knowledge would be appropriate to their chosen field. In most cases they accept this situation without protest or query, even when an outside observer might consider these justified. No doubt other parts of the enquiry will consider in detail how far this trust is warranted. One very important effect of validation is that it encourages the production of a clear scheme and regulations, which should help students to tackle their course effectively.

As noted above, I encountered several instances where students felt that their course was biassed towards theoretical considerations, where they would have preferred a more practical orientation. This was expressed most strongly by two groups of practising teachers working towards part-time degrees in education: their interest, naturally, is in how to teach rather than the theóry of teaching and they would have liked to start their seminars from the basis of their own classroom experience. The staff confirmed that the CNAA had, indeed, insisted on a more theoretical flavour than the staff had initially intended before these particular courses were validated.

Similar sentiments were expressed about a BEC business studies course where the students wanted a larger practical element and, less forcibly, about courses in management and computing and other areas. There appears to be some tension between academic and professional needs over a wide range of subjects. It may not be so simple as it was presented to me, however. In some cases it was the course committee which inserted the theoretical bias, either to satisfy its own dynamic or to meet what it thinks the validating panel requires, rather than what is actually required. 'The CNAA forces an orthodox approach.' And in some cases the students may have failed to appreciate what the course was intended to achieve. There is room for better communications all round. At least half a dozen members of staff asserted that the content of courses validated by professional bodies was antiquated and backward looking and militated against the students for this reason.

ASSESSMENT AND COURSE STRUCTURE

The assessment pattern for a course is always of considerable concern to students: both the type and the amount of assessment come in for considerable criticism whenever students are consulted about a course. Many staff also expressed the opinion that their students are over-assessed and that there is an obsession with standards. All validating bodies appear to expect a large amount of formal assessment and this gets written into the course scheme and is thereafter difficult to alter. In addition, there is a long standing battle between those who would prefer more informal, continuous assessment and those who insist on rigid, formal assessment. This is a complex issue in which the arguments are by no means all on one side: many students prefer an end of term exam to regular assessed exercises: both students and staff (who may not have tried it) fear that continuous assessment can distort the teaching or impede staff-student relationships. Since, however, the assessment pattern, more than any other single factor, determines the impact of the course on the student, there does seem to be a case for more flexibility and a greater readiness to experiment on the part of the validators and on the part of the course committees. Again, there may possibly be a discrepancy between what the validators require and what they are believed to require. I was also told that the intentions of both course committee and validating panel are sometimes frustrated by external examiners, who insist on more formal and rigid assessment than was originally envisaged. 'More emphasis on exams due to pressure from externals — the students are not overjoyed.'

The CNAA, in particular, has done a good deal to encourage modular courses and this obviously increases the range and flexibility of student choice, which seems to be widely appreciated by both students and staff. The need to attract students forces staff to keep improving their modules in light of student criticism. But the benefits of modularity have to be paid for. Modular schemes tend to be complicated and students must receive first-rate counselling if they are to choose their options sensibly: counsellors are not always available when required and may not always give the best advice when they are. As Gutterridge (1975) rather acidly remarked 'Counselling to resolve artificially created problems is wasteful and undesirable'. Extremely modular courses may get so fragmented, despite the intentions of the authors, that students cannot identify themselves with either the discipline or the course and as a result fail to develop a healthy esprit de corps. Their knowledge may also remain fragmented.

Even the validating panel may find it difficult to come to grips with the overall course structure, so that 'too much validation of modular courses is concerned with administration rather than content'. I have already noted that arbitrary restrictions on allowable combinations of modules can cause resentment among the students and further disappointment can arise if desired options fail to run, either because of lack of demand or because of staff shortages. Modularity intensifies the problems which arise when students fail part of their course. Should they resit (and if so, when?), carry on, repeat the year, have a fallow year etc? TEC moderators must approve such decisions. CNAA examiners are appointed by the colleges, so the CNAA, as such, has no influence on these matters.

I was told that CNAA panels usually pay considerable attention to the overall structure of the course proposal, whether modular or not, and attempt to make sure that it is likely to make sense to the students and to lead to their progressive development. By contrast, the other validators concentrate much more on the outline syllabus with reference to standards and acceptability to employers and sometimes approve courses which turn out to be fragmented and incoherent.

I do not know to what extent course committees consciously attempt to match the demands of the course to the existing knowledge and abilities of the students coming on to it, or the extent to which the validating bodies attempt to check up on this. My experience at the Open University is that this is an important aspect of course design. I am sure it is not overlooked by the validating bodies, but I suspect it may not be done very systematically. Possibly there is room here for further research both into what goes on and into strengthening procedures.

## FACILITIES AND ADMINISTRATION

The CNAA was widely praised for looking beyond the syllabus content of a course to its administrative arrangements and to the facilities available for its implementation. Both staff and student officers acknowledged the value of CNAA leverage in making a case for improvements in equipment, staffing and general facilities. This has helped to raise sights and improve the standards and status of the colleges, to the considerable benefit of the students (not only those on CNAA courses). While this worked well during the period of expansion, it remains to find out whether CNAA pressure will be so effective during a period of contraction: some departments told me they were already finding it difficult to continue courses or options as specialist staff leave and cannot be replaced, and that was before the cuts had really begun to bite. I fear both colleges and the CNAA will be forced to reduce their expectations during the coming decade and this, in turn, may bring profound changes in the impact of courses on students — not to mention the whole process of validation. With hindsight one may suspect the CNAA encouraged some departments to be over-ambitious and over-lavish and this may accentuate the problems in a bleaker climate.

The other validating bodies generally take the facilities for granted, especially if the college has taught similar courses before. This generates much less pressure to maintain and improve facilities and may result in courses being approved with insufficient resources available to teach them well. (Though I was given no specific instance of this happening, only a generalized complaint.)

With accumulated experience the CNAA has learnt how to check course proposals to make sure they can be taught satisfactorily in terms of student workload, timetabling, timing of assessments and numerous other practical details which vitally affect student progress. The ability to check these details (and the recognition that they are important) is also being acquired by the colleges, many of which have set up machinery to vet these matters (and also the academic content of the proposed course) for themselves before submitting a proposal to a validating body. This has been recognized by the CNAA, who put forward the *Partnership in Validation* scheme in 1975. A number of staff put it to me that much validation is perhaps too concerned with the minutiae of course mechanics, with the danger of an over rigid scheme which cannot respond to experience. Opinion differed as to whether the move towards internal validation will increase or decrease this danger.

An important spin-off of this move is that similar methods are beginning to be applied to non-CNAA courses, even though this is not required by the other validators. Rather more than half the colleges I visited said this is now happening, though not uniformly through all their departments. I was only given one specific instance of another body taking an initiative on a matter of course management — a BEC panel which wrote in a 'learning to learn' conversion module for ex-HND students entering a business studies course. But this same panel imposed the same workload on full-time students and on part-timers with only half the scheduled study time!

However carefully a course may be planned, difficulties which can affect students, individually or as a group, are bound to arise during its implementation. A humane and enlightened system should be able to make adjustments to cope with these. Any form of external validation tends to impede attempts to do so. The next section considers the mechanisms by which students are able to complain or seek redress. Here I am concerned with whether or not there is a possibility of redress once a difficulty is recognized. A great deal appears to depend on the closeness of the links between the college and the validating panel. Where there is personal contact — via external examiners or assessors who visit the college regularly — it is usually fairly easy to get agreement to small changes in, or relaxation of, the rules. Where there is no contact, the system becomes much more rigid, so that in the worst case validation is scarcely distinguishable from external examination. Some professional bodies were heavily criticised in this respect.

The regulations for a validated course constitute a legal contract between the validating body and the students, which can only be changed during the course by mutual agreement. Even one dissenting student can nullify the change for his cohort. This is not a situation which often arises, since proposed changes are generally widely welcomed and reluctant students can often be persuaded by their peers. Nevertheless, there may be need for clearer, and possibly modified, definition of the contract in order to establish how course regulations may be altered in midstream.

INDIRECT EFFECTS

The, on the whole, greater flexibility and sensitivity of the CNAA compared to other validating bodies is bought at a price. Many staff complained about the amount of time they have to spend preparing and revising proposals, which they feel detracts from their primary task of teaching (though one head of department said he felt this effort was necessary and beneficial by improving standards. 'It had made a good college first-rate, criticisms of time wasted on submissions comes from the "failures" on the staff'). One student complained bitterly that his lectures had been totally disrupted for four weeks prior to a CNAA visitation and he asked, very pertinently, why this could not have taken place in the vacation. It is possible, too, that some staff spend so much time on panels visiting other institutions that their own teaching and preparation suffers, though I did not encounter any allegations of this.

There were also complaints from the staff about the financial cost of preparing submissions, about the excessive development time of many courses and the long and sometimes tortuous chain of communications between college and validating panel, about the lack of personal communications between development team and panel (with consequent uncertainty about what the panel would require), and of panels which appear to change their minds during negotiations. All this leads the team to try to produce a bland proposal which they hope will meet all eventualities and is hardly in the best interests of the students. 'The CNAA requires catch-all proposals to suit any conceivable assessors instead of educational validity. It's like negotiating with a black box.' There were also unfavourable comparisons between CNAA validations and previous validations by a neighbouring university which, although less thorough and often less innovative, were held to establish a long-term understanding between the two sides. Similar complaints were made about TEC, which was accused of involving staff in more bureaucracy than previous HND validations by professional bodies.

The process of validation can also impose demands directly on students' time if they are to be consulted about new proposals or the progress of their course. This cost is generally not excessive — certainly not as serious as the cost to staff — but it is necessary for all concerned to be aware of the danger and to keep the demands in proportion. It was also evident that many students are reluctant to devote much time to participating in (re)validation processes, particularly when the benefit will accrue to their successors rather than themselves.

Validating bodies are generally concerned much more with students who will eventually succeed in gaining their accolade than with those who fall by the wayside. While this attitude is understandable, it is not necessarily defensible since failure can lead only too easily to personal trauma and waste of talent. Perhaps they should enquire into the numbers of drop-outs. It can also be argued that so far as possible, all students undertaking a course of study should be provided with an alternative course to follow if they fail to achieve the required standard: honours to ordinary, ordinary to HND or DipHE, etc. — whichever seems appropriate. Some departments told us they do try to arrange their courses so that this is possible, but apart from CNAA honours and ordinary paired courses and a few TEC and BEC courses, validating bodies do not seem to pay much attention to escape routes or the lack thereof. No doubt the plethora of different validating bodies in itself creates barriers to the interchangeability of partial qualifications. I encountered one department dealing with seven different validating bodies. There is at least a prima facie case for saying that students might benefit if this matter came within the validation process. It is a matter which student representatives on course committees might take up.

## CONSULTATION WITH STUDENTS DURING A COURSE

No matter how carefully a course has been planned, there will always be difficulties arising in its presentation and improvements which can be made in future presentations. There is therefore a need for some mechanism for identifying the faults and to evaluate a course. Practice and attitudes on this vary enormously. A few staff still adhere to the old notion that students have to make the best of what they are given; a few departments have gone to enormous lengths to consult their students in every conceivable way, both formally and informally. Most come somewhere in between.

The mechanisms used to consult the students include a bewildering mixture of informal contacts, meetings, representation on course committees (and higher bodies) and questionnaires. The biggest dichotomy of opinion comes between those who prefer informal contacts and those who believe in formal representation. Both methods can work successfully and both can fail to achieve real communication. Personalities, size of department, college organization and type of course all seem to contribute to the practice which evolves. On the whole, the smaller institutions are more likely to rely on informal encounters and it is clear that often there is close contact and trust between students and staff, so that if difficulties arise over workload, the availability of books in the library or the intelligibility of a particular lecturer, they are quickly reported and dealt with. Both students and staff in these institutions are emphatic in preferring this approach.

On the other hand, some of the larger institutions have developed a complex system of course, faculty and polytechnic committees on which students are involved at almost all levels. Typically, each year of a course will be represented by one or more students on the course committee and there will be representatives of the whole student body on the higher committees. This type of structure may be more suitable for discussing matters such as the cost to students of having their project reports typed, and to iron out the creases in the course and improve its overall effectiveness, but in several institutions doubts were expressed about it. Common complaints were that students frequently fail to attend the committees on which they are supposed to serve (holding such meetings during the lunch period or other times when there is no formal teaching helps to encourage attendance), that 'they lose interest in formal boards once the course is running smoothly', that they find the proceedings confusing and 'very boring — four to five hours with little of concern to students', that they are out of touch with their fellows and that students generally do not know their representatives. These difficulties can be overcome, since other institutions spoke highly of their student representatives, who were held to make a significant contribution to the proceedings. It is not clear how much of this success is attributable to the sensitivity of the institutions and how much to the personalities of the students involved. An opinion expressed more than once is that informal contacts are preferable for the majority of problems, but there should be formal machinery available if an informal approach fails to produce results.

Some departments (mainly engineering and kindred disciplines) offering TEC or BEC courses have a more paternalistic attitude going back to old HND days. They see their primary clients in the employers who send their apprentices on the courses and they maintain close liaison with the industrial training officers, who quickly report any difficulties their students may encounter. Several staff opined that these students show little interest in formal consultations and are loath to become involved, so the indirect route is justified.

The ongoing evaluation of a course requires a different sort of consultation with students. Obviously representatives on course committees can say what they think about the course, but it is difficult for them to speak for others, so it is essential to seek the views of at least a large sample of the students on each course. The two methods most commonly employed are meetings between staff and students — which may be formal or informal at regular or irregular intervals — and questionnaires. Ideally, a combination of both should be used. A meeting is good for identifying important points which need consideration: the questionnaire may give a better indication of the extent to which different views are held, as well as some very revealing comments if open-ended responses are allowed. 'Written criticisms from students may go deeper than verbal.' But questionnaires are difficult to devise and to interpret and many staff lack the requisite skills. Really effective systematic evaluation of courses is probably still a rarity. There is need for more staff training in methods of course evaluation: more good books on the subject, plus workshops, plus at least one consultant expert in each college. Perhaps Coombe Lodge could do something about this.

One group of students made the very good point that they are regularly asked to complete questionnaires, but they are never told the results or what action will stem from them. 'Course reviews don't seem to have much result.' Students are likely to co-operate in evaluation exercises more enthusiastically if they are given some feedback. One or two staff said they found evaluation exercises during the autumn, when there is still time to modify the current year's teaching, are far more effective than similar exercises at the end of the academic year. This leaves a gap in the evaluation of the end of the course.

Most CNAA panels (although certainly not all) demand a statement of the arrangements made for consulting students about a course submitted for validation and this obviously provides a powerful incentive to set up formal committees with student representatives and there is some machinery of this kind in all the institutions offering CNAA courses, although the vigour with which they operate varies. The CNAA has, therefore, certainly contributed to the practice of student representation but it was probably not the prime mover in this: student unrest and a change in the climate of opinion were already impelling colleges in that direction before CNAA started.

Informal enquiries at nine universities revealed that they, too, had all evolved formal student representation, both at course level and above, without any prompting from an outside validator. Details varied from one to another. Two said that they circulated agendas and minutes to students and held preliminary meetings on matters of particular concern to enable students to submit recommendations, but they did not normally have students present at their committee meetings. In case of dispute, the students had a right to appear before the committee. This practice appears to work well and promises to overcome some of the difficulties with student representation outlined above. One polytechnic had tried a similar method at one level. Perhaps others should follow suit.

Other validating bodies are less concerned about consulting students, although it was reported that some BEC and one or two TEC panels had suggested some rudimentary consultation. Some TEC assessors make a point of talking to students when visiting colleges. Other bodies, however, discourage or even forbid direct student involvement in course committees. One or two of the larger institutions, having set up student representation on CNAA course committees, are coming to regard this as a normal state of affairs and are encouraging or even requiring non-CNAA courses to do likewise. The move towards internal validation also seems to encourage consultation, since students are often able to make a valuable contribution to the evaluation of current courses and the evolution of new ones.

As might be expected, all institutions bar students from participating in any discussion of course results or personal matters: in some instances this is achieved by separating the functions of examining and course administration, in others by requiring student representatives to withdraw when these matters arise. Students accept this state of affairs: there is not yet any demand for union representatives to observe examiners' meetings to see that justice is done! One matter they might investigate is the distribution of results and how this compares with other courses. Most CNAA students are aware that they have a right of appeal if they think they have been unfairly examined, but this seems to be invoked very rarely — of the order of three appeals per institution per year. I have no knowledge of appeals procedures on other courses.

## STUDENT INVOLVEMENT IN THE VALIDATION PROCESS
In the past, the majority of new courses were planned and validated without any direct consultation with actual or potential students, for the very good reason that in most cases there were no students studying the subject accessible to the institution. It was therefore assumed that there was no point in attempting to discuss a proposal with potential students; even if they could be found they would lack the knowledge to make pertinent comments until they had studied the subject. The attitude is now changing, partly because revalidation rather than initial validation is becoming more common, and partly because of the growing movement towards internal validation.

There is general agreement that students can comment usefully on the administrative aspects of a new proposal. For example, one group of full-time students were quick to point out that the library was inadequate both for their course and for a proposed part-time course in the same subject. Staff should, of course, foresee these problems, but they do not always do so, so it is a useful long-stop to have students associated with the planning. It is also valuable to be able to sound out preferences before choosing between alternatives. Students might also ask pertinent questions about the demand for a course and the subsequent job opportunities, but I have no evidence that they do so up to now.

Three mechanisms of consultation are used: full-time officers of the students' union may be invited to sit on all course approval committees, representatives of students taking cognate subjects (or precursor courses) may be invited on to a particular course committee or the course proposals may be circulated to all students on similar courses for comment. All three have their strengths and weaknesses. Co-option of full-time student officers has the advantage that the officer concerned gets a lot of experience on the design of courses and eventually learns what sort of general questions to ask but inevitably is out of his depth whenever academic questions arise. It also has the advantage that the officer is paid, in part, to participate in the discussion and is therefore more likely to attend than active students. One disadvantage is the severe discontinuity when the officer is replaced. 'Sabbatical officers take a term to find their feet.' Another is that the students' views may not be expressed until it is almost too late. In a few institutions this method appears to work well and is valued by both sides, but in others it obviously generates some doubts. In one polytechnic the union policy is for officer representation, but the staff are not convinced that this is the ideal method. In another, the polytechnic drafts somewhat reluctant officers on to the committees.

Active students from cognate subjects on the committees can participate in at least some of the academic arguments and they have personal experience of where the shoe is likely to pinch but they are less likely to develop an instinct for searching out administrative flaws. To take a continuing interest in the ramifications of the interminable arguments which go on during the development of a course imposes a heavy load on the student concerned. If he is interested, the experience may be valuable to him in later life, but the success of this method is heavily dependent on finding the right kind of co-operative students.

Circulating course documents to cognate students at critical stages of development is possibly the most economical and effective method of gauging student opinion, since it invites comment at just those moments when the course team should be most receptive and it should generate a range of opinions. (It may also benefit the students; one group found the documents invaluable in understanding the structure of their own course.) But if no student has any specific responsibility to respond, response many not be forthcoming, or important points may be overlooked. Students in general do not always know what kind of points to raise, even when they are interested. For maximum effectiveness, circulation of papers probably needs to be accompanied by co-option of a student or officer who can go round soliciting responses, or by holding a meeting of students to discuss the proposals.

When I started my investigations one polytechnic, enthusiastically setting up its internal validation procedures, was going to great pains to involve the students at all stages. Two years later the mood had changed to one of disappointment on the part of the staff — though the student officers concerned still thought they played a worthwhile role. It was felt that the expenditure of time and money in consulting the students had yielded little in the way of tangible improvements to the courses and the various difficulties discussed above loomed large. No doubt a more satisfactory procedure will evolve with experience. Possibly a less formal approach would yield greater dividends, perhaps coupled with machinery to seek student views on specific aspects of course proposals at specific points in their development rather than expecting token involvement at every stage.

Student representatives — particularly union officers — are likely to be more effective if they are given some training for the job. The NUS tell me they are thinking of compiling a handbook of hints for students serving on course and college committees — in particular listing the sorts of questions they should be asking. In addition, each union could usefully prepare briefing notes to hand on to incoming officers. Finally, the colleges might find it would pay them to brief student respresentatives on college (or departmental) procedures and on the current state of play in committees which have been running for some time. At one polytechnic an assistant director had taken on this role, which was obviously appreciated by a student officer still quite new to the job.

The foregoing remarks apply particularly to consulting students over the administrative arrangements for new courses. Opinion varies as to how far it is valuable — or possible — to consult students over academic content. A common belief is that students cannot properly assess the value of their course until a year or two after graduation (and even then they may not be cognizant of the whole range of activities to which it relates) and that staff must beware of accepting too readily the views of those still in statu pupilari — views which may change after graduation. While this is a necessary caveat, it does not mean that students' views should be ignored. They are perfectly competent and entitled to express an opinion about the general features of their course and in particular about the options and subsidiary subjects on offer. One group of law students campaigned to have a section on sociology altered from a discussion of Durkheim to a study of family relations, against bitter opposition from the staff concerned. Whenever students complain that part of a course is dull or irrelevant or unreasonably difficult, there is at least a prima facie case for seeing whether it is really necessary, or could be replaced by something more appropriate.

If students on a course are not always competent to advise on content, possibly recent graduates could do better. They can offer a greater maturity, a wider outlook and some work experience. One member of staff said they received valuable suggestions from former students returning on social visits and a few departments attempt systematically to consult their alumni with varying success. Teachers are generally willing to co-operate if still living in the area — industrial personnel less so. There can be no guarantee of success in attempting to obtain feedback from this source, but it might be more likely if those invited back could at least receive their travelling expenses. A graduate could be a valuable member of a course committee if there happens to be someone suitable living nearby, or a research student might fill this role.

Gaining feedback from students is obviously a necessary part of evaluating a course coming up for revalidation and most panels recognize this, at least to the extent of talking to students informally while on visitations or oral examinations. Many CNAA panels arrange a formal meeting with at least a few students during their visitation. They enquire about workload, exams, time for reading, seminars, problems, coping with difficulties and the corporate identity of the course. A usual experience on these occasions is that the students defend their course quite vehemently against any perceived attack. Certainly all the colleges I visited had great confidence that their students would acquit themselves well and be a credit to their department.

These formal occasions, however, are probably less useful as a means of assessing the real impact of the course than the consultations described above which go on earlier. Certainly most, if not all, CNAA panels will expect to see a written report on the impact of the course on students at the start of a revalidation proposal and polytechnics often require such a report at the start of their own internal revalidation proceedings. Hence CNAA validation provides a powerful incentive to consult with students both on course administration and on content and to pay serious attention to their desires and difficulties. Again this spills over into courses validated by other bodies which are less concerned about the student point of view. It is perhaps a little ironic that the one place students have not yet infiltrated is the CNAA itself. One exciting suggestion is that CNAA panels might include a recent graduate in a cognate subject from another college.

I will not attempt to sum up this chapter, but let the narrative speak for itself. I thank all those who gave me some of their time for discussions and pay tribute to the high morale and enthusiasm I encountered amongst both staff and students, in all the institutions I visited.

REFERENCES

Alexander, R. (1979) What is a course? Curriculum models and CNAA validation *Journal of Further and Higher Education* III (1) 31-45

Chambers, A. (1975) Approaching change with caution *Education for Teaching* 97, 12-18

Gutterridge, W. (1975) Too many modules can spoil the mixture *THES* 188, 23 May p. 11

Murray, R.G. (1978) Planning for diversification *Journal of Further and Higher Education*, II (1) 57-65

National Union of Students (1980) *The Academic Affairs Manual* London: NUS

Parlett, M. and Simons, H. (1976) *Learning from Learners* London: Nuffield Foundation

Ridler, A.M. (1974) Course validation and approval — the CNAA *Coombe Lodge Reports*, VII (5) 276-83

Suddaby, A. (1978) The CNAA: a growing cause for concern *THES* 364, 3 Nov, p.10

Squire, K.H. (1980) Assessing TEC *Education in Chemistry* XVII (1) 10-12

# 8  THE LEGITIMATION OF VALIDATION

Ron Barnett

'Validation' has, over the last twenty years, slowly crept into the language of British higher education. Sufficiently familiar as a term to be comfortable to many associated with the public sector of higher education, it probably still remains unfamiliar or registers unease with many connected with the university sector of higher education as other conributors have observed. There is an obvious reason for this disparity across the binary line; the development of the public sector as a deliberate part of public policy has seen the establishment and growth of quasi-academic bodies, with no students of their own, but with responsibilities of various kinds towards students and courses in the polytechnics and institutions of higher education. These so-called *validating* agencies, while establishing considerable diversity in their powers and in their operating styles and procedures (FEU 1981), are a dominant characteristic of the public sector of higher education. It is not the case, however, that validation is wholly foreign to universities: in Chapter three, Church has shown how courses within universities are subject increasingly to assessment, sometimes by other bodies. At the same time, it is not clear whether, or rather to what extent, universities can be said to have implicit or informal processes by which their own internal academic programmes are 'validated'. But it remains the case that universities are not subject like the public sector of higher education to the powers of external bodies with responsibilities for the academic validation of their work. It is not surprising therefore if those whose experience and understanding of higher education is confined to the universities have only a vague understanding of the idea of validation.

However, there seems to exist a much more general vagueness about the idea of validation. This vagueness about the term has its own characteristics which will be explored below, but it is perhaps explicable. For, as has already been made clear, the general notion of validation has lacked a serious debate to clarify its meaning, to excavate some of its conceptual underpinnings, to assess the value of the processes for which it stands, and to offer some justification of it in principle. This chapter begins the first two tasks, avoids the third (taken up by other contributors in this volume), and attempts the last. The chapter goes on to sketch out a particular concept of validation, and to indicate the implications of that concept for the processes of validation.

## THE INEFFABILITY OF VALIDATION

Validation has, as is often remarked, an increasingly significant part to play in British higher education, especially in the public sector. It exists as an institutionalized process. Yet it appears from other contributions to this volume (notably Alexander & Wormald and Church & Murray) that even those engaged in the process are unable to give a coherent account of the enterprise. And this would appear to hold not just for those whose courses and institutions are being validated, but even for those who bear the immediate responsibility for conducting the validation process. In short, validation seems to be generally mysterious.

It might be countered, however, that the mystery is more apparent than real. It might be claimed, for example, that the concept of validation is like the concept of cycling. In each case it is very difficult to give a completely unambiguous description of the activity, but many people either can achieve it or can recognize the relevant performance as such. In other words it might be said that validation is more a matter of knowing-how rather than knowing-that, and that the difficulties associated with giving a verbal account of validation provide no testimony for believing there is no consensus as to what counts as validation (Ryle 1949).

This argument will not do, however. For even if it is granted that validation is more a matter of knowing-how than of knowing-that, unlike cycling, it is clear that a potentially wide range of activities could be present as candidates for the description 'validation'. More than that, those different kinds of activity might be so different in character that even as a form of knowing-how, validation could turn out to be a disputed concept. Unlike cycling, there is prima facie no consensus as to what constitutes a valid form of validation. The activity of validation is different from cycling in various other senses too. Many people can engage in the same act of validation at once; and it necessarily leads to some end-point. Validation is therefore significant in the double sense that something hangs on the outcome for many people.

Beyond reflections of this rather inconclusive nature, is it possible to give a more positive account of validation in the context of higher education, which fleshes out the concept yet retains the allegiance of those who use the term? If it is possible, the task will be more difficult than indicated so far; and this is due to the nature of higher education as practised in general in Great Britain. Higher education is here in a paradoxical state: it sustains theory without theory. It is constituted essentially by the acquisition on the part of the learner of various kinds of elaborated discourse. Yet, in Great Britain at least, higher education has not systematically attempted to understand itself: it has not generated an elaborated code (or set of codes) in which higher education itself is the focus of the enquiry. Consequently the activities which constitute higher education are conducted primarily through a restricted code, understood more or less tacitly by their practitioners (Bernstein 1970). Validation is one such activity: those who conduct it have their own tacit assumptions of which even they are unaware (Gouldner 1976, 1979).

Validation is a microcosm of higher education. It takes on the largely unreflected nature of higher education, and is a stage on which are exhibited rival concepts of higher education. As an unreflected activity within and yet outside higher education it posesses a mysterious, ineffable quality. It remains to be seen whether a general justification of validation can be elaborated.

## THE CONCEPT OF VALIDATION

Validation implies that something is judged to be valid. The act of judgement in turn implies that validation is conducted by some person or body competent so to judge. Questions then arise as to what is being judged, by whom, by what criteria, and by what means. There are conceptual connections between each of these. The competence of the adjudicator is specific to that which is being judged, and is exhibited through the use of a restricted set of methods employing a limited range of criteria. As a corollary, certain means and criteria of validation will be inappropriate to the object being judged.

The concept of validation, in the context of higher education, is non-specific. It does not, in itself, supply definite answers to the four questions (raised above) about competent judges, the focus of their judgements, their methods or their criteria. Different views can be, and are, held on each of these aspects of validation in higher education. Views differ, for example, as to who constitute the authorities competent to conduct validation, and on the foci of the validation process itself. These differences of view will be explored below. For the moment, the point is that there exist, often quite marked, differences of understanding of validation. In other words, the concept of validation is susceptible to various interpretations. Validation, in the context of higher education at least, is a contested concept (Ryan 1974 as contrasted with Wilson 1981). However, as I shall attempt to show, not all possible interpretations are legitimate in the context of higher education qua higher education.

Validation in the context of higher education is parasitic upon higher education: it provides an investigation into and a judgement of the extent to which the process of higher education has come up to some kind of standard. It is therefore both a task and an achievement concept (Peters 1967). Validation is conducted by non-specific activities (tasks) which, in order to warrant the appellation 'validation', must contain some precise outcome or achievement (the judgement or series of judgements). The tasks are related to the achievement: the kind of judgement sought will influence the nature of the process of validation. Validation is an achievement concept in a double sense. It implies the validators have succeeded in their task of assessing the degree to which the object of their attention has succeeded. Validation necessarily presupposes that something, or someone, of value is being evaluated (Hirst and Peters 1970).

## PROCESSES OF VALIDATION

The validation process is usually a conglomerate of different processes. Processes of validation may be explicit: they may be institutionalized with a bureaucratic apparatus. Or they may be implicit, not formalized to any real extent (as within universities). The foci of the process vary considerably: they may include the students, their courses, the staff, or the institution.

The validation process takes a variety of different forms, employing different models. Three axes seem to be dominant, which superimposed could be used to locate different kinds of validation practice. Validation can be conducted within an institution or by an external agent, or utilize a blend of both in varying proportions, that is to say it can vary along an internal-external axis; the style in which it is conducted can vary from the consensual to the confrontational; and its focus can vary along an axis from the individual student to the institution as a whole.

Once the processes of validation begin to fill out, further questions present themselves, of both a conceptual and an empirical kind.

Conceptual questions arise in particular over the foci of validation. For example, if the course is to be the object of the validation process, what is to be meant by 'the course'? Is it the syllabus, or the material (in whatever form), to which the student is deliberately exposed, or the course as assessed? The development of curricular innovations makes the concept of a course even more problematic: modular course designs, independent learning, distance learning, open learning systems, and credit-based structures all, in separate ways, render 'the course' less visible. In a similar fashion, the institution of higher education, were that to be the object of validation, can be subjected to a parallel kind of analysis: its ethos, capacity for self-management, resourcing, and staff might all be considered as worthy objects of assessment. Neither the course nor the institution are 'given': for the purposes of validation, what counts as the course or the institution is the result of prior assumptions on the part of the validators.

If the institution and the course are not a myth, they are at least very elusive. And so it might turn out to be the case for all potential objects of validation. Validation, however, does not take place in a vacuum: and its institutional setting presents problems. We do not, for example, know what implicit curriculum models, or indeed what concepts of higher education, are held by those who conduct validation, or what assumptions are held about the development, distribution, and transmission of knowledge. Nor do we know, a fortiori, the social effects of validation on these and other aspects of higher education. The processes of validation constitute a potentially rich area of research for the sociology of knowledge: serious research of this kind into validation is long overdue.

## WHO VALIDATES THE VALIDATORS?

I suggested earlier that validation necessarily implies an act of judgement by some person or body competent to judge, an act from which something of consequence follows. Validation therefore contains aspects of power, authority, and accountability. The element of power resides in the act of judgement from which something of significance follows. The element of authority is found in the competence of those conducting the validation, and also, by extension, in the nature of the judgement. And the element of accountability is found in the process of validation, since an assessment of validity is an appeal to impersonal standards, by which if necessary the adjudicators can be held to account (although if pressed the adjudicators would find it difficult to elaborate those impersonal standards under which the process of validation was conducted).

Teasing out the concept of validation in this way merely serves to raise other questions. Who has the authority to conduct validation in the realm of higher education? From where are such authorities to be found? Are they to be 'the great and the good'? And by what criteria would they be determined?

The Council for National Academic Awards has prima facie avoided such invidious problems by opting for validation by 'academic peers'. The justification for such a policy presumably takes the form that 'the great and the good' might operate by standards which were so atypical that unreasonable expectations might be exerted upon the institutions and courses in question. The cynic might comment that such authorities were being thought unsuitable to conduct the validation process because they would be too competent. That would be a tendentious argument however; for in turn it would prompt the further question 'competent at what?'. It does not follow from the fact that $x$ is a Nobel prize winner, that $x$ will be competent in conducting the validation process.

Yet the alternative strategy (of the CNAA) of judgement by academic peers is not without its conceptual difficulties. Who is to count as an academic peer? Presumably the rationale is that the standards of validation are to be those of the academic community in general: the academic peers are therefore to be drawn from the relevant academic community. But what is to count as the relevant academic community? Are students, for example, members of it? It might be said that they are not fully competent members of the academic community and therefore would not constitute 'authorities'. Yet is it then being suggested that perhaps all academic staff being members of the community are ipso facto members of the pool from which the validators are drawn? If it is the generally held standards that are sought as the criteria of validation then efforts should presumably be made to ensure that a representative cross-section of that community comprises those who conduct the validation process, including those 'academic peers' who are felt to be the weaker members of that community.

In short, the community of 'academic peers' is not unambiguously given as such. It would seem that some criteria of selection must be adopted in order that the validators (the validating team) be produced. The term 'academic peers' is not, therefore, a neutral term: its boundaries are a function of prior evaluations as to what constitutes not only an 'academic peer', but even an 'academic' (Gellner 1970).

The third aspect of validation picked out above, that of accountability, raises further questions (Church 1981). To whom are those conducting the validation process accountable? What constitutes the relevant public? Is it the students (present and/or potentially future), or the academic world, or the civil public (the taxpayer), or the relevant professional bodies, or the state? And is it logically necessary for those to whom higher education is to be accountable themselves to conduct the act of validation? The criteria of validation, the personnel conducting the validation, and the process and language of validation reflect the public to which validation is addressed.

The authority and the accountability of those who validate in the context of higher education are not then 'given'. They are a function of the interests sustained by the process itself. They may be largely unintended consequences: the validation process may not carry the kind of authority, or be accountable, to meet either needs felt when the validation machinery was first established, or which had arisen since that time.

To put some flesh on these abstract remarks, I suggest that if, as might have been expected, following the 1966 White Paper on *A Plan for the Polytechnics* and Crosland's (1965) Woolwich and Lancaster speeches, a validation system had been designed for the public sector of British higher education which both sought parity of esteem with the universities as perceived by the general public and demonstrated the social responsibility of the public sector, the validation system could have been markedly different from that which emerged. It might however be argued in turn that the two objectives (of parity of esteem and demonstrated social responsibility) would have pulled the validation process in different directions, and that the system which actually emerged was a rational response in the British political and cultural contexts (DES 1981). It could be argued that the relatively low level of recognition accorded CNAA in the establishment of machinery for planning the public sector of higher education was caused by the Council's disinclination since its inception to address itself positively either to the consumers of higher education or to the defined needs of the state.

To return to the general theme, it appears to be the case that the outcome of the validation process is inherently suspect. Given different objectives, different kinds of personnel, and different criteria of assessment, not only different judgements but even different objects of judgement might have emerged. (The objects offered for assessment are in part a function of the criteria of assessment as perceived by those responsible for what is assessed.)

This indicates to me that validation can be used by different interest groups to legitimize different ends. There is an urgent task to investigate the extent to which the validating agencies which have been recently established in British education are parts of the ideological state apparatus

(Althusser 1972; Russell 1981). Such an investigation would need to examine what I believe are quite significant differences between the various agencies. I suggest that the CNAA, for example, would demonstrate a domination (though not total) by the 'educational class' (Dahrendorf 1978); rather than any significant interpenetration with the state.

At this point in the analysis arises the temptation to ask the question: who then validates the validators? It is not entirely a rhetorical question, but the general difficulty with it is well-known: it leads to an infinite regress. A more serious question is this: given the often hidden context of interests and presuppositions within which validation takes place, is it possible to structure validation in such a way that those interests can be neutralised and validation itself legitimized?

## VALIDATION AS IDEOLOGY

All social activities, including that of validation, presuppose particular values (even if, as for validation, it is often quite difficult to pick them out). But values are themselves suspect on the grounds of possible subjectivism, relativism, or ideology (Larrain 1979). The questions can therefore be levied against any particular validation process: what values are enshrined within it, and what or whose interests do they serve? The values sustained by the validation process will reflect the implicit ideologies of higher education held by those responsible for the process (which will include those responsible for establishing and organizing the activity, as well as those actually conducting it).

Ideologies of higher education, themselves part of the restricted code of validation and therefore seldom formulated, are both high level and low level in character. High level ideologies are conveyed in abstract concepts of, for example, academic freedom, knowledge, rationality and relevance. The actual conception of each such notion embodied by any particular validation process will depend upon the values of the relevant social actors. The formulations of academic freedom and relevance (for example) sustained by a validation system which underpins state capitalism will tend to be different to those sustained by a system which furthers the interests of the educational class. In each case, the differences are a function of the different kinds of value promoted by the validation system. In practice, the actual system will be the result of a negotiation of those different values. Low level ideologies of higher education encapsulated by the validation process operate at the level of the curriculum, and the operation of the process itself. For example, there may be an easy familiarity amongst the validators with terms such as 'honours standard', and the 'integration' or 'coherence' of the course. What precisely these are is seldom if ever made clear. They are assumed to be 'a good thing'.

Ideologies sustain values at two levels: surface and hidden. The hidden function, for example, of a proclaimed or alleged belief in academic freedom may be an attempt to legitimize the autonomy (and thus the interests) of the educational class. In other words, the real value of 'academic freedom' as an ideology may be much less 'idealistic' than it appears, and more a matter of promotion of hidden interests. Correspondingly, when the validation process seeks to improve the 'integration' of a course, the real value of more 'integration' may not be an enhancement of the educational experience, but a diminution of it. For it may well be that the effect of greater integration is to reduce the student's access to the kind of fundamental concepts that would make possible for the student an educational outcome which is both critical and autonomous (Barnett 1981).

Further possible ways in which validation might sustain higher education as ideology can be briefly indicated: 'rationality' in higher education may function to promote modes of thought which are conducive to a bureaucratic society (Zijderveld 1974); 'relevance' may function to produce the managers of both production and consumption required by advanced capitalism (Stedman Jones 1969, Shaw 1975); and talk of 'the educated man' may function to promote the separation of manual and mental labour (thereby emasculating the concept of polytechnic education) (Garz 1977, Castles and Wustenberg 1979).

Higher education is inescapably ideological in character, both in terms of its rhetoric and its processes (Grant 1975, Marx 1975). Both can and do sustain a range of values, many of which are hidden from view. Validation mirrors this situation. The values for which any validation process stands are not merely disputable; on examination, it may turn out that the actual process is fulfilling quite different values. In so far as validation is sustaining hidden unreflected interests it necessarily takes on ideological characteristics.

These reflections do not necessarily undermine validation as such. They suggest, however, that validation will be legitimized only if it can offer a process of critical reflection which brings to the surface the hidden assumptions, values and interests present within the curriculum of higher education, but without imposing further implicit ideologies of its own. In short, can validation neutralize the ideological aspects of higher education without itself being ideological?

## THE EPISTEMOLOGY OF VALIDATION
Higher education is concerned essentially with the transmission and acquisition of elaborated discourses containing corpuses of knowledge claims. Validation is accordingly the assessment of the extent to which a valid acquisition of such discourses or corpuses is being or is likely to be realized. Validation necessarily needs to operate with some concept of knowledge.

The key aspect of knowledge underlying the process of validation is the extent to which knowledge is asssumed to be objective. This is not the place for a systematic examination of various non-objectivist accounts of knowledge. What needs to be said here, however, is that the debates over the nature of knowledge need to be recognized, and that it cannot be assumed that objective knowledge is available within higher education and, by extension, in the validation process. On the contrary, it needs to be recognized that the belief in objective knowledge ('objectivism') constitutes an ideology of its own, barring the way to an excavation of possible 'knowledge-constitutive interests' embedded within different forms of enquiry (or knowledge) (Habermas 1978). This account of knowledge of course represents an attack on Popper's (1972) view of objective knowledge, although 'knowledge-constitutive interests' may not necessarily be 'invariant' as Habermas claims.

In short, it should not be assumed within the process of validation that objective knowledge is available, since that assumption is itself on the agenda for philosophical examination within higher education. Yet if this reflection seems to begin to undermine the rationale for validation, at the same time it also strengthens the case. For if the processes of higher education are themselves operating under assumptions of objectivity, exhibited in both the formal curriculum and the learning/teaching processes, it becomes incumbent upon validation to generate forms of systematic reflections to bring those undisclosed assumptions to the surface. It becomes 'incumbent' on a particular view of higher education. If higher education is seriously to be liberal, then the learner must be free from dependence upon the modes of thought into which he or she is initiated (Wegener 1978).

This aim certainly points to the need to ensure that the processes of learning are sufficiently opened for the student to be able autonomously to learn for himself and make critiques of the corpus of knowledge to which he is exposed. But it also points to the need for systematic critical reflection on the curriculum as a whole if the presentations of knowledge it provides and the forms of learning processes are not to be frozen into hypostasized structures (McCarthy 1978). In theory, both knowledge and higher education are emancipatory in character (Habermas 1978b). However, the suspected hidden interests and assumptions of what passes for knowledge and its organization undermine the emancipatory potential of both knowledge and its supreme institutional embodiment in higher education. The possibly contaminated nature of the curriculum needs therefore to be exposed through critical examination, and its hidden dimensions brought to the surface. Validation becomes criticism of critical discourses; in a word: metacriticism.

## VALIDATION AS CRITICAL DIALOGUE
Higher education purportedly offers an open-ended exploration of the objects (aspects of knowledge) which form the staple of the curriculum. Higher education, taken seriously, declines to accept them as given: every aspect of what passes for knowledge is potentially on the agenda for critical examination.

Yet if knowledges, as they are constituted, are potentially ideological and interest-bound, higher education seems undermined. It seems that its emancipatory promise can only be assured through a process of critical scrutiny (or validation). Yet, the snares that befall higher education befall validation itself. For the acts of assessment and judgement of courses and their curricula seem to presuppose access to just those authoritative criteria of validity which are already held in doubt (in respect of higher education). There seems therefore to be no secure redoubt from which the act of validation can take place objectively: it seems to imply privileged access to uncontaminated knowledge, the availability of which is in question (Gellner 1974). Validation thus finds itself in a double-bind: higher education requires validation to ensure its legitimacy, but the very reasons which undermine higher education, and thereby point to the need for validation, also in turn undermine validation.

The premise is correct, but the conclusion does not follow. There is no pure vantage point available from which unchangeable judgements can be made; but this is not only a problem for validation. It is also, and critically, the problem faced by any attempt to produce a liberal theory of higher education. Validation is no more than the institutional embodiment of higher education as metacriticism, that is a higher education which recognises that the offerings put before each student are not 'given', and that the emancipatory promise of higher education accordingly requires that those offerings themselves be subject to critical scrutiny.

Validation is not merely justified, but is literally the logical outcome of the concept of higher education, taken seriously: it is part of the logic of higher education, or at least a particular concept of higher education. At the same time, the concept of validation secreted by the concept of higher education mirrors the 'non-givenness' or non-authoritarian view of higher education here suggested. Critical reflection, whether termed higher education or validation, has no end-point. It is the process of inquiry that is significant, and not any particular claim. Indeed, it is the purpose of the critical enquiry to question the knowledge claim, or the curricular practice, or the values and assumptions within it, and not to counterpose incommensurable rival claims and assumptions.

It follows that the confrontation model of validation is inappropriate, when by confrontation is meant the opposition of competing viewpoints. Rather, the appropriate model is that of an extension of Habermas's 'ideal speech situation' in which participants of more or less equal competence generate a critical discourse which is unconstrained by any relation of domination (McCarthy 1978, Habermas 1978). The result of such an interaction is no end-point but merely a temporary stopping-place.

The dialogue needs to be real, and the depth and scope of the critical explorations need to be significant. A priori the participants within the processes of higher education could conduct that kind of validation themselves; but there is good reason to suppose this will be unlikely. For the targets of critical reflection are just those matters (values, assumptions, unreflected interests and practices, latent functions) which lie hidden to the participants. External validators can at least bring other knowledge claims, other values, other assumptions to bear. They will not be any less 'interested', and certainly not disinterested; but the presence of their interests will not be an overriding constraint, provided that the open, undominated character of the dialogue is sustained. The discourse will thus sustain, naturally, dialogic relationships between the participants (Freire 1972).

On this account of validation, Juvenal's question 'Quis custodiet ipsos custodes?' becomes redundant, or at least is easily enough answered. At one level the guardians, or the validators, do not need guarding, for they are not imposing their authority: they are essentially asking critical questions. At a second level, in so far as they are providing a counter set or sets of claims, values and assumptions which require justification, they in turn are submitting those claims to the forum of debate validation provides. Their critical comments are offered in the Leavis-like stance of 'this is so, isn't it?' (Leavis 1969), where the 'isn't it?' reflects the non-authoritarian status of the claim. The external validators provide a further claim, the offering of which indicates the non-givenness of that against which it is offered as a critical comment; in turn it is potentially subject to scrutiny. Validation is thus an essentially interactive process: the validators are themselves subject to the reflective critical comment of those they validate. Validation therefore has no real end-point: it is institutionalized critical dialogue between equals ('peers') who recognize themselves as such.

## PROBLEMATICS

This chapter has explored the concept of validation. It started by suggesting that as commonly understood, the concept of validation stood for a judgement that something with academic pretensions had come up to standard. The chapter went on to suggest that the bases for the twin aspects of that concept, of judgement and standards, were not available either empirically or theoretically. Empirically, those conducting the processes of validation were unlikely to be able to give a proper account of the basis of their judgement, or define the relevant standards. And, theoretically, there was no privileged access to presuppositionless knowledge and values by which a pure, unchallengeable judgement might be made.

Although those reflections appeared to undermine the concept of validation, it was also argued that liberal higher education rested on a foundation of critical reflection which, if taken seriously and institution-alized, would be a form of validation. The logic of the concept of higher education presupposes self-reflective strategies: validation is accordingly legitimized as critical dialogue.

The critic may say that the argument contains a contradiction: for, surely, the aspects of judgements and standards which were earlier picked out as necessary conditions of validation, have now been discarded. For, it may be suggested, validation as critical dialogue, on the account developed here, neither contains judgement (the dialogue is, in principle, never ending) nor is it underpinned by assumptions about determinate standards, for such standards would themselves be open to criticism.

This objection is in fact soundly based: for what is being offered here is a particular concept of validation which recognizes the philosophical and social problematics of both validation and higher education. Whether higher education would be prepared to adopt such a concept of validation is a different matter, however. For under this concept, validation is shorn not only of its characteristics of imposition and domination but also, as a corollary, of its more obvious laudatory aspect. Under this form of validation, those in institutions of higher education might feel that the public seal of approval was no longer available to them and might therefore be reluctant to engage in the process of critical dialogue. The sentiment would be understandable but misguided: for the process of critical dialogue is a dialogue between recognized equals. It is implicitly but necessarily a seal of recognition by both sides. However, the doubts might well remain: in which case one set of problems of the legitimation of validation would have been exchanged for another.

REFERENCES
Althusser, L. (1972) Ideology and ideological state apparatuses. In Cosin, B.R. (Ed.) *Education, Structure and Society* Harmondsworth: Penguin pp.242-280
Barnett, R. (1981) Integration in curriculum design in higher education *Journal of Further and Higher Education* (3) 33-45
Bernstein, B. (1970) in Rubinstein, D. and Stoneman, C. (Eds) *Education for Democracy* Harmondsworth: Penguin
Bernstein, B. (1971) in Minnis, N. (Ed.) *Linguistics at Large* London: Gollancz
Castles, S. and Wustenberg, W. (1979) *The Education of the Future* London: Pluto
Church, C.H. (1981) The impossible contract: the pitfalls of validation as accountability *Educational Policy Bulletin* IX (1) 83-177
Crosland, A. (1965) *The Role in Higher Education of Regional and other Technical Colleges engaged in advanced work*, Woolwich Polytechnic Speech, Department of Education and Science, 6 May
Crosland, A. (1966) *A Plan for Polytechnics and Other Colleges* Cmnd 3006. London: HMSO
Crosland, A. (1967) *The Structure and Development of Higher Education,* Lancaster University Speech, 20 January, reprinted in Robinson, E. (1968) *The New Polytechnics* Harmondsworth: Penguin
FEU (1981) *Curriculum Control* London: Further Education Curriculum Review and Development Unit

Dahrendorf, R. (1978) The rise of an educational class *Times Higher Education Supplement* 14 July

Dahrendorf, R. (1975) The educational class In Seabury, P. (Ed.) *Universities in the Western World* London: Collier Macmillan

DES press notice, London, 20 November (1981) *Arrangements for the Management of Local Authority Higher Education in England*

Freire, P. (1972) *Pedagogy of the Oppressed* Harmondsworth: Penguin

Gellner, E. (1964, 2nd imp. 1969) *Thought and Change* London: Weidenfeld and Nicholson

Gellner, E. (1970) Concepts of society. In Emmett, D. and MacIntyre, A. (Eds) *Sociology Theory and Philosophical Analysis* London: Macmillan

Gellner, E. (1974) *Legitimation of Belief* London: Cambridge University Press

Gorz, A. (1977) Technical intelligence and the capitalist division of labour. In Young, M. and Whitty, G. (Eds) *Society, State and Schooling,* Lewes: Falmer

Gouldner, A.W. (1976) *The Dialectic of Ideology and Technology* London: Macmillan

Gouldner, A.W. (1979) *The Future of Intellectuals and the Rise of the New Class* London: Macmillan

Grant, G. (1975) The university curriculum and the technological threat. In Niblett, W.R. (Ed.) *The Sciences, the Humanities and the Technological Threat* London: University of London Press

Habermas, J. (1978) *Knowledge and Human Interests* London: Heinemann

Habermas, J. (1978b) *Knowledge and Human Interests: A General Perspective* Inaugural lecture. In op.cit. pp.300-317

Hirst, P.H. and Peters, R.S. (1970) *The Logic of Education* London: Routledge and Kegan Paul p.19

Leavis, F.R. (1969) *English Literature in our Time and the University* London: Chatto and Windus p.47

Larrain, J. (1979) *The Concept of Ideology* London: Hutchinson

Marx, L. (1975) Technology and the study of man. In Niblett, W.R. (Ed.) *The Sciences, the Humanities and the Technological Threat* London: University of London Press

McCarthy, T.A. (1976, reprint 1978) A theory of communicative competence. In Connerton, P. (Ed.) *Critical Sociology* Harmondsworth: Penguin

McCarthy, T.A. (1978) *The Critical Theory of Jurgen Habermas* London: Hutchinson pp.87-89

Peters, R.S. (1967) What is an educational process? In Peters, R.S. (Ed.) *The Concept of Education* London: Routledge and Kegan Paul

Popper, K. (1972) *Objective Knowledge* Oxford: Oxford University Press

Russell, T.J. (1981) *The State, Vocational Curricula, and Curriculum Agencies* Unpublished. Outline of a talk given to The Politics, Education and Society Research Group at the Polytechnic of Central London, 13 March

Ryle, G. (1949) *The Concept of Mind* Harmondsworth: Penguin, pp.31, 41
Ryan, A. (1974) An essentially contested concept *Times Higher Education Supplement* 1 February
Shaw, M (1975) *Marxism and Social Science* London: Pluto
Stedman Jones, G. (1969) The meaning of the student revolt. In Cockburn, A. and Blackburn, R. (Eds) *Student Power* Harmondsworth: Penguin
Wegener, C. (1978) *Liberal Education and the Modern University* University of Chicago Press
Wilson, J. (1981) Concepts, contestability, and the philosophy of education *Journal of Philosophy of Education* XV (1) 3-16
Zijderveld, A.C. (1974) *The Abstract Society* Harmondsworth: Penguin

# 9 THE RELEVANCE OF EVALUATION RESEARCH FOR VALIDATION

Roy Cox

Recent closures and threatened closures of colleges have raised the question of the validity of validation procedures in a particularly virulent form. Lecturers at Chelsea College are disturbed by doubts about the quality of many departments and there is little in the Swinnerton-Dyer Report on London University to assure them that, if the College is closed, it will be on the best possible evidence. Lack of faith in ill-defined peer review systems — 'simply asking a few experts ... for their assessment of a person or department' — and visitations is likely to prompt questions about methodology and validity which parallel controversies in the field of evaluation research. Neither evaluation research nor educational research generally has been well integrated into educational practice at any level, so it is not surprising that there has not been a traditional link between evaluation research and validation activities. In the past, moreover, the classical 'agricultural' paradigm of research often meant elaborate, highly controlled, set piece projects which seemed remote and not responsive to the problems and constraints of validation.

They were two quite different operations, but are we now seeing greater openness and variety in both validation and evaluation research which means that more serious reappraisal of the relationship is needed? On the surface at least the more illuminative styles of research look as if they could be more responsive to the sort of problems raised by those engaged in validation. On the other side we find the CNAA in its *Partnership in Validation* (1979) exercise expecting that when a new course has produced its first cohort of graduates those responsible for the course will write reports analysing its success and these will be part of the validation. As long as validation was concerned only with new courses and hence with proposals and resources, evaluation in terms of research was marginal. But when courses are actually running the situation is quite different and analyses become crucial. Are these analyses evaluation research? Does the new partnership have any parallels with the even newer participative styles of evaluation? Is the concern of the researchers that 'much of the debate about evaluation is ideology disguised as technology' relevant to the concern of many lecturers that the disappearance of their jobs may have as much to do with disguised ideology as with objective validation? Validating bodies are not yet set up to do extensive evaluation research but the 'analyses of success' are needed. But is it only about success? The difficulty for institutions is that evaluation research is as much about failure as success, but how is this related to validation?

Plainly validation is different from research but so much is changing on both sides that a review of developments in the very confusing field of evaluation may be a useful contribution. This chapter, which is adapted from a recent book on evaluation in medical education (Cox et al 1981), is not meant to be an attempt to analyse the relationship between the two. That can be done better by those who are more experienced in validation. I hope, however, that it will raise issues that are worth raising and perhaps help to broaden the scope of validation activities. What then has been happening?

In the past few years there has been growing interest in evaluation research due partly to the international economic crisis, but more generally to the increasing demand for more accountability in many areas of public life. Although funds for many types of research are being cut back, there is, nevertheless, a growing realization that the amount spent on research and development in education has been pitifully small in relation to that normally expected in industry and commerce. But at the same time, there is a greater willingness to innovate in education and this naturally calls for systematic reflection on the nature and effectiveness of these innovations. Rapid social and technical changes have meant that simply spending more money might be ineffective; new methods of teaching and even reappraisal of goals are called for — whereas only a decade ago academics were often of the opinion that "the firmest and most easily used criterion of what ought to be done is what has been done" (MacIntyre 1964).

During the nineteenth century, however, there was a disastrous experiment of paying school teachers in proportion to the achievement of their pupils and this failure may have been related to the disproportionate outcry in 1968 against the Prices and Incomes Board's suggestion that university teachers should be paid in accordance with the ratings of their teaching by their students. In recent years, however, there has been considerable sympathy with, or at least lip-service to, the idea that teaching ability should be taken into account in promotions and appointments in higher education. Now there is encouragement to make this more than lip-service from the agreement between the University Authorities Panel and the Association of University Teachers which requires systematic support and appraisal of the teaching of probationary staff before tenure is granted. Many staff are still suspicious but it seems that the time is now right for setting up systems of evaluation of teaching and courses, provided they can be both effective and yet clearly sensitive to the complexities and subtleties of teaching, avoiding the distortions, injustices and alienating effects of over mechanistic inspections.

A useful way of beginning this review of evaluation research is to attempt to clarify the problems, to look at the language, to outline the traditional approach and to mention the various styles which have developed and the prominent issues and dimensions which have featured in the discussions. Next I shall look at the criticisms of traditional evaluation and review some of the newer more integrated approaches. Finally, I shall briefly consider recent doubts about the desirability of any evaluation and suggest the possibility of a collective or participatory style which may avoid some of the dangers of manipulation and suppression of spontaneity.

## PROBLEMS AND LANGUAGE

Although there have been discernible trends in thinking about educational evaluation over the last thirty or forty years the general impression of the newcomer to the field is still of complexity and confusion. He can read of evaluation as formative, summative, intrinsic, pay-off, comparative, goal-free, bureaucratic, autocratic, democratic, exploratory, responsive, utilization focussed, ethnographic, illuminative, and still find many subtle distinctions within any of these labels. These terms reflect very different approaches and yet the words themselves are not clearly defined. In Britain evaluation has been associated with educational processes, course design and the curriculum and the word 'assessment' has been generally used to refer to measuring the attainment of the students. The performance of students has, of course, been recognized as an important aspect of evaluation of any teaching but the problems involved in evaluation by results — even if it is not payment by results — have been more influential on this side of the Atlantic than they have in the States.

Bloom (1970) has used the word 'assessment' in a very broad way including analysis of the environment and the psychological pressures it exerts together with the roles and demands made upon individuals. Those who do the assessment attempt to collect many different types of qualitative and quantitative evidence using interviews, observation, self-reports, projective situations, role-play, situational tests, free association and so forth, combining information to make general judgements. The validation for such assessment is taken to be construct validity — the different evidence relating characteristics of individuals together and to those of the environment must be consistent with an acceptable construct theory or model which relates and makes explainable those otherwise disparate pieces of information. The emphasis is on what is needed to cope with the environment.

But we could be less interested in the environment and more in the various changes it induces. Here we would be engaged in what Bloom calls 'evaluation'. Objectives would be very important and different objectives require different measures. Improving these measures, determining priorities and encouraging change are important issues and content validity is central. But Bloom is using ordinary words in a rather special way and perhaps the language of evaluation styles is more appropriate. Let us then look at some of these and begin with the traditional.

## THE CLASSICAL OBJECTIVES MODEL

Perhaps the clearest form of criterion-reference mastery testing is in the field of individualized or personalized systems of instruction which are becoming very popular now. But the objectives model of curriculum development actually began in the States in the 1930s largely under the influence of Ralph Tyler (1977). In general it had five steps:

1 Researching, and reaching agreement on, the aims of the course or curriculum
2 Expressing these aims in terms of behavioural objectives expected of the learner
3 Devising and implementing learning experiences with which to lead students to behave in the appropriate ways
4 Assessing the degree to which pupils have achieved the intended learning objectives
5 Changing the course of 'treatment' or student selection until the performance does match the objectives — or perhaps changing the objectives themselves

This model was taken up particularly enthusiastically by the funding agencies in the United States in the 1960s. In their extremely valuable reader in educational evaluation *Beyond the Numbers Game* Hamilton and his colleagues (1977) suggest that the model was influential in the curriculum reform movement and enabled the funding agencies to demand pre-specified intended performance gains and proof of 'pay-off'. They choose Tyler's contribution as an historical starting point because they believe 'all subsequent approaches to curriculum evaluation have either evolved or recoiled from Tyler's proposals'. We shall not be taking up the issue of the value and limitations of the objectives model in detail, but it is clear that it would have an attractive simplicity to anyone wanting a straightforward and uncomplicated answer to the question as to whether or not money was well spent.

## STYLES AND DIMENSIONS OF EVALUATION
Before we go on to look at some of the criticisms of the traditional evaluation model, however, it may be worth setting out some of the issues which we have touched on in a diagrammatic form. To explain fully the meaning of Figure 1 would take more space than can be devoted to it here. What is intended is to give some indication of the various issues which writers have suggested are important in understanding what is involved in educational evaluation and we shall only make a few comments now.

The distinction between 'purposes' and 'roles' (boxes 1 and 4) is Scriven's (1967). Unfortunately, these words are not used as clearly in ordinary language as Scriven would wish, so it is difficult to make the distinctions by using these words but we have kept them since the idea behind the distinction is a useful one. Under 'subject of evaluation' (box 3) the boundaries of 'the environment' are not easy to draw. Here the more limited

# Figure 1   STYLES AND DIMENSIONS OF EVALUATION

Tentative links for traditional mechanistic-behavioural style illustrated

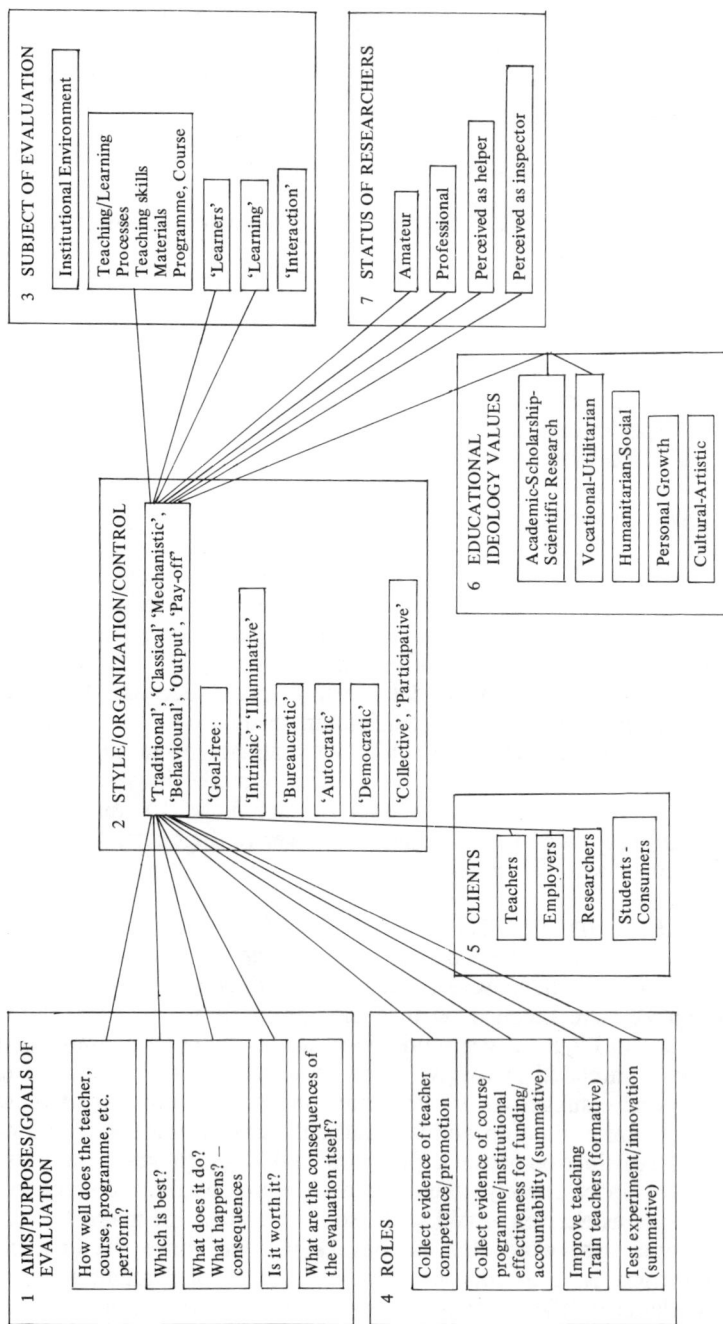

**1   AIMS/PURPOSES/GOALS OF EVALUATION**

- How well does the teacher, course, programme, etc. perform?
- Which is best?
- What does it do? What happens? – consequences
- Is it worth it?
- What are the consequences of the evaluation itself?

**2   STYLE/ORGANIZATION/CONTROL**

'Traditional', 'Classical' 'Mechanistic', 'Behavioural', 'Output', 'Pay-off'

- 'Goal-free':
- 'Intrinsic', 'Illuminative'
- 'Bureaucratic'
- 'Autocratic'
- 'Democratic'
- 'Collective', 'Participative'

**3   SUBJECT OF EVALUATION**

- Institutional Environment
- Teaching/Learning Processes
- Teaching skills
- Materials
- Programme, Course
- 'Learners'
- 'Learning'
- 'Interaction'

**4   ROLES**

- Collect evidence of teacher competence/promotion
- Collect evidence of course/programme/institutional effectiveness for funding/accountability (summative)
- Improve teaching Train teachers (formative)
- Test experiment/innovation (summative)

**5   CLIENTS**

- Teachers
- Employers
- Researchers
- Students - Consumers

**6   EDUCATIONAL IDEOLOGY VALUES**

- Academic-Scholarship-Scientific Research
- Vocational-Utilitarian
- Humanitarian-Social
- Personal Growth
- Cultural-Artistic

**7   STATUS OF RESEARCHERS**

- Amateur
- Professional
- Perceived as helper
- Perceived as inspector

use is in the box 'Institutional Environment' — which concerns the physical environment, libraries, qualifications of staff, etc. — but the teaching/ learning processes might also be thought of as the learning environment of students. The distinction between 'learners' and 'learning' is Wittrock's (1970).

In the introduction to *Beyond the Numbers Game* the authors state that 'much of the debate about evaluation is ideology disguised as technology'. 'Disguise' is an important word in this context. Scriven's description of 'goal-free' evaluation (1977) (in the 'Style' box 2) is an interesting example of how an explicit attempt to avoid bias by refusing to be contaminated by any knowledge of goals of a particular project may itself introduce values which are not made explicit. It may be, however, that underlying the more obvious values and ideologies set out in the diagram in box 6 are more subtle and yet equally important more general philosophical assumptions about the nature of values and the language of description and evaluation. It may be that beneath the controversies about 'intrinsic' evaluation and 'pay-off' or 'output' evaluation lie philosophical problems of idealism and utilitarianism and these may benefit from a little philosophical analysis. This,however, would be a subject in itself — for the moment we might simply look at the meaning of some of the lines on the diagram.

The lines linking the boxes are not meant to represent anything more than tendencies towards association so that those with double lines might be expected to be more closely associated than those with single or with no line at all, but within any evaluation style there will be many variations not dependent on factors mentioned in the other boxes, so the diagram itself is perhaps not very useful in characterizing styles. But it can — in a rather oversimplified way — draw our attention to influences and associations which are worth considering.

## THE CRITICISMS OF TRADITIONAL EVALUATION

Much of the criticism of traditional evaluation has centred on the appropriateness of the objectives model for curriculum development. Myron Atkin (1977) puts the point very forcefully. 'These ideas (equilibrium, symmetry, entropy) are taught with the richest meaning only when they are emphasized repeatedly in appropriate and varied contexts. Many of these contexts arise in classroom situations which are unplanned but that have powerful potential. It is detrimental to learning not to capitalize on the opportune moments for effectively teaching one idea or another. Riveting the teacher's attention to a few behavioural goals provides him with blinders and may limit his range. Directing him to hundreds of goals leads to confusing mechanical pedagogic style and loss of spontaneity'.

Atkin sees the classroom activity as complex and subtle but the traditional perspectives of researchers have often been narrow in relation to the richness of real behaviour. As a result of the research bias 'we usually find that problems in education that are investigated turn out to be either trivial or they bear little relevance to classroom practice'. Much of the triviality is often the result of using only 'hard' measures of behavioural change: 'inasmuch as we have not yet learned to assess behaviourally some other most important educational changes for which we strive the sophisticated research models that are used often manipulate insignificant variables .... An elaborate research methodology was evolved around the investigation of inconsequential events.'

Similar criticisms are developed in Parlett and Hamilton's (1977) influential paper 'Evaluation as illumination, A new approach to the study of innovatory programmes'. They feel that this research is divorced from the real world by studying 'parameters' and 'factors' rather than 'individuals' and 'institutions'. The 'before and after' design tends to assume no change in teaching during the period of study and can in fact discourage change. Such research tends to require large samples and so is insensitive to local idiosyncrasies which might be particularly valuable and they feel in general that this type of research fails to respond to the very different problems and questions which can be raised by different interest groups.

Other critics rather more sympathetic to the traditional line such as Scriven (1977) have criticized the exclusive 'pay-off' emphasis from a more moral point of view. He feels that neither injustice nor even cruelty very easily shows up in terms of effects, and yet these may have very serious long-term consequences for society. It is no use waiting for these effects to show up; we need to observe the process in the classroom. On the more positive side education takes time and is not only there for the effects it produces but as an experience in its own right and as such should be enjoyable. The effects of enjoyment are similarly difficult to detect but the enjoyment itself is not. The point is made briefly by Scriven but it is an important one and one that reflects the underlying utilitarian philosophy which is encouraged by 'pay-off' evaluation — a point developed by MacIntyre in 'Against Utilitarianism' (1964). This type of criticism was behind the development of so-called 'expressive' objectives concerned with the processes and experiences rather than the outcomes (Eisner 1969).

THE NEWER INTEGRATED APPROACHES
Since the 1960s there have been attempts at developing more integrated approaches, or at least seeing the problem of evaluation in more comprehensive terms. *Bloom* (1970) criticized the narrow approaches of what he termed 'Measurements', 'Evaluation' and 'Assessment' leading to only partial solutions to the complex general problems he defined under the heading of 'Testing'. His main thesis in that paper was that 'Testing' is now ready for a major effort to create a synthesis out of what has hitherto been a series of unrelated approaches. Such a synthesis is necessary if it is to adequately deal with 'the very complex problems of describing, explaining, and predicting human characteristics'. He illustrates the new approach by

taking the problem of change, which he says is one which the 'Evaluation Approach' has dealt with in the past. He defines the problem of change in this new, more comprehensive way as:

$$\text{Change} = \frac{\text{Final}}{\text{Status}} - \frac{\text{Initial}}{\text{Status}} + \frac{\text{Strategy}}{\text{Employed}} + \frac{\text{Effective}}{\text{Instrument}} + \frac{\text{Related}}{\text{Changes}}$$

Under 'strategy employed' he wants a really specific description of the learning experiences so that they can be clearly differentiated from other strategies, and the context in which the strategy is used must be included in the description. With the 'effective instrument' he notes that ways of testing can be as 'powerful as the instruction or strategy in producing changes'. He suggests that these must be separated. Under 'related changes' he sees the importance of not only looking at the objectives but defining the consequences as well and suggests that the 'assessment' approach may be useful in exploring these. He feels that 'a problem of the type suggested above could only be attacked by a combination of the resources and techniques of all three of the existing test approaches'.

*Wittrock* (1970) looked at three types of evaluation: of the environments, of learners, (ie the relative achievements of different learners) and of learning, (ie the change which occurs during learning). The evaluation of instruction is essentially looking at the interactions between these three types. The essential questions to him are 'what are the important effects of the assignments, curriculum and experiences on learners of different abilities and 'in future what are the results of similar instructional experiences for different learners likely to be?'

He is essentially looking for 'cause and effect' relations amongst learners, instructional environments and learning. He feels that 'teachers, administrators, evaluators and researchers have been only modestly helped by the data and methods of many evaluation studies. One reason for this lack of help is that these data and methods were designed to evaluate learners, learning or learning environments, but not for the more comprehensive problems of relating the learner's interactions with his environment to his learning.' This sounds encouraging, but his insistence upon the use of quantitative methods and his language of 'cause and effect' appear to be rather restricting. 'Cause and effect' language seems to be most appropriate where we have a known set of systematic relationships between variables, but we do not know which are operative at a particular time.

It is most useful in a fault-finding operation where we may want to know whether the breakdown is caused by a flat battery, a broken switch or a blown fuse. Causal language can cope with more complex situations than this, but where we are looking for an explanation of complex behaviour, then disentangling apparent causes from background conditions can be difficult or dangerously arbitrary, where 'last straws' become 'the cause'. The multi-variate statistical techniques which he advocates can no doubt be extremely useful in evaluation research but they generally require largish samples and the data which can fit into such studies is limited by the resources available for collection and the difficulties of quantification.

## GREATER EMPHASIS ON CONSEQUENCES THAN ON GOAL ACHIEVEMENT

Although earlier writers have not ignored the unintended consequences of educational practices — there are very few new ideas in this field — later writers began to give these a great deal more attention and so moved away from the traditional approach. As we have seen, Scriven took a really firm stand — 'it seemed to me in short that consideration and evaluation of goals was an unnecessary and also possibly contaminating step. I began to work on an alternative approach — simply, the evaluation of actual effect against (typically) a profile of demonstrated needs in this region of education (this is close to what Consumers Union actually does). I call this Goal-Free Evaluation'. He felt that the language of 'side effects' or 'unintended outcomes' tended to be a down-grading of what might in fact turn out to be the most crucial achievement. 'Worse, it tended to make one look less hard for such effects in the data and to demand less evidence about them — which is extremely unsatisfactory with respect to many of the potentially harmful side effects that have turned up over the years'. In his very provocative paper 'Goal-Free Evaluation' (quoted at length in Hamilton et al 1977) he puts the case in an extreme form and we are not too sure just how we should take it, but it is clear that it is an approach which *could* lead to a serious undervaluing of interaction between evaluators and teachers.

Samuel *Messick* (1967) comes to similar conclusions about the need for assessing possible, not just intended, outcomes from a different point of view. In a paper in Wittrock and Wiley's book (1967) he discusses 'cognitive styles and affective reactions as two major classes of criterion variables which should be taken into account in the evaluation of instruction. These two types of variables are emphasized because of their bearing on questions that stem from particular views about the diversity of human performance and about the role of values in educational research'. He feels that many studies have produced 'answers that are either wrong since they summarize findings "on the average" in situations where hypothetical "average persons" do not exist, or else are seriously lacking generality because they fail to consider the multiplicity of human differences and their interactions with environmental circumstances'. He makes the obvious but often neglected point that a particular innovation in teaching might be better for certain kinds of students and another type of teaching better for other kinds, but because of the failure to make the distinction between the students the two approaches might exhibit negligible differences on the average while producing widely different effects on individuals. He outlines nine different cognitive styles including 'field dependence versus field independence', 'scanning', 'breadth of categorizing', 'reflectiveness versus impulsivity', 'levelling versus sharpening' and others which might be considered as cognitive styles but are often described as intellectual abilities such as speed, flexibility, divergence and fluency.

He cites evidence to show that, unlike the more conventional ability dimensions, one extreme of the stylistic dimensions is not uniformly more adaptive than the other. Styles of intellectual and perceptual functioning moreover are part of the 'total personality and are intimately interwoven with affective, temperamental and motivational structures'. He wishes to see an extension of the assessment of mental performance 'beyond the crystalized notion of achievement levels to a concern with patterns of cognitive functioning'. The importance of cognitive styles of understanding not only pupil/teacher interactions but also teaching styles and different testing styles (later called Trait-Treatment Interaction) opens up a whole complex set of questions about the matching of styles and whether or not cognitive style flexibility can and should be encouraged. Certain types of teaching and assessment may have a whole range of unintended outcomes which are likely to be ignored if we fail to take notice not only of the diversity of different effects upon different students at the end of a course, but of the complex and only partially understood processes of teaching and learning during the course.

Robert Stake (1977) is one of the earlier writers to systematize evaluation in a way which took into account a much wider range of variables than the classical model. Despite many evaluators' rejection of judgement he felt that both description and judgement were likely to be important in any evaluation study and each would be concerned with three distinct areas: the antecedents, the transactions and the outcomes. The descriptions would be concerned with both the intentions or objectives of the teachers or programme organizers and what actually happened. This would include not only what happened in relation to particular intentions, but what happened in spite of intentions or incidentally to them. The judgements can be divided into the general standards of quality and judgements specific to a given programme. The evaluator could be expected to organize his data in relation to the cells set out in Figure 2.

On the descriptive matrix there should be a logical relationship or contingency between intended antecedents, intended transactions and intended outcomes but an empirical relationship or contingency between observed antecedents, transactions and outcomes. To the extent that what actually happens is what was intended there would be congruity between the intended and the observed at each level. The data relevant to any of these cells can be collected in formal or informal ways and might be general or detailed (the model is very abstract). However, to lay it out in three levels is useful in drawing attention to a possible mismatch or lack of congruence which can suggest changes which may not otherwise be made, or could have been made in the wrong area. In general we might say that

Figure 2    STATEMENTS AND DATA FOR THE EVALUATOR OF AN
EDUCATIONAL PROGRAMME

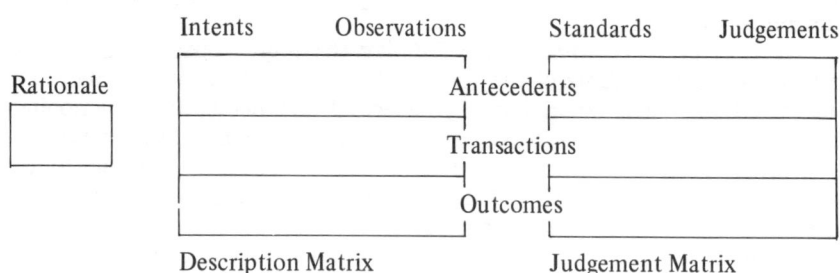

| | Intents | Observations | Standards | Judgements |
|---|---|---|---|---|
| Rationale | | Antecedents | | |
| | | Transactions | | |
| | | Outcomes | | |
| | Description Matrix | | Judgement Matrix | |

From Stake 1977

there is nothing very profound about the model but it does represent a very
important change of emphasis away from the traditional model.

'ILLUMINATIVE' EVALUATION
It may now perhaps seem a little unfair of Parlett and Hamilton (ibid.) to
have suggested that despite all the criticisms of the traditional approach
'little attempt has been made to develop alternative models'. Their own
approach might be seen as another definite shift of emphasis rather than
as a completely new approach. 'Illuminative evaluation' they say is primarily
concerned 'with description and interpretation rather than measurement and
prediction. It stands unambiguously within the alternative and anthropologi-
cal paradigm. The aims of illuminative evaluation are to study the innovatory
programme: how it operates; how it is influenced by the various school
situations in which it is applied; what those directly concerned regard as its
advantages and disadvantages; and how students' intellectual tasks and
academic experiences are most affected'. The emphasis is very much on the
educational processes, what it is like to actually participate as a teacher
or as a student. The illuminative evaluator is not simply using a different
methodology, his starting point is different. The formalized plans or
descriptions of the course or programme or 'instructional system' are not
taken as serously by the illuminative evaluator, since what actually happens
in practice is often very different from what is specified.
    The central pre-occupation is the 'learning milieu'. This represents 'a
network or nexus of cultural, social, institutional and psychological
variables. These interact in complicated ways to produce in each class or
course, a unique pattern of circumstances, pressures, customs, opinions and
work-styles which suffuse the teaching and learning that occur there'. The
research methods are both adaptable and eclectic. Both formal and
informal methods might be used to throw light on a particular aspect of

EVALUATION RESEARCH AND VALIDATION     173

the programme. Studies have three characteristic stages: investigators observe, enquire further and then seek to explain. Besides observation, interviews and questionnaires, tests and documentary background information might be used. They seek to be useful but it could be that in acknowledging the complexity of educational processes the illuminative evaluator is likely to increase rather than lessen the sense of uncertainty in education. Nevertheless, they hope that it will lead to moving 'beyond helpless indecision or doctrinaire assertions'. Many of these ideas are developed by Patton (1978) in his earlier 'utilization focused' approach, in which he lamented the dominance of physical science paradigms. Later he made a more thorough analysis of the qualitative methods which must be developed if evaluation is to be really effective in decision making (1980).

## THE NEWER CRITICISM OF EVALUATION
It is now many years since Scriven (1967) was writing: 'professional evaluators may simply exude a kind of sceptical spirit that dampens the creative fires of a productive group. They may be sympathetic but impose such crushing demands on operational formulation of goals as to divert too much time to essentially secondary activity'. The second part of this criticism may be less relevant to modern evaluators and certainly is not applicable to illuminative evaluators although their work has been criticized for being too demanding in terms of length and complexity, raising more problems rather than producing neat answers and often leaving serious doubts about subjectivity — and sometimes confidentiality. But criticism in terms of dampening creative fires is not so old-fashioned. Brian Lewis of the Open University is sceptical of much evaluation research for very similar reasons. It may not be coincidental that in recent years there has been a growing interest in techniques such as brainstorming and synectics where the suspension of criticism and analysis is seen as a necessary condition for the production of original, unusual and imaginative ideas, associations and solutions which could never have emerged without an initial suspension of disbelief. But perhaps more important than the destructive or inhibiting effects of some evaluations is the association with authoritariansim. An evaluation is something which is done by a superior to an inferior.

But this can be taken further than the earlier arguments about professional and amateur evaluation. Even where the evaluator is the amateur teacher, it can still, from the point of view of participants on the course, appear to be something which is entirely under the control of someone else and they are only guinea-pigs, filling in questionnaires and giving opinions, but not really feeling that they themselves are part of the evaluation processes. Being treated as consumers may be better than never being asked to express an opinion at all, but there is still something fundamentally inappropriate about treating participants in a course in the same way as a buyer of a motorcar; the buyer does not make the motorcar,

174    COX

but the student in a very important sense does make his own education.

In *Evaluating the New BEd* (Collier 1978) many of the contributors, but especially Alexander, stress the need for evaluation to be more participative and democratic 'to provide all participants in courses with information on a wide range of aspects of a course's operation', with emphasis on perceptions and meaning, and on creating a climate where evaluation is a continuous process of reflexion for improvement. But still the impression is that the main point of student involvement is that they contribute to improvement on the course and even here little is said about the need for students to learn how to reflect and comment and what such learning can mean to them apart from improving the course.

COLLECTIVE OR PARTICIPATIVE EVALUATION

On the other hand, in the study at Essex University of different patterns of student response to various forms of examination and other assessment (Cox 1975), it was clear that the development of a sense of personal and professional identity was closely bound up with the student's perception of the value of the work he produced. But where the judgements about his work were seen as arbitrary and authoritarian the relationships between academic work, intellectual or professional competence and personal identity were so strained that in many cases their formal academic work would not become an important part of their conception of themselves as developing individuals. It was very rare to find students who thought they had been helped in any way to become better judges of their own work. They were not in other words autonomous learners in the full sense, even though this is commonly thought of as the main purpose of a university education. In his book *Handbook of Academic Evaluation* Paul Dressel (1976) says 'the central goal of education is to inculcate in students the ability to make wise judgements — to evaluate. Only when the students become competent evaluators of their own goals, experiences and accomplishments, do they become truly educated (liberally educated one might say) and capable of engaging in the individual judgemental processes essential to a democratic society'.

John Heron in his concept of the peer-learning community (1974) similarly stresses the importance of self-evaluation for attaining adult autonomy. If we extend this concept of self-evaluation beyond knowing what level of academic achievement we have reached to becoming aware of our own cognitive styles, and to acquiring an ability to learn and develop in relation to other people and other learning resources, then perhaps we need to think of going beyond illuminative evaluation and towards a genuine participative style of evaluation where all those involved in the educational process become evaluators, not simply as interviewees or respondents or test takers but as active students of education.

This is not as yet a widely researched field, but in the medical field Cox (Cox et al 1981) and Heron (1974 and 1977) have been active and

John Rowan (1981) gives an outline of 'New Paradigm Research' which takes a broad perspective. This is discussed in depth in a new book which looks at the new paradigm in relation to many areas of human inquiry (Reason and Rowan 1982).

CONCLUSIONS
This chapter was meant to be a review of issues and developments in the confusing field of evaluation research and not an analysis of the relationship between validation and evaluation. But there do seem to be two important questions which perhaps deserve more attention than they are getting. The first concerns lessons which can be drawn from the ways in which the more recent illuminative style researchers work and the other concerns participation.

The earlier evaluation researchers were seeking rigour and academic respectability by moving closer to the methods of the established experimental sciences. These methods led them away from the practical world of validation but the newer researchers seek rigour through becoming more sensitive and more responsive to the wide range of issues and influences which determine events in natural settings. Their academic respectability comes less from accurate measurement and more from being close to what actually happens, more sensitive to the thoughts and feelings of those involved. Their ways of observing and talking to students and staff attempt systematically to avoid the many pitfalls of this type of inquiry, and subjectivity may have more to recommend it to staff who know the complexities, than the hard objective indices, which are often seen to be unproblematic only by those who are not close to the reality from which they were derived. Illuminative research, however, is time consuming and it would be unrealistic to suggest that all validators transform themselves into illuminative researchers. But familiarity with such research may well help them to evaluate their own validation activities and become more acceptable to the students, staff and administrators involved.

As I said at the beginning, the CNAA envisages 'partnership in validation' developing so that institutions 'analyse the success' — or otherwise? — of their courses, and this raises the question of the relevance of this participative or co-operative style of research to validation procedures. The problem of evaluation research being, and being seen to be, 'superiors' investigating 'inferiors' is even more apparent with validation — even if it is also more appropriate. But as with the debate about assessing individual staff competence the most promising direction may be less in improving the competence of the assessors and more in encouraging and developing the skills of *all* involved in education to be more sensitive, perceptive and *articulate* about all the experiences by which they learn.

Not only would this fit better with the view that education is now essentially about future learning and the capacity to adapt to change without institutional supports, it would also make the validation process a more

176     COX

genuine partnership. Participative research is still relatively undeveloped but
if it becomes integrated as a constant and personal reflective element in
all areas of education and is less dependent upon the professional
researchers, it could make a very significant contribution to the validation
process, and one which might lessen rather than encourage the suspicions
and anxieties which threaten to distort all atempts at evaluation and
validation in times of closures and redundancies.

The validation demands of the CNAA have in many ways encouraged
constructive thinking but there has always been the danger of ritualistic
formalities which bear very little relationship to what actually happens, of
plans which conform to the pattern but do not reflect the style of teaching
of the department. Formal, traditional, quantitative approaches to
evaluation of ongoing courses may equally be open to manipulation to
produce acceptable answers. Formal surveys can produce valid, useful
information but the will has to be there. With participative styles evaluation
is not a mere appendage to the main purpose of the course, it is
an important part of it. Learning to become sensitive critics of education
does not go well with validation window-dressing and can be one of the
best defences against the alienation which can so easily accompany
evaluation which does not grow out of a shared desire to understand.

REFERENCES
Atkin, M. (1977) Research styles; Stamp out non-behavioural objectives.
    In Hamilton, D. et al. (Eds) op.cit.
Bloom, B. (1970) Towards a theory of testing which includes measurement-
    evaluation-assessment. In Wittrock, M. and Wiley, D. (Eds) *The
    Evaluation of Instruction: Issues and Problems* New York: Holt Reinhart
    & Winston
Collier, G. (Ed.) (1978) *Evaluating the New BEd* Guildford: SRHE
Council for National Academic Awards (1979) *Developments in Partnership
    in Validation* London: CNAA
Cox, R.J. (1975) *Students and Student Assessment — a Study of Different
    Perceptions and Patterns of Response to Varied Forms of Assessment —
    the University of Essex* University of Essex PhD Thesis
Cox, R., Kontiainen, S., Rea, N. and Robinson, S. (1981) *Learning
    Teaching: An Evaluation of a Course for Teachers in General Practice*
    London: UTMU
Dressel, P. (1976) *Handbook of Academic Evaluation* San Francisco:
    Jossey-Bass
Eisner, E.W. (1967) Instructional and expressive objectives: their formula-
    tion and use in curriculum. In Stake, R.E. et al. (Eds) *American
    Educational Research Association Monograph Series on Curriculum
    Evaluation III* Chicago: Rand McNally
Hamilton, D., Jenkins, D., King, C., MacDonald, B. and Parlett, M. (1977)
    *Beyond the Numbers Game* London: Macmillan

Heron, J. (1974) *The Concept of a Peer Learning Community* Guildford: University of Surrey
Heron, J. (1977) *Behaviour Analysis in Education and Training* London: British Postgraduate Medical Federation
MacIntyre, A.C. (1964) Against utilitarianism. In Hollis, T.H.B. (Ed.) *Aims in Education* Manchester: University Press
Messick, S. (1967) The criterion problem in the evaluation of instruction: assessing possible, not just intended, outcomes. In Wittrock, M. and Wiley, D. (Eds) *The Evaluation of Instruction: Issues and Problems* New York: Holt Reinhart & Winston
Patton, M. (1978) *Utilization Focused Evaluation* Beverly Hills: Sage
Patton, M. (1980) *Qualitative Evaluation Methods*, Beverly Hills: Sage
Reason, P. and Rowan, J. (Eds) (1982) *Human Inquiry: A Source Book of New Paradigm Research* New York: Wiley
Rowan, J. (1981) New paradigm research *Training Research Bulletin, Air Transport and Travel Industry Training Board*, IX (1)
Scriven, M. (1967) The methodology of evaluation. In Stake, R.E. et al. (Eds) *American Education Research Association Monograph Series on Curriculum Evaluation I* Chicago: Rand McNally
Scriven, M. (1977) Intended and unintended effects — Why distinguish?; Goal-free evaluation; Legitimate and illegitimate cases of evaluating the treatment rather than the effects. In Hamilton, D. et al. (Eds) op.cit.
Stake, R. (1977) The countenance of educational evaluation. In Hamilton, D. et al. (Eds) op.cit.
Tyler, R. (1977) Evaluating learning experiences. In Hamilton et al. (Eds) op.cit.
University of London (Swinnerton-Dyer) Reports (1981, 1982) Committee on Academic Organization Discussion Documents, Jan 1981, May 1981, Jan 1982, University of London
Wittrock, M. and Wiley, D. (Eds) (1967) *The Evaluation of Instruction: Issues and Outcomes* New York: Holt Reinhart & Winston

Roy Niblett

The consultation on validation, of which this book is, in part, an outcome, took place under the joint auspices of the Society for Research into Higher Education and the Higher Education Foundation. The concern of the Foundation, as has already been said, is to analyse and seek to understand the values and objectives of higher education more thoroughly than is usual. It regards higher education as having a responsibility for the production of knowledge and for its communication to students, but also for helping those students to be feeling and choosing, as well as thinking, men and women. The scope and practice of validation are problems of central concern to it. What follows is a personal attempt to outline and assess the scope of the operation as it appears through the preceding papers and the deliberations of the consultation.

PROPER PLACES AND PURSUITS

Validation involves the approval, whether more consciously or less consciously arrived at, of subject offerings and courses; and the determination and standardization of results so that the courses approved maintain their currency. Should it involve the approval of the institution and departments in which they are taught? Should it also cover the methods used to teach subjects in lecture room and lab? The more searchingly one considers the implications of the validating process the more difficult it is narrowly to limit its range, the more arbitrary it appears to draw an absolute line between the factors it is permissible and not permissible to include. Be that as it may, what can be taken into account must often be determined by what it is practicable to measure. The immediate aim must certainly be to encourage courses that are coherent and of educational worth, and to ensure that the standard reached by those who are deemed to pass in them compares reasonably with that attained by others taking courses that are roughly equivalent.

That is presumably accepted, but one has to go on to say that environment, custom and habit are subtly but immensely influential in judgements about what is practicable and in the decisions arrived at. The verdicts we pronounce on the worth of courses or examination are framed by a long tradition of judgements which is largely unrecognized and simply taken for granted.

In his illuminating chapter on the legitimation of higher education Ron Barnett rightly insists that no validation takes place or can take place in a vacuum: those who conduct it make many assumptions about the nature of knowledge and the nature of higher education itself, whether they are conscious or not of what the assumptions are. 'The criteria of validation', he says, 'the personnel conducting the validation, and the process and language of validation reflect the public to which validation is addressed. The authority and the accountability of those who validate in the context of higher education are ... a function of the interests sustained by the process itself.' And such 'accountability' includes the prejudices, the more temporary as well as the more permanent goals and standards of the society in which it takes place. Approval of a course, and of the climate and amenities of the institution in which it is to be given, is a mark of the acceptance by surrounding society of what is deemed a sufficiency for the achievement of the purpose in question.

Whoever the validators are — members of CNAA boards and panels or of the Council itself; members of university and college staffs; external examiners of subjects; members of professional associations keen to uphold the standards of entry to the territory they guard — all of them will be imbued with many of the values and traditions of the society they belong to and, always in the background, there is the fact that validation must in some sense win the approval of the society in which it is carried out or it will not prove acceptable. Courses that are too conservative, too 'advanced', or appear too tendentious, are likely to find approval difficult to get, though the understanding of what is 'advanced' and what is 'tendentious' is a very relative matter. (I was present at a discussion in the early sixties at a meeting of the Senate in a New Zealand University where I was at the time a Visiting Professor. There was a proposition that a new course in the Sociology Department should involve the study of New Zealand Social History from 1890 to 1920. 'Getting rather *close*, isn't it?' said the Professor of Classics.)

The idea that some institutions are fit to be places of higher education, in contrast to others that are not, embodies, of course, an evaluation of what higher education consists of in distinction from further education and secondary education. The universities are not in doubt about this, though they may not always be able to define the differences, and at times during their history have in fact themselves been more like places of secondary education than anything else. Today both universities and the CNAA want the courses they approve to be taught in places which encourage reason, scholarship and research. 'The Council', says the CNAA, 'recognizes that environments offered by different institutions will vary according to factors such as location, size and range of work. The institution as a whole should be sympathetic to the objectives and requirements of study at the appropriate level, and should provide a cultural environment which stimulates a wide-ranging interest among students, and in which rational debate is encouraged. The Council considers that students should have the opportunity of mixing with students who are pursuing courses different from their own and that the staff of an institution should be able to engage in debate within a wide academic community ... Advanced work can only flourish in an institution which has made considerable progress towards becoming an academic community, and this is not normally achieved unless there are opportunities for the staff and student body to contribute in an informed way to the formation of academic policy, to the determination of priorities between the various activities in the institution, and to the discussion of other major issues.'

The climate of an institution has, in other words, a considerable influence on the kind of education it can give. It may affect what a particular subject can *mean* not only to students but to members of staff in both the depth at which its teaching can be done and at which it comes home to the students being taught.

The idea of what an institution for higher education should be like has a very long and varied history. Judgements are embedded in validators' minds about the sort of place in which learning of the kind they approve can flourish. Ideally it must be one through which, in Matthew Arnold's phrase, 'a current of true and fresh ideas' is blowing. Socrates teaching in the Athens market place and its gymnasia was not merely conducting a colloquium but furthering a tradition of enquiry which has influenced the western concept of a university ever since. Among the presuppositions his practice embodied were the importance of a free search for truth, of a respect for the principles of logical argument, of a reverence for facts, of treating one's students as equally — or almost equally — human beings with oneself. Each of these presuppositions involves an evaluation and each has been a fertilizing element in higher education in the west as it has developed over the centuries.

Even objectivity itself as a criterion is a value, belief in which always has limits — limits which may be drawn in the west by, for example, a conviction of the sacredness of human life or of the rights of animals and by the certainty that some ends will not justify a number of the means which might be employed to attain them. Some courses which would secure validation in Britain would not do so in communist countries or, for different reasons, in Muslim ones. On the other hand, some courses highly respectable today in the universities of the Arab world would not obtain validation in the west — which has a deep emotional investment in an assumption, not in the last resort objective, that we live in a universe whose rules have an ultimate authority quite independent of social, moral or religious values. This assumption is so unconscious, and so profound, that we refuse to credit that it is only an assumption.

Even taking this overall assumption for granted, however, the pursuit of some kinds of knowledge over the centuries has had throughout Europe to be defended again and again against those with particular vested interests. And here the degree of independence allowed to places of higher education in British has been a great asset. The independence of universities from the state or from local education authorities, from over-dominance by churches or big business, has helped to defend them from many threats and temptations. The possession of such independence has indeed had numerous subtle consequences. It may be said that it is because of their own ease of mind, springing in part from an intimate sense of their own independence, that Oxford and Cambridge have by and large been able to set the example of treating their students as independent men and women, immature of course, but once inside the walls possessed within remarkably wide limits of rights and liberty, including liberty of spirit.

It is thus within a concept of what is really proper for its purposes that an institution will be deemed fit to have any courses at all validated within it. In Britain it will not be licensed as a place for degree studies if it is too narrow in its range of interests; not interested in the life of the mind; too small in size or impoverished in the quality of its staff and students. But of course it is not only the concept of an institution fit to be a place of higher education which is in the minds of validators but — and perhaps more consciously — the concept of what are subjects suitable for it to teach. Not 'peculiar' subjects — astrology, say, or acupuncture, or chess playing, or psychical phenomena. Not subjects concerned only with practical training — plumbing, for example, or hairdressing. Into the concept of what is an acceptable subject will enter considerations of whether that subject can be recognized as having an autonomy or separateness of its own, of its scope, of the detachment with which it can be taught.

In a notable but now largely forgotten essay Lord James of Rusholme, then merely Eric James (1949), said some acute things about the acceptability of subjects suitable for the purposes of higher education — eligible as it were for validation. The first of these principles of subject selection is that a subject should be readily related to the whole body of knowledge by the generality of its principles. As he says,

'We are saved from being overwhelmed with vast accumulations of fact only by the emergence of new principles of synthesis. And these can be forthcoming only when it is possible to find common methods of approach in quite different subjects. This, in turn, is possible only if these subjects are of a certain breadth, or, rather, if they have the potentiality for providing relationships with other fields...'

'We must look', he goes on, 'for some element of a quality that we may call importance in the subject-matter of higher education ... A research which determined the number of pebbles on a square foot of the path outside my window would undoubtedly be adding to the sum of knowledge. The low view which we should take of such a piece of research arises partly from the absence of this quality of importance. The idea derives mainly from a concern with fundamental questions. Thus the study of chemistry is more important than that of cosmetology, since it deals with the ultimate structure of matter, from an understanding of which a multiplicity of results follow, including the development of new cosmetics. The idea of permanence is also present when we say that a subject is important. An aspect of knowledge that may become rapidly and completely irrelevant to any of our needs because of some technological change cannot be held to be really serious unless it has other pressing claims.

We may also demand of a university subject that it shall extend fully the intellectual capacity of the most intelligent men and women. The phrase "most intelligent" is, of course, an ambiguous one. The point is, however, that if we fix the level of intelligence in terms relative to accepted subjects, the claims of new subjects for admission must be judged by that standard. They must be capable of eliciting a full intellectual response from individuals who are of the calibre to study the more orthodox subjects.

Finally, we may ask that the universities shall be concerned with living and developing studies that will claim the attention of original minds in disinterested research. By using the word "disinterested" ... I wish ... to indicate that a subject should attract first-class minds to find out the truth about it, and not simply for financial profit or social prestige. It is this kind of consideration that links the highest intellectual effort with moral value, and which makes it clear that the criteria by which we seek to distinguish between university and non-university studies are related to spiritual worth of a particular kind, though spiritual value of other kinds is to be found, or course, associated with work at a much lower intellectual level.'

Had Eric James been writing today instead of in 1949, he might well have put polytechnics into the same sector as universities, though he might not have included some of the studies leading to national certificates.

Yet his discernment of the kind of studies for validation for degree purposes in fact is still not as objective as he supposed. For it is limited — whether desirably or not — by the traditions inside which he worked and thought, perhaps too by a narrower understanding of 'objectivity' than is acceptable. 'Creative English', for example, a subject permitted in many American universities even for MA work, would hardly meet his criteria. He might conceivably have found a musical composition submitted for a Masters degree not acceptable, or the performance of a musical work not a suitable substitute for a written paper in a BMus degree. It must be granted that a great problem is posed in the examining of any such composition or performance, for experiential factors are involved. In such judgements, much more obviously than in most, one is drawing upon a civilized tradition of perception whose objectivity is not to be tested by logic but rather by the representativeness incorporated in the judge. The criterion by which an examiner decides the merit of the performance or composition springs from a vital tradition of value judgements which must still be growing in his own mind, nourished by the centrality, as it were, of his humanity. It is upon that centrality rather than on any external proofs that his real objectivity will depend. But, to rule out of count all creative work in subjects which cannot be marked conventionally on a points system, is to narrow the scope of the academic unduly and of reason itself irrationally.

It may be worth noting here, incidentally, that attainments widely recognized both by universities and the CNAA for the award of honorary degrees would by no means always satisfy the requirements for an earned degree at any level. A remarkable variety of distinguished human beings — statesmen, politicians, administrators, authors, artists, musicians, sculptors — may have an LLD, DLitt, or DMus, even a DSc, deservedly conferred on them. Is the judgement of their worth any less objective than that included in what might be called 'normal' academic tradition? No tests are imposed: the criterion here is the consensus of as representative a committee of as mature and seasoned members as a university can assemble that so-and-so deserves the award.

In the validation of most subjects for earned degrees, however, the criteria used tend, I suggest, to be confinedly cognitive. The area allowed to be 'proper' to a subject is of course very much wider in some subjects than others — English for example has potentially a much wider range than anatomy and will legitimately exercise many more of the modes of knowing than anatomy does — the historical, aesthetic and moral as well as the factual and analytic. But in both cases what is innovative in a new syllabus will often only be accepted by outside opinion — including the opinion of potential validators — if a very considerable part of the structure and content follow a traditional pattern. Such following of tradition is indeed often taken as in itself evidence of objectivity!

It is in part because of this that combined or 'integrated' subjects are notoriously difficult to get validated the first time an attempt is made to float them. Validators have to get used to the idea that such mixtures are desirable, even possible. They will usually be able to adduce cogent and apparently objective arguments to rule them out. And even when authorized, some Combined Study degrees suffer from sufficient disapproval inside the institution to make them of less worth and attractiveness than was expected by their advocates. In several universities which have for forty years or more had joint degrees in some combinations of two subjects a shrewd counsellor may advise a student against trying to take them: for he will rightly point out that it will be harder to get a 'First' in them, the student may be no one's real baby, he will find the amount of work called for excessive, his academic future may be endangered, and so on. Within a faculty or sector of a polytechnic or university a quiet sort of internal validation may thus be going on, even less objective than the official one but having much authority and effectiveness all the same.

Bearing the needs of our civilization in mind the most valuable type of multi-disciplinary degree in future may well be one which involves both the 'confinedly cognitive' criteria for validation in which we are more practised and the searching out and testing of 'tacit' forms of knowledge whose importance we tend so much now to down-play. The authority of fact and the authority of insight both need to be acknowledged if higher education is not to become still more narrowly professionalized. It is easiest to see the necessity of insight and feeling if our concern is with the validation of literature or musical appreciation — which should test, inter alia, the student's capacity to discern and evaluate the experiences given him by music or literature. But many experiences not brought by the arts also need to be recognized as educationally indispensable and to have their recognition acknowledged and validated — among them the ability to read character, situation and mood. If this does not happen the authority of such intuitions (and their supply also) will be diminished. If a man or woman is imperceptive of the values embedded in human and social behaviour; or of the assumptions about values which he is conveying to the children he may be teaching in a classroom; or of the values embodied in the office blocks he is designing with such admirable skill; his education is defective.

Types of multidisciplinary course (some of them postgraduate or for the mature student) we need might include, among many others, medicine and ethics; architecture and social purpose; literature and human development; electronics and the evolution of society. Each of these could at its best call for types of validation which reckon with cognitive (external) and tacit (inward) knowledge. Validators need to widen their concepts and extend the scope of their art — not least if the alternative life styles urgently required by our civilization are to be fostered.

## THE BRITISH TRADITION

The objectivity of the judgements we make in validating the standards and classifications of the degrees we award is as subject to embedded assumptions as the objectivity of those we make in validating the institutions and subjects in which those degrees can be taken. This second stage in the validating process in the completion of the earlier stage, for a degree has licensing power in our society — partly because of its approved content, but partly because it offers some guarantee that the approved content has been educationally effective.

It used to be said that the academic standard required for the attainment of a degree in Britain varied little between institutions, however different they might be in the social composition of their student entry. It was also maintained that a 'First' in university X was academically pretty nearly equivalent to a 'First' in university Y and that its attainment would demand roughly the same standard of intellect and knowledge in the student irrespective of the subject in which it was awarded. We are less confident about such matters than we were; it is widely suspected that the academic pecking order between institutions has lengthened. It is also difficult to credit that honours classifications can mean the same thing when the competition for acceptance in some places and on some degree courses is so much greater than in others and growing fiercer, that the proportion of 'Firsts', 'Seconds' and 'Thirds' differs so much from subject to subject everywhere, and that investigation strongly suggests that the proportion in each class in the majority of honours schools in a good many places, remains more or less constant in the same subject not merely over periods of, say, three years, but ten, twenty or even fifty with some subjects habitually having a far higher proportion of 'Firsts' than others irrespective of their standards of entry or of teaching. Tradition rather than objectivity seems to have a strong hand to play in this business.

Though there is a highly significant difference in the concept of an honours degree as between normal British university practice and that of the Open University and the CNAA — a point to which we will return — the principle of classifying degrees and ordinarily of validating them in a I, II, III and Pass categorization is normal in the award of honours in first degrees in contemporary Britain. The curiosity of the structuring (with the First and Third classes usually kept small, a Fourth class now almost unknown and a Fifth class completely so) goes unremarked, its sanctity being presupposed. The OU and the CNAA took it over without perhaps giving too much objective thought to the matter. Yet the whole tradition is more peculiarly British and more recent than often supposed.

It may be worth spending a paragraph or two upon the historical background. In the consultation too little attention was devoted to the history of the development of validation processes. It was not until 1722 that even written examinations were introduced for the first time in an English university — Cambridge — and then only in some subjects. Twenty-five years later the first classified 'Tripos' list was published there — in mathematics, the only subject to be classified either at Oxford or Cambridge until the nineteenth century. At Oxford in 1800 new Public Examinations Statutes introduced written examinations both for degrees and classified honours degrees, though for many years after that the majority of students continued to read for pass BAs. Basically, if a student was studying for honours he was studying with an examination in mind; and students who were at a university for social purposes tended to regard those reading for honours as their social inferiors.

The entry of the University of London into the field in 1838 as an examining body, and the fact that from 1863 onwards it began to award classified honours degrees in a range both of arts and science subjects, added to the competitive element. At the 'modern' universities in big cities, founded during the latter part of the nineteeenth century, classified honours degrees were given from the start in arts, science and applied science subjects and, though the proportions of candidates opting to take them was at first small, it steadily increased, largely, no doubt, because of the growth of industrialization, with its concomitants of competitiveness and personal ambition. The idea of classifying degree results owed much to the need for encouraging students to work harder, but something also to the growing scientific spirit of the age — which encouraged a looking for results and results that could be measured. Even in the 1870s though, when the foundation of a university in Manchester was being advocated, *The Times* still thought the danger to be that its degrees, though attainable with honours, would count for little because they would carry little social cachet. The principle of proof of merit by competitive and classified examination results very much went in fact with the stirrings against privilege of the growing middle class; and the introduction of examinations of 1872 for posts in the highest administrative grades of the Civil Service, with half the marks awarded upon the results obtained in them and only half on interview, was significant.

The direction of development of civilization in Europe from the seventeenth century onwards has in general been towards the further individualizing of men; and the process of classifying degrees can perhaps be seen as a contribution within this sequence. University students became less and less treated, as they once were, as members of a group with a right to graduation as a result of years spent as members of a university community (their alma mater); instead it came to be agreed that they ought to be judged and classified 'objectively'. University examiners were thus increasingly required to become more external in their attitude, and to grade candidates on behalf of society, of the nation, indeed of civilization itself, so that their ability and qualifications could be more objectively depended upon. The nation was in course of evolution from aristocracy to meritocracy.

All the same, the objectivity was to be exercised within a tradition which ascribed lower standing to a pass than an honours degree; which in general approved of the classification of such honours degrees but not of pass degrees; and which gave high status to a new help to 'correct' validation — an external examiner brought in from another place of higher education to act as umpire and if necessary as arbiter of the final result. A subject into which there has been little research is that of the choice of external examiners for first degrees. There is evidence to suggest that they are selected for their reputation primarily as representative 'professionals' within their subject field — their objectivity in validating the work of the candidates whose work they sample being assumed because they incarnate a scholarly tradition themselves.

One significant difference in the concept of an honours degree between most university practice and that of the CNAA and the OU is that some of the latter can regard the honours year or years as added to those spent in studying for a pass degree whereas traditionally a University honours 'school' has been selective in choosing its entrants, those proving unfit for its rigours often being relegated after a year or two years to a pass course (no undergraduate pass course being called, nor regarded as fit to be called, a 'school'). It may well be that the normal English university attitude to the classified honours degree still has an element of the aristocratic about it, though now the aristocracy concerned is an intellectual not a social one.

The greatest strength of a good, if now somewhat old-fashioned, university honours school lay perhaps in its very capacity to bind people together as students of a subject. Once you belonged, you belonged to a community with an ethos and a direction of looking — one which might owe a lot to a particular professor or a tradition, but an orientation which mattered and was recognizable. In other words the honours school had quite an element of fraternity within it. Once a member of it, you might have to sacrifice a good deal of freedom to choose what you should study. And your chances of getting say a 'First' or an 'Upper Second' depended very much of course on the custom in that particular honours school. Some indeed have produced year after year, over half a century or more, a very different percentage from others of 'Firsts' and 'Seconds' — and there was and still is no one to compel them to behave differently.

In examiners' meetings for the validation of candidates for classes of honours there is often considerable reliance upon the 'sense of the meeting' in deciding what class shall be awarded to a candidate, especially a 'borderline' candidate. It is, in my experience, rare for particular internal examiners in universities to plead for a certain candidate to pass rather than fail or to be awarded a higher class of honours or some form of distinction than the majority opinion of the meeting would favour — more unusual than it was for internal examiners in training colleges to do so. This practice of pleading the merits of particular candidates is, I think, much more rare in colleges of higher education than it was their predecessors, though still more common than in universities. The concept of objectivity in the two sectors is still different. But I would not be prepared to say that the rough-and-ready objectivity of adding mark totals together to secure an indisputable consensus, as can happen in some examiners' meetings, is necessarily superior to a knowledgeable pleading for a known candidate!

The basic American system of first degrees, with its multiplicity of possible offerings and combinations, has more flexibility than the English. But the courses or units taken tend to be seen by the students (as in many modular degrees in CNAA courses in Britain) as discrete in themselves, their interconnectedness with one another and other areas of knowledge rarely being revealed in the students' work. Fissiparous tendencies are indeed inevitable perhaps in any degree system built and validated on a modular principle. The absence of final 'classes' in the United States system is in accord with the American disinclination overtly to label a student's intellectual attainments. Even the term 'grades' is less socially conscious or divisive than 'classes of honours'. But in many American colleges there is a tendency to work within a fairly fixed range of proportions for the various grades; so that a student can raise his position only at the expense of his fellow students. The emphasis for many students tends to be on securing a sufficiency rather than on excelling. The practice of checking students' attendance at classes and giving them relatively frequent and apparently objective tests are realistic devices to ensure that justice is done. There is nothing like the stigma attached to being 'a drop-out' from an American university that there still tends to be for those who fail at any stage during a first degree course at a place of higher education in Britain.

In the American tradition there is in fact much less attempt than in Britain to identify an intellectual elite as such. The aim rather is to train and underwrite a professional cadre — made up of those able to serve the community usefully as technologists, scholars and administrators. The explanation of the lack of desire in the USA to identify, in the English way, either a social or an intellectual elite is to be found in the anti-aristocratic strands present in United States society generally and in the strong tendency to make a proved capacity for long-maintained, reliable hard work a considerably greater asset than cleverness. Normality is respected; to get the reputation for being an egghead can be disastrous either to one's advancement or to any hope of really being trusted. In addition, there is a powerful desire not to classify, or validate, a man at one stage of his life in a way that might give him either a permanent privilege or a permanent handicap.

There are limits to the objectivity which it is proper for examiners in any country to assume, however distinguished, representative or professional they may be. They must remember that at best their objectivity will be temporary and that even as objectivity it will be limited by the presuppositions built into the stances they take as examiners, the rating they give to general education as compared with specialized scholarship, to hard knowledge as compared with imagination, to intellectual precision as compared with moral responsibility. All validation whether at the first stage of approving institutions and courses or at the second stage of underwriting results is apt to be more time-bound, subject to contemporary consensus and fashion than we may wish to think. This is no reason for not seeking to be as objective as possible in our judgement and judgements; but it *is* a reason for bringing up into consciousness as many of our assumptions as we can and taking them with some humility into consideration.

## THE SOCIAL SHAPE OF THINGS TO COME
And yet ... when we have done that, are we much further on? No doubt raising further into consciousness the prejudices, the biases, the elements of fashion, within our judgements may help us to lessen their fallibility. But a good deal more may be needed if we are to distance ourselves enough from the validation effort itself to ask some of the more fundamental questions that need asking in a late twentieth century uncertain of itself and its direction of development.

There was a point in this consultation when such questions came near to being asked. The determination to achieve and validate sensible courses and to achieve justice in rewarding success in them had led it was suggested, to a 'consolidation of the bureaucratization' of education. The whole business of course planning had become as it were a kind of learnable game. The very concentration upon the validation process may have hastened the transition from thinking of knowledge as tacit and personal in character to being overt, written and point by point examinable.

What is important about the teacher in this view is no longer his effectiveness as a person communicating but his ability to put his knowledge on to paper, to handle it so that it can be discussed at arm's length. 'It is a change', said David Edge in discussion, 'from a charismatic notion of the man of knowledge, what I like to think of as the Isaiah Berlin effect, the lecture where you see the man's brain functioning ... to a routinization of the charisma, which is all boiled down. Can you answer questions on the second law of thermodynamics? Are the aims specified?'

Several papers presented to the consultation emphasized that, if validation was to be sufficiently sensitive to need, the consideration of courses must involve the institution and the institution as a community. 'Those responsible for validation internal or external', said Alexander and Gent, 'should be keenly aware that what is being appraised includes not only individuals — as persons, academic, managers — but also the network of relationships between people which welds the community together'. And Roy Cox suggests the need for validation procedures which involve a knowledge more intimate than that with which the present ones are satisfied. Validation must not be regarded only as a utilitarian exercise but as one which, without losing its rigours, is in touch with students actually learning. He pointed to the work of the new researchers whose 'academic respectability comes less from accurate measurement and more from being close to what actually happens, more sensitive to the thoughts and feelings of those involved'. Participative research of this kind might in future, I believe, make a very significant contribution to the validation process, broadening its scope and enabling it to take account of insights and individuality in a less limited way than is at present the case. What is involved, however, is some change in the *expectation* of what higher education should do for people. We need, in Edge's view, to 'get back from what looks like a dehydrated approach to the teaching process towards thinking in terms of people' ... and 'to more direct interaction between validators and validated'. What he is at bottom pleading for is, of course, a concept of knowledge itself that is more dynamic, more human and personal, than that which tends to be encouraged by the validation process today.

Yet there can hardly be so great an evolution without a major reorientation of social demand. During the consultation it was pointed out that the approval of college courses by the Secretary of State was given 'not on political grounds' but 'purely on the grounds of demand and resource'. But what creates the demand and who decides what resources should be made available? Though types of course and of testing which are unacceptable to society are not likely to be validated, those who approve, and those who validate, courses are not wholly without power to modify what society wants. Marketing and publicity could certainly affect the popularity of (and therefore the demand for) course X rather than course Y. So, at a deeper level, could a new perception of what is important to social progress at a particular juncture. Public opinion is not a fixed entity. It can be changed by pressure from a number of points — as a wheel can be made to rotate faster by pressure exerted on many different places on its circumference, provided that they are consistent in direction. 'Who validates the validators?' was a question never far beneath the surface in the consultation. Behind it is the still larger question: who can cause the values of the validators to evolve? And if the answer if 'social opinion' we are back to the question of what can effect an evolution there; and to the same answer: the process of change can be influenced, and at many points, by new perceptions. If policy makers are keen that courses for an age of leisure should be introduced in greater numbers and at times examined in some unconventional ways, they can do something to help this to happen.

How? Not directly, but by means that are traditionally British. One of these is still through encouraging the creation of working parties and committees which are likely to recommend changes of the sort desired. A major power indeed of a government or of the great departments of state is so to choose the composition, and particularly the chairman, not only of Royal Commissions but of lesser bodies, that an impetus will be given to a change in social opinion. Of course the members of such bodies or commissions must be selected 'fairly' — that is with a reasonable spread of view and of representation. This does not mean that they must be so composed that their report is likely to call for no development of social view, or for a development which those who chose the members would deplore.

But in the last resort it will be individuals with convictions and prophetic power who, through their books and through the media, are most likely to influence and change social opinion. If several of them in what they say point in more or less the same direction of advance, an impetus to opinion to move in that direction is powerfully given. Both people and institutions may well follow such a lead.

This is in no way to deny the freedom of any institution to initiate changes in its curriculum or to seek validation of courses of the kind it desires. But it will almost always be found that the kind of initiative shown in introducing the new courses it wishes to have approved will, if acceptable, be fairly well in accord with the direction in which the society that supports it is itself moving. Obviously this is the case where the course covers territories which are in clear contemporary need of exploration and cultivation: computer studies, for example; micro-processing; institutional planning and management. But it may be the case, too, where the underlying direction of social movement, though real, is less obvious. There is good reason to think that art and design, music, even religious studies, may figure more rather than less conspicuously in the curricula of places of higher education in the next quarter of a century. And if this is so it is an additional argument for searching for the wider (but not less rational) forms of sensitivities in examining of which I spoke above.

The freedom of an initiator of new types of course for validation will rightly be limited by his need to cater for a nascent or actual social demand. But, if he is sensible, he will not feel this as unduly constrictive. The chances are we do not want a freedom that is quite complete anyway. 'Me this unchartered freedom tires', said Wordsworth. Too complete a liberty will tire and de-energize any man.

A CNAA visit or a staff discussion in a university department about a new course — which can be in some ways more and in some ways less adequate than such a visit — can compel a concentration and orderliness of mind that are productive. But too confined a concentration can yield the wrong results. The task of validators is not only to reckon with immediate needs but, as Hugh Sockett emphasized during the consultation, to shape higher education for a post-industrial society tomorrow. Our immediate industrial and economic needs understandably bulk large. But vocational courses which demand only 'the facts' and the attainment of 'expertise in skills' can be antipathetic to the development of knowledge and judgement. Places of higher education which seek to foster these last two qualities do not necessarily deserve to be branded as more 'elitist' than the larger number which seem, sometimes against their will, to have become chiefly selection-and-training grounds for the socially mobile in search of status or of well-paid occupations.

Validation, as this whole investigation has brought out, involves decisions which are based upon perceptions of the nature of what is to be validated. At a time of social questioning it is more than ever necessary that such preceptions should be raised into consciousness. Validation, as now practised, may involve following quite a lot of traditions with too unconsidered an acceptance of current ideas about what ought to be in the curriculum, what can or cannot be taught, what can or cannot be examined. It does not take enough into account the scope of what will and ought to be validated in higher education in coming years if social and individual needs are adequately to be catered for. Thinking at some depth can do much to enable both new types of course to be created and approved and to ensure that existing courses evolve further; research can do much to make more varied, humane and imaginative the recognition of what is meritorious in the achievement of those who are examined.

REFERENCE
James, E. (1949) *Essay on the Content of Education* London: Harrap pp.65-7